WILD
Montana

Bill Cunningham

FALCON®

GUILFORD, CONNECTICUT
HELENA, MONTANA
AN IMPRINT OF THE GLOBE PEQUOT PRESS

A FALCON GUIDE®

Cover photo: Medicine Mountain, Absaroka-Beartooth Wilderness,
    by Michael S. Sample.
Back cover photo: Expedition Lake, Lee Metcalf Wilderness,
    by Bill Cunningham.
All black-and-white photos by author.

Library of Congress Cataloging-in-Publication Data
Cunningham, Bill.
    Wild Montana : a guide to 55 roadless recreation areas / by Bill Cunningham.
        p.   cm.
    "A Falcon guide."
    ISBN 1-56044-393-6 (pbk.)
    1. Outdoor recreation—Montana—Guidebooks. 2. Wilderness areas—Montana—Guidebooks. 3. Montana—Guidebooks.   I. Title.
GV191.42.M9C86 1996
796.5' 09786--dc20   95-52631
                                                                              CIP

Manufactured in the United States of America
First Edition/Fourth Printing

CAUTION
Outdoor recreational activities are by their very nature potentially hazardous. All participants in such activities must assume the responsibility for their own actions and safety. The information contained in this guidebook cannot replace sound judgment and good decision-making skills, which help reduce risk exposure, nor does the scope of this book allow for disclosure of all the potential hazards and risks involved in such activities.

Learn as much as possible about the outdoor recreational activities in which you participate, prepare for the unexpected, and be cautious. The reward will be a safer and more enjoyable experience.

♲ Text pages printed on recycled paper.

CONTENTS

Northwest: Cabinet-Yaak/Greater Glacier/Bob Marshall

West-Central: Bitterroot-Upper Clark Fork

Southwest: Upper Missouri/Greater Yellowstone

Central: The Island Ranges

East: Lower Missouri and Yellowstone

FOREWORD—THE BALANCING ACT

I believe most people would agree with this statement: If something is rare, it's precious. The truism certainly applies to wilderness. It's rare. It's threatened. And it's invaluable.

We, the People, have tamed almost all the wilderness. Only 2 percent of the continental United States remains roadless; only 10 percent of Montana has gone untamed: 4 percent as designated wilderness, and an additional 6 percent currently hangs in the balance as de facto wilderness. Of the fifty-five wild areas covered in this book, only five have received the full protection of Wilderness designation—twenty are partially protected and thirty have no protection at all. At least fifty of the fifty-five areas are currently threatened with development.

In the early 1970s I worked hard as a volunteer board member of the Montana Wilderness Association. We were trying to pass a wilderness bill; the same legislation has been proposed annually ever since. The legislation, meant to save the last 6 percent of Montana from development, has been a political football for decades with the end of the game nowhere in sight. Tragically, the name of that game is "The Balancing Act."

Here's how it goes. A politician or a developer will get up to the podium and say, "I'm in favor of more wilderness, but we need some balance. We can't have all wilderness." But only 10 percent of Montana (10 million acres) has any chance of remaining wild.

I'm not sure anybody could agree on how "balance" should be defined, but if we preserved every square inch of wilderness left in Montana today, we would not even be close to balance. We certainly are not going to achieve a balance by protecting only part of the last 10 percent. We need all of our remaining wilderness.

—Bill Schneider, Publisher

DEDICATION

In gratitude to all those who are helping to defend Montana's wilderness heritage, and to those who set the example for others to follow in no-trace wilderness recreation.

ACKNOWLEDGMENTS

I must first thank my publisher, Bill Schneider, for the prompting needed to begin what turned out to be a monumental project. "Go for it, Bill," he said, "for you this book will be a layup." Well not quite, Bill, but I sure enjoyed it. Guidebook editors Randall Green, Christian Sarver, and the other good folks at Falcon Press deserve a lot of credit for magically transforming piles of rough maps, photos, and electronic data bits into a final product worthy of publication. Certainly I could not have completed such an effort without current information provided by numerous Forest Service and Bureau of Land Management offices throughout Montana. All of the agency folks who helped had lots of other work to do, so their assistance is especially appreciated. I am deeply indebted to my friend Polly Burke whose cheerful companionship on reconnaisance trips, meticulous proofreading, and boundless enthusiasm salvaged this project from unmitigated disaster. And lastly, I must salute those conservationists before my time whose vision and foresight helped secure much of the wild country portrayed in this book, without which there would be nothing to write about. Although they are too numerous to name, I feel their spirit whenever I venture beyond the road.

LEGEND

Trailhead or
Starting Point **(T)**

Continental Divide
National Scenic Trail **(CD)**

Trail, Trail Number,
Trail Junction – – – *102T* O – – *319T*

Interstate **(15)**

US Highway **(12)**

State Highway **(43)**

County Road **(32)**

Forest Road **(401)**

Railroad

State or
International
Boundary
MONTANA
IDAHO

Site Location

Mountain ▲ Granite Peak 12799'

Campground Λ

Mine ✕

Ranger Station ✚

City or Town ⊙ **Butte**

Pass

Lake, River

Distance to
Town or Road
**Town
00 Miles**

Scale and
North Arrow
0 1 2 3 **N**

STATEWIDE OVERVIEW MAP

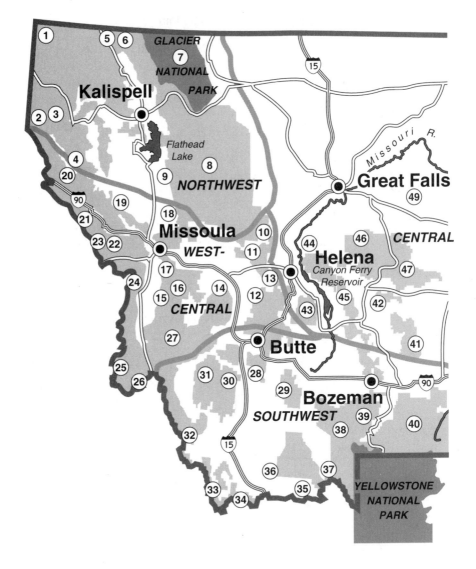

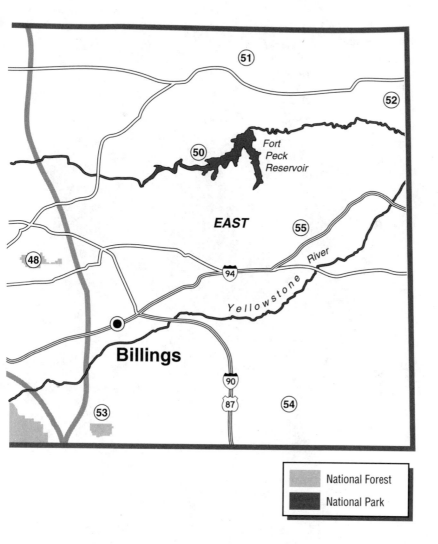

LOOKING SOUTHWEST TO BLACKROCK PEAK ALONG THE RESERVATION DIVIDE.

INTRODUCTION

This guide to Montana's wild country is but a snapshot in time in the on-going debate between preservation and development of the last of our publicly owned wildlands. As I write these words the "snapshot" consists of nearly 12.4 million wild acres in 89 wildlands (or clusters of wildlands) that contain 197 separate roadless areas. By focusing on larger wildlands better suited to non-motorized backcountry recreation, this book covers 10 million acres spread within 55 of Montana's nearly 200 roadless areas. Just as floods, fire, earth-quakes, wind, and decay constantly change the face of the land, so do politics. The 15 federal Wildernesses, along with the single tribal Wilderness in Montana, add up to about 3.5 million acres, so that only 28 out of every 100 wild acres are legally protected as Wilderness. About half of the total lacks any kind of legal or physical protection.

With popular support Congress can be persuaded to safeguard some of what remains wild, but it cannot "create" more wilderness. With continuing pressure for resource extraction and other non-wilderness uses, we will never again have as much wilderness as existed when this "snapshot" of *Wild Montana* was taken.

LOOKING NORTH FROM PINE BUTTE TO CHOTEAU MOUNTAIN AND THE MAJESTIC SWEEP OF THE ROCKY MOUNTAIN FRONT.

RIVER BOTTOMS RISE TO RUGGED BADLANDS IN THE MISSOURI BREAKS.

Those of us who know and love wild country have our own personal definition of wilderness, heartfelt and often unexpressed, which varies with each of us. But since Congress reserved the exclusive power to designate Wilderness in the landmark Wilderness Act of 1964, it is important that we also understand the legal meaning of Wilderness. The fundamental purpose of the Wilderness Act is to provide an *enduring* resource of Wilderness for this and future generations so that a growing, increasingly mechanized human population does not occupy and modify every last wild niche. Just as important as preserving the land is the preservation of natural processes, such as naturally ignited fire, which shape the land. Before 1964 the uncertain whim of administrative fiat was all that protected wilderness. During the 1930s the "commanding general of the wilderness battle," Wilderness Society cofounder Bob Marshall, described wilderness as a "snowbank melting on a hot June day."

The act defines Wilderness as undeveloped federal lands "where the earth and its community of life are untrammeled by man, where man is a visitor who does not remain." In old English the word "trammel" means a net, so "untrammeled" conveys the idea of land that is unnetted or uncontrolled by humans. Congress recognized that no land is completely free of human influence, going on to say that Wilderness must "generally appear to have been affected primarily by the forces of nature, with the imprint of man's work substantially unnoticeable." Further, a Wilderness must have outstanding opportunities for solitude or primitive and unconfined recreation, and be at least 5,000 acres in size or large enough to preserve and use in unimpaired condition. Lastly, Wilderness may contain ecological, geological, or other features of scientific, educational, scenic, or historical value.

In general, Wilderness designation protects the land from roads, timber cutting, motorized vehicles and equipment, and commercial uses except preexisting livestock grazing, outfitting, and the development of mining claims and leases validated before the 1984 cutoff date in the Wilderness Act. The act set up the National Wilderness System and empowered three federal agencies to administer Wilderness: the National Park Service, the Fish and Wildlife Service, and the Forest Service. The Bureau of Land Management was added to the list with passage of the 1976 Federal Land Policy and Management Act. These agencies can make wilderness recommendations, as any of us can, but only Congress can set aside Wilderness. This is where politics enters in, epitomizing grassroots democracy. In Montana, with six million unprotected national forest roadless acres and close to a million acres of qualified Bureau of Land Management wildland awaiting a long-elusive resolution, the formula for conservationists continues to be "endless pressure endlessly applied."

Wilderness is the only land use with a biocentric emphasis. It is off-limits to intensive human uses with an objective of preserving the diversity of nonhuman life. As such, its preservation is our society's highest act of humility. This is where we deliberately slow down our impulse to drill the last barrel of oil, cut the last ancient tree, dam the last wild river. The wilderness explorer can take genuine pride in reaching a remote summit under his or her own power, in guiding a well-balanced packstring over rough mountain trails, in catching native cutthroat far from the madding crowd. Mules and misery whips replace pickups and chain saws, allowing us to find something in ourselves we feared lost.

Chronology of Congressional Wilderness Designation in Montana

1964—Establishment of the Wilderness Act, with instant inclusion of the Bob Marshall, Selway-Bitterroot, Cabinet Mountains, Anaconda-Pintler, and Gates of the Mountains Wilderness Areas. The act also required wilderness review of the Mission Mountains, Spanish Peaks, Absaroka, and Beartooth Primitive Areas.

1972—Designation of the Scapegoat Wilderness as the nation's first citizen-initiated Wilderness.

1975—Designation of the Mission Mountains Wilderness.

1976—Designation of the Red Rock Lakes, UL-Bend, and Medicine Lake National Wildlife Refuge Wilderness Areas, and the Elkhorn and Great Bear Wilderness Study Areas.

1977—Passage of Senator Lee Metcalf's Montana Wilderness Study Act (S.393) giving wilderness study status to nine national forest roadless areas totaling one million acres.

1978—Designation of the Absaroka-Beartooth, Great Bear, east side Birch Creek addition to the Bob Marshall, and Welcome Creek Wilderness Areas in three separate acts.

1980—Designation of the Rattlesnake Wilderness and National Recreation Area.

1983—Designation of the Lee Metcalf Wilderness, with Bear Trap Canyon (the country's first Bureau of Land Management Wilderness), and the Cabin Creek Recreation and Wildlife Area, along with removal from wilderness consideration of the Mount Henry WSA, portions of the Taylor-Hilgard WSA, and the Tongue River Breaks roadless area.

THE BEARTOOTH PLATEAU OF THE VAST ABSAROKA-BEARTOOTH WILDERNESS— "MONTANA'S ROOFTOP."

BULLWHACKER CREEK, DEEP IN THE MISSOURI BREAKS.

Leave No Trace Wilderness Manners

Proper respect for wild country and its wild denizens makes it unthinkable to leave evidence of having been there. The Leave No Trace ethic begins with reverence, is applied through common sense, and is refined with experience. Here are the eight principles of backcountry manners to help you "stay together / learn the flowers / go light" in the words of poet Gary Snyder:

1) Plan and prepare ahead to prevent the kind of problems that can impact wildland. Start with this book and good maps, and check with the local land management office to see if conditions have changed or if any new regulations may be in effect.
2) Keep the noise down, recognizing that the key wilderness values of quiet and solitude go hand-in-hand.
3) Pack it in, pack it out; plus pack out whatever litter you may find in the backcountry.
4) Dispose properly of anything that can't be packed out. For human waste use a cat-hole several inches deep, then carefully replace the dirt and duff.
5) Leave the land as you found it—or better, if possible. Ask yourself, "When I leave will there be no trace that I camped here?" If camping in a popular site try to actually improve it by picking up litter, cleaning out fire rings, and scattering ashes.

6) In popular sites, concentrate use so as to confine activities to areas already damaged by past use.

7) In pristine sites, disperse use by spreading out or by using durable sites such as dry meadows.

8) Avoid sites that are just beginning to show signs of use, to allow recovery.

Some other tips:

Respect wildlife by observing from a distance with binoculars. You're too close if an animal changes its behavior because of your presence.

Be courteous to and tolerant of other visitors you encounter in the backcountry, keeping in mind that they are there for similar reasons and that you have more in common than you may at first realize. In fact, I would go a step further and state that we're all in it together, regardless of our chosen mode of transport, and that we'd best get along with each other if we are to hold onto the wild country we still have. For example, when meeting packstock on the trail, hikers should step off to the downhill side while speaking calmly, so the animals can identify you as humans.

The proper use of packstock in the wilderness requires special preparation, beginning with knowing your animals, your equipment, and all pertinent regulations. Keep the number of packstock to a minimum by packing lightweight gear, and by all means keep the animals away from campsites. Many areas,

WEST BIG HOLE NEAR THE CONTINENTAL DIVIDE.

LOOKING SOUTH FROM NORTHWEST PEAK IN EARLY JULY.

such as the Bob Marshall, require certified weed-free seed. Move stock fre-
quently to avoid overgrazing any one area. Use a hitchline between two trees
instead of tethering directly to a tree. Scatter manure piles when breaking
camp. Every backcountry stock user should become familiar with an informa-
tive book by outfitter Smoke Elser and Bill Brown called *Packin' in on Mules
and Horses*.

Mountain biking is one of the fastest growing forms of recreation on public land. The responsible biker seeks to eliminate conflict with other trail users, which is accomplished through common courtesy. Slow down when
approaching others, give a friendly greeting, yield the right-of-way at all times,
and give lots of room for others to pass. For more information contact the
International Mountain Bicycling Association at (303) 545-9011.

For the bible on no-trace outdoor recreation see Falcon's *Wild Country
Companion* by Will Harmon. Booklets on no-trace camping skills for specific
ecosystems are available from the National Leave No Trace Program at 1-800-
332-4100.

Preparedness and Safety

To survive and actually enjoy the wilderness experience, wanderers must
know how to cope with grizzlies, lightning, hypothermia, avalanches, rock
falls, high water, hantavirus, giardia, being lost, and a host of unpredictable
medical emergencies. With all of these pitfalls, why would anyone give up the

security of home for the hazards of wilderness? Truth is, I feel a lot safer in the wilderness than I do in cities and towns. The key to this self-confidence is preparedness.

Statistically, the most dangerous part of your trip is the drive to and from the trailhead. Nonetheless, the inherent danger of being several hours or even days from the nearest 911 service fosters self-reliance—an integral part of the wilderness experience. So don't let paranoia rob you of the ecstasy of experiencing wild country. Instead, focus on the rewards of safe practice: increased self-confidence, personal growth, and a healthy, vigorous outdoor life. Choose your own acceptable level of risk. Calculate the risk by knowing your limits. Here are a few preventative tips with respect to some of the potential dangers but, again, I refer you to the definitive work on wilderness safety, *Wild Country Companion*.

Changeable weather

Montana is well known for sudden changes in the weather, so prepare yourself with extra food and clothing, rain gear, and waterproof matches. When leaving on a trip let someone know your exact route, especially if traveling solo. If you do get lost, stay put and keep warm.

Hypothermia

Wear layers of clothes, adding or subtracting depending on conditions, to avoid overheating or chilling. A warm hat is the single most important garment to wear. Snack throughout the day on high energy foods and drink lots of fluids.

Grizzly country

Both grizzlies and black bears roam much of Montana's wildlands, so keeping a clean camp. Storing food out of reach is crucial. Travel with at least one other person and make enough noise to avoid surprising females with cubs, bears at close range, and bears when they're feeding. Bears will protect themselves in all three instances.

Giardia

Any surface water, with the possible exception of springs where they flow out of the ground, is apt to contain *Giardia lamblia*, a microorganism that causes severe diarrhea and dehydration about two weeks after it gets into your digestive tract. Again, prevention is the best approach. Boil water for at least 5 minutes or use a filter system. Iodine and other chemical additives are not reliable shields against this pesky parasite.

Lightning

Lightning storms can build up at anytime but are most prevalent during summer afternoons. As these storms develop, stay off exposed ridges and peaks and away from isolated trees and metal objects. Shallow overhangs and gullies should also be avoided because electrical current often moves at ground level near a lightning strike.

Avalanches

Anyone who ventures into the backcountry during winter should enroll in an avalanche safety course. Snow slides can occur on any slope but are most common on 30- to 50-degree inclines. Eighty percent of all avalanches happen during or just after a fresh snowfall, particularly one that drops a foot or more snow at a rate of an inch or more per hour. Usually the safest route in snow country is on the windward side near the top of a ridge.

FORDING ROSS CREEK IN THE SCOTCHMAN PEAKS ROADLESS AREA.

How to Use This Book

Think of this book as a broad-scale, textual map to be used for the initial trip planning overview, only with more information. You can sit back and say to yourself, "Where should I explore this weekend?" Or, perhaps, "Which Montana wild area do I want to learn more about?" Start with the statewide locator map to assess the geographic setting, select an area, then focus for greater detail.

The book divides Montana into five regions: northwest mountains, west-central mountains, southwest mountains, central island ranges, and eastern prairie-canyon country. Boundaries between regions are imprecise, but each wildland falls logically into one of the regions based on its topography, plant communities, and geographic location.

Each of the fifty-five Montana wildlands in this book is a contiguous, unroaded expanse of undeveloped (mostly federal) land. But of these, only fifteen have been formally designated by Congress as Wilderness under the 1964 Wilderness Act. A given wildland is managed by one or more of four federal agencies: the National Park Service, Fish and Wildlife Service, Bureau of Land Management, and the Forest Service. Portions of some of the areas also contain tribal, state of Montana, and individual or corporate private land. In terms of number of areas and acreage controlled, the USDA Forest Service is by far the major player.

Trip planning information for each wildland is presented as follows:

The maps - The statewide locator map on pages viii-ix shows the fifty-five areas covered in the book. A more detailed map accompanies the information blocks for each wildland, distinguishing between Wilderness and non-wilderness, showing major trails and access points, and indicating the driving distance from featured trailheads to the nearest highway or town. These maps are an important reference for trip planning, but they are no substitute for the applicable topographic and travel plan maps listed in the Information Blocks.

Information Blocks - These contain quick facts, including—
1) Location—the direction and straight-line distance to that portion of the wildland closest to the largest and/or nearest town. This is intended only to give a general idea as to where the area is in this vast space we call Montana.
2) Size—measured as the total contiguous roadless area in acres, regardless of ownership or land status, based upon the best available information.
3) Administration—names the federal, state, or tribal agencies and offices responsible for management. See Appendix C for addresses.
4) Management status—reveals the area's designation as Wilderness, Wilder-

ness Study, Park, non-wilderness roadless, etc. Since status changes continually, this gives some idea as to whether a portion of the roadless area is slated for future resource development. I encourage you to obtain more detailed information from the managing agency and to then work with the agency, conservation groups (Appendix B), and Congress toward improved management and protection of our wildlands.

5) Ecosystems—based largely on the broad Kuchler classifications used by the Forest Service for ecosystem management.

6) Elevation range—the minimum and maximum elevations, to give an idea of vertical relief.

7) System trails—estimated distances of designated or numbered trails that may or may not be regularly maintained.

8) Maximum core to perimeter distance—is the longest straight-line mileage that you can be from the closest road while inside the roadless area. Exceptions abound, but this figure gives you some idea of the wildness of the country in terms of remoteness and solitude.

9) Activities—those non-motorized pursuits for which the area is best suited, from both a legal standpoint (in the case of Wilderness) and the physical lay of the land. Hiking is the common activity of all the areas. Hunting is not mentioned as one of the activities only because this book is not a hunting guide, which would be a major book in its own right. Legal hunting in season takes place in most of these wildlands, including designated Wilderness, except for in National Parks, certain tribal lands, and specially restricted areas.

10) Modes of travel—refers to how you can travel through the country. These modes, in turn, are dependent on terrain, trails, legal status, stream characteristics, snow depths, and access. For example, mountain biking is not a primitive mode of transportation, so is disallowed in Wilderness, yet is appropriate within or to the edge of many other roadless lands. Other low-elevation wildlands may not have reliable snowpack for skiing, but do have gumbo wheel tracks ideal for mountain biking when dry.

11) Maps—a listing of the applicable agency travel or management plan map, which is usually small-scale (0.5 inch/mile planimetric), the applicable wilderness map on a contour base, and all the 1:24,000 scale USGS topographic maps that cover the wildland, starting at the northwest corner. A topo map listing is also provided in Appendix D.

12) Overview—captures a bit of the "personality" of the country, including flora and fauna, geology, and major points of interest.

13) Recreational uses—expands on suitable activities and seasons, with occasional trip ideas woven into the text. In keeping with the idea of helping to redistribute use, the more heavily visited trails and sites are indicated, where applicable. Your route may still include these locations, but at least you'll know ahead of time that your chances for solitude will be reduced.

14) How to Get There—contains detailed driving instructions to the trailheads or jumping off points for the sample trips. Road designations are abbreviated as follows: FR - Forest Road; I - Interstate; MT - Montana highway; US - U.S. highway.

15) Sample Trip Ideas—one or more trips are suggested within each wildland into mostly lightly used locations, to help redistribute use. These suggestions cover a variety of activities, travel modes, and seasons. Most of the sample trips are on established trails because they are prescribed routes with less impact on pristine areas. Those who plan to do any of the suggested bushwhacks through trackless terrain must know how to use a compass and topo map, and do everything possible to travel lightly in a fragile environment while minimizing disturbance to wildlife. The rating from "easy" to "strenuous" is subjective, but is based on the author's firsthand experience on each sample trip. For example, a short hike on a level trail would be easy for most people, whereas a lengthy off-trail bushwhack through heavy brush and cliffy terrain would be strenuous for all but the most fanatically fit.

Near the end of the book is a roadless area monitoring form. You are invited to reproduce it and use it on future trips as a means of keeping track of the wildlands you visit. To help with future updates of this book I would be delighted to receive a copy, care of Falcon Press, of any of your visitation records.

Northwest Peaks

Location: 55 miles northwest of Libby in extreme northwest Montana.
Size: 20,330 acres.
Administration: USDAFS—Kootenai National Forest.
Management status: Roadless recreation with about 15 percent of the area allocated to development in the forest plan.
Ecosystems: Northern Rocky Mountain coniferous forest/alpine meadow province characterized by glaciated mountains with moraines; Precambrian metasedimentary rock; Douglas-fir forest type; and numerous streams.
Elevation range: 5,120 to 7,705 feet.
System trails: 17 miles.
Maximum core to perimeter distance: 1.5 miles.
Activities: Hiking, backpacking, fishing, horseback riding, cross-country skiing.
Modes of travel: Foot, horseback, skis.
Maps: 1994 Kootenai National Forest Visitor Map; Northwest Peak-MT and Canuck Peak-ID/MT (1:24,000 topo maps).

OVERVIEW: The loftiest mountains in the Purcell Range rise within the Northwest Peaks Scenic Area and surrounding roadless lands. This wild setting drapes the slopes of a prominent north-south ridge where Montana touches Idaho and British Columbia. The heavily tree-covered ridge reaches its apex at 7,705-foot Northwest Peak in the heart of the roadless area. Here the remnants of a 1930s fire lookout offer unlimited vistas of the nearby Yaak River wildlands and far to the north into Canada. The alpine core of Northwest Peaks is managed as a scenic area for non-motorized recreation. Moderate glaciation has sculpted pockets for seven high lakes, three of which support rainbow and cutthroat trout.

RECREATIONAL USES: If this small but highly scenic alpine gem were anywhere else it would receive lots of hiking and fishing pressure. But because the wild Purcell Mountains are so far from anywhere, in Montana's extreme northwest corner, recreational use is generally light. The big attraction is quick, easy access to glaciated peaks and mountain lakes for hikers, anglers, horseback riders, berry pickers, and hunters. An occasional hearty cross-country skier will venture up to the higher ridges above the lake basins.

I NORTHWEST PEAKS

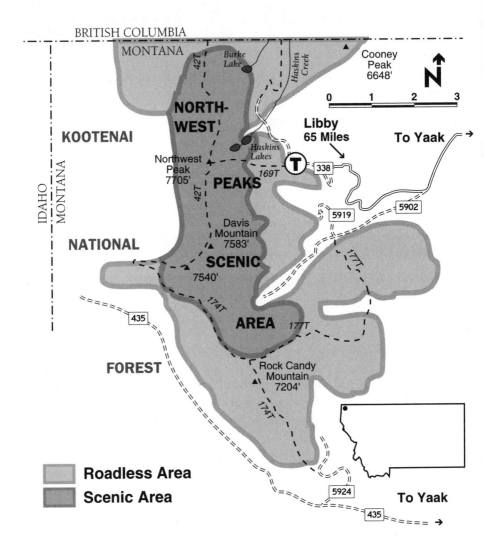

THE FUN OF CATCHING FROGS IN BLUEBIRD LAKE, NORTHWEST PEAKS.

HOW TO GET THERE: From Libby head north to Yaak by driving about 40 miles on the Pipe Creek - S. Fork Yaak County Road 68. From Yaak, drive 2.5 miles west on MT 508. Turn right on FR 338 (the Pete Creek Road) and drive about 13 miles north. Turn left on FR 338 and head 2 miles up the West Fork of the Yaak River. Then turn right up Winkium Creek and go 7 miles to the signed trailhead for Trail 169 at an elevation of 6,300 feet. The trail takes off on the left (west) side of the road.

Day Hike

Northwest Peak
Distance: 4 to 5 miles out and back; or 9- to 10-mile loop; or 10 to 12 miles point to point.
Difficulty: Moderately strenuous.
Topo map: Northwest Peak-MT.

Ridgeline Trail 169 climbs steadily, gaining 1,400 feet over a distance of 2 miles to the rocky, narrow summit of 7,705-foot Northwest Peak. The top is graced by a rustic old lookout cabin reminiscent of the early firefighting days of the Forest Service. Scree slopes drop into three sparkling lake basins with the steepest headwall cirques on the north and west sides. The Northwest Peaks area is heavy snow country, and the lakes and upper basins are often frozen and snowbound well into July. The main up-and-down, north-south ridge can be hiked cross-country north (toward Canada) or south. A 9- to 10-mile loop hike with some cross-country travel can be made by hiking north from the peak along the main ridge to 7,461-foot Burke Point, which is only 1 mile south of the border. Descend 1,300 feet to Burke Lake. Bushwhack through dense forest and brush east to the Hawkins Creek road and then walk 2 to 3 miles south on the road back to the trailhead. A slightly longer 10- to 12-mile point-to-point route is possible if you continue about 6 miles south from the peak along the main divide to 7,204-foot Rock Candy Mountain, which also has an old lookout. You'll be wrapping around the broad, forested upper head of Davis Creek. From there Trail 174 can be taken a couple of miles south and down to FR 5924 on Spread Creek. This exceptional high-ridge traverse would require a lengthy car shuttle.

Scotchman Peaks 2

Location: 20 miles south of Troy and 5 miles northwest of Noxon.
Size: 86,250 acres, 64,580 acres of which are in Montana.
Administration: USDAFS-Kootenai and Idaho Panhandle national forests.
Management status: Roadless non-wilderness, with about 10 percent of area allocated to future development in the forest plan.
Ecosystems: Northern Rocky Mountain coniferous forest/alpine meadow province characterized by glaciated mountains with moraines; Precambrian metasedimentary rock; Douglas-fir and western ponderosa pine forest types, old-growth cedar-hemlock forests in low elevation valleys; and numerous streams.
Elevation range: 2,280 to 6,906 feet.
System trails: 42 miles.
Maximum core to perimeter distance: 4 miles.
Activities: Hiking, backpacking, horseback riding, cross-country skiing, fishing.
Modes of travel: Foot, skis, and horseback.
Maps: 1994 Kootenai National Forest Visitors Map; Benning Mountain-ID/MT; Spar Lake-MT; Scotchman Peaks-ID/MT; Sawtooth Mountain-MT; Heron-MT; and Smeads Bench-MT (1:24,000 topo maps).

OVERVIEW: Extending from the Idaho Panhandle to Montana's Bull River, the Scotchman Peaks harbor some of the wildest country in the Cabinet Mountains. The Scotchman area is unusual in that it has remained roadless to the very edge of its natural landforms—from peaks to valleys. Even though the summits on the Montana side of this large interstate roadless area fail to reach 7,000 feet, the rugged landscape contains striking glacial cirques and cliff faces at the heads of Savage and Ross creeks.

Above the cirque headwalls, hillsides of alpine vegetation plunge sharply into the West Fork of Blue Creek, while the south slopes of dramatic Sawtooth and Billiard Table mountains send cascading snowmelt through parks and down waterfalls to the East Fork of Blue Creek. To the north the U-shaped valley of the South Fork of Ross Creek winds through meadows and rockslides to stately stands of ancient cedar, hemlock, and white pine, cutting through a jumble of moss-covered boulders and devil's club to the magnificent Ross Creek cedar grove—home to the largest and oldest western red cedar still standing in northwest Montana.

2 SCOTCHMAN PEAKS

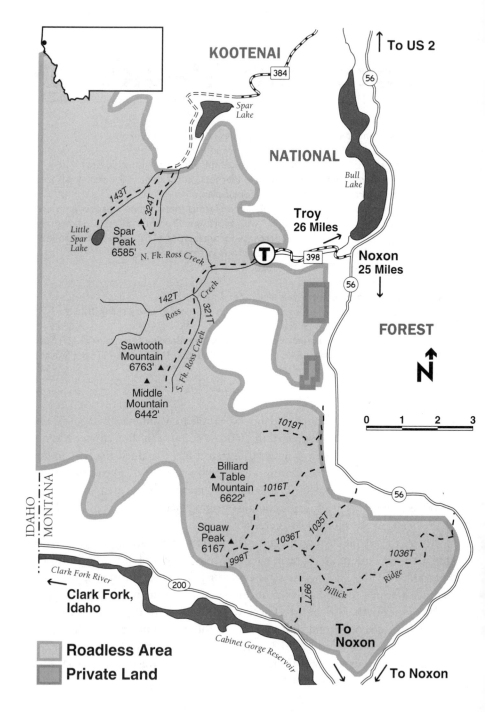

MIDDLE FORK OF ROSS CREEK.

For 10 miles the rocky south-facing slopes of Pillick Ridge fall nearly 4,000 feet to the Clark Fork and lower Bull River valleys. The cooler north aspects of the ridge display an unbroken forest canopy to the lower canyons. Pillick Ridge offers grand vistas as well as living space for grizzly bears, bighorn sheep, goats, and elk. Cutthroat trout dwell in the icy depths of Scotchman's only named lake—Little Spar.

RECREATIONAL USES: The extremely rugged terrain and relatively few trails provide the challenging opportunity for a true wilderness experience. Roadless hunting, hiking, backpacking, horseback riding, and cross-country skiing are light to moderate in intensity. A deep sense of solitude prevails, especially in the north-central reaches of Ross and Blue creeks, which have deep valleys forested with ancient cedar, hemlock, and white pine, sharply defined cirque basins, and heavy brush along the streams. There are no mainline trails and only Little Spar Lake holds fish. Because of this, recreation use is well dispersed, as opposed to many of the big-name wildernesses with destinations that concentrate use. For example, the scenic Pillick Ridge trail is more than 10 miles long, but does not have a particular destination that draws visitors. Much of the travel in Scotchman is cross country during both summer and winter. Ski mountaineering challenges, requiring steep climbs to high ridges, abound, with good highway access close to Pillick Ridge on all sides. The Cabinet Ranger District rents the five-person capacity Squaw Peak lookout cabin on Pillick

Ridge from September 1 to June 30. It is at least 5 miles by trail to the lookout—the only humanmade structure in this large, wild core of the west Cabinets.

HOW TO GET THERE: From Troy drive 22 miles south on MT 56 and turn right (west) on FR 398. Or, from the south, drive 16 miles north from MT 200 on MT 56 and turn left on FR 398, which is signed for the Ross Creek Cedars Scenic Area. Take this paved road about 4 miles to where it ends at the edge of the cedar grove and the jumping-off point for Trail 142 up Ross Creek. Trail 142 begins at the outer loop of the Ross Creek Cedars nature trail (a barrier-free 1-mile loop).

BACKPACK - BASE CAMP

Ross Creek
Distance: 5 miles round-trip.
Difficulty: Easy; with moderate to strenuous side trips.
Topo map: Sawtooth Mountain-MT.

From the Ross Creek Cedars Scenic Area along the east-central edge of the roadless area, take Trail 142 through one of the more majestic old-growth

STAIR STEP FALLS MARK THE END OF THE TRAIL ON THE SOUTH FORK OF ROSS CREEK.

Ancient-western red cedar grove in Upper Ross Creek, Scotchman Peaks.

cedar forests in the Northwest. After about 2.5 miles of level walking through ancient groves of 500-year-old cedar, on a soft trail cushioned with moss, you'll reach the mouth of the South Fork of Ross Creek. There are good log crossings over both Ross Creek and the South Fork. At this point you'll be at the signed junction of the South Fork Trail 321 and the main Ross Creek Trail 142. If you're staying overnight look for a flat spot to pitch your tent, then take a day hike up the steep South Fork Trail 321 through a magnificent mixed conifer forest. After gaining 600 feet in more than 1.5 miles, the trail drops to a small tent campsite next to a sparkling bridal veil falls. The trail is a bit narrow and side-sloping for stock, but great for hiking. Although the map indicates otherwise, the trail ends here. A faint path overgrown with devil's club follows the streambed up for about 0.25 mile before disappearing altogether.

For another day hike head up Ross Creek on Trail 142. This well-maintained trail climbs gently for 2.5 miles through the most stately monarchs of the extensive Ross Creek cedar grove before ending at a horse camp, just after crossing the second sizeable side stream. For a strenuous extension of an otherwise easy hike you can climb higher for a grand view of Sawtooth Mountain. Look for old blazes and log cuts of a long-abandoned trail that goes straight up without relief. This punishing, largely overgrown path gains about 1,400 feet in 1 mile before ending in a large, open subalpine park bounded by layered sedimentary rock, heavy brush, and a flowing spring. The tough ascent is well rewarded by overwhelming views of Sawtooth and the glaciated head of Ross Creek with cliffs, snowfields, and waterfalls.

Cabinet Mountains Wilderness Complex

Location: 5 miles west/southwest of Libby; 2 miles north of Noxon.
Size: 203,512 acres.
Administration: USDAFS—Kootenai National Forest.
Management status: Cabinet Mountains Wilderness, 94,272 acres; 109,240 acres of roadless non-wilderness, 33,200 acres of which are allocated to future development in the forest plan.
Ecosystems: Northern Rocky Mountain coniferous forest/alpine meadow province characterized by glaciated mountains with moraines; Precambrian metasedimentary rock; Douglas-fir forest type; and numerous lakes and streams.
Elevation range: 3,000 to 8,738 feet.
System trails: 135 miles.
Maximum core to perimeter distance: 5 miles.
Activities: Hiking, backpacking, horseback riding, mountaineering, cross-country skiing, fishing.
Modes of travel: Foot, horse, and skis.
Maps: 1992 Cabinet Mountains Wilderness 1"/mile contour map; 1994 Kootenai National Forest Visitors Map; Kootenai Falls-MT; Scenery Mountain-MT; Crowell Mountain-MT; Treasure Mountain-MT; Little Hoodoo Mountain-MT; Ibex Peak-MT; Snowshoe Peak-MT; Cable Mountain-MT; Elephant Peak-MT; Howard Lake-MT; Noxon Rapids Dam-MT; and Goat Peak-MT (1:24,000 topo maps).

OVERVIEW: The Cabinet Mountains Wilderness occupies the higher reaches of the northern Cabinet Range southwest of Libby. A narrow line of snowcapped peaks, glacial lakes, valleys cut by icy streams, and cascading waterfalls runs north to south for 40 serpentine, up-and-down miles. Two major north-south ridges divide the north Cabinets, sending Lake Creek north to the Kootenai River while spilling the Bull River south to the Clark Fork. A dramatic vertical mile separates lush stream bottoms from the rocky crest of centrally located Snowshoe Peak—the apex of the range at 8,738 feet. These pointed pinnacles challenge technical climbers in a primeval setting.

From an ancient shallow sea, sedimentary basins were thrust upward. After the mountains were built they were shaped by extensive glaciation, leaving today's myriad of sharp peaks, 80-plus cirque lakes, wet meadows, hanging

3   CABINET MOUNTAINS WILDERNESS COMPLEX

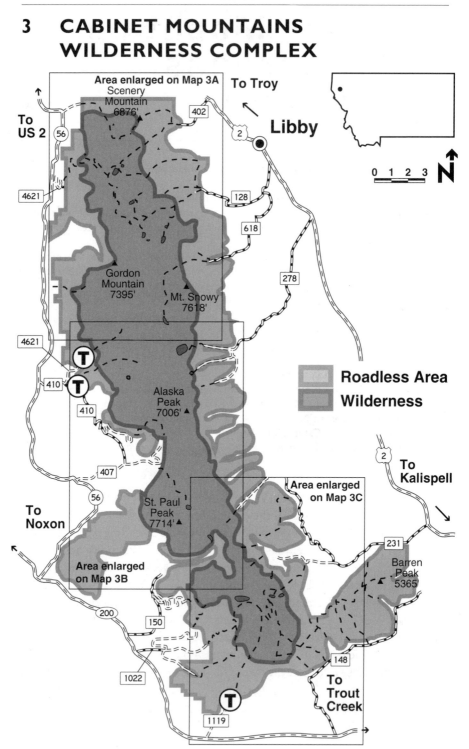

valleys, U-shaped drainages, and scoured slopes. As the loftiest mountain barrier directly east of the Cascades, the Cabinets receive up to 100 inches of annual precipitation, with snow depths exceeding 800 inches in high, sheltered basins. The maritime climate produces vegetation on every acre, from giant old-growth cedar and hemlock to delicate little harebells blooming from rock fissures as late as September.

Denizens of this wild, wet land include wolverine, deer, elk, moose, mountain goat, bighorn sheep, black bear, and a small but threatened grizzly population that hangs on despite development pressures from nearby roads, logging, and mining. Potential large-scale mining, permitted by a grandfather clause in the 1964 Wilderness Act, is likely in the southern, narrow Rock Creek portion of this linear wildland. With most trails only 3 to 5 miles long, dead-ending in high basins, the impact of industrial mining on solitude and other wilderness values could be severe.

Contiguous wildlands larger than the designated Wilderness core encircle the Wilderness on all sides. The east face runs the length of the range in a row of rugged canyons, from which the Cabinets get their name. Along the northwest face a roadless band of forested sidehills extends for 16 miles. Mountain goats winter here in Camp Creek and in the dramatic Goat Rocks, with bighorn sheep common near Ibex Peak. A roadless flange of high ridges and steep, forested gullies around Government Mountain juts out and down to the Bull River. Mosaics of conifers and hardwoods from a 1910 burn provide forage for grizzly bears and wintering elk. The southwest face, containing McKay and Swamp creeks, is important fall range for both mule deer and grizzlies.

RECREATIONAL USES: More than 90 percent of the recreation use in the Cabinets occurs on less than 10 percent of this rugged mountainous region. And some 90 percent of the visitors travel on foot, with the remainder riding horses or hiking with packstock. The area's mostly short, steep trails combined with a lack of forage explain the low level of horse-borne recreationists. Some 75 percent of the visitors are Montana residents, and two-thirds pack into the high lakes to fish, with an average trip duration of only 1.6 days, which tends to fall on weekends. Thus, a picture emerges of the typical Cabinet Mountains visitor: the local weekend angler. Most of the eighty-five lakes in the wilderness contain fish and, as such, are the focal points of use. Centrally located Granite Lake is the only lake in the wilderness known to have historic native cutthroat. By 1970 fish had been planted in most every lake capable of supporting populations.

Generally, the thirty trails are well maintained. Most of the trails are less than 5 miles long, penetrating east or west and ending in subalpine basins. There are few loop trails so most visitors come and go on the same trail, thereby increasing the chances of encountering other parties. Most of the avail-

3A CABINET MOUNTAINS WILDERNESS COMPLEX

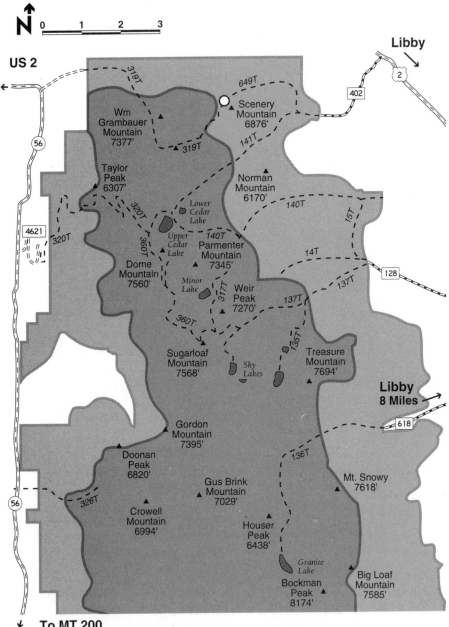

N

0   1   2   3

Libby

US 2

2

402

319T

649T

Scenery
Mountain
6876'

Wm
Grambauer
Mountain
7377'

56

319T

141T

Taylor
Peak
6307'

Norman
Mountain
6170'

140T

15T

320T

Lower
Cedar
Lake

4621

320T

360T

Upper
Cedar
Lake

140T

Parmenter
Mountain
7345'

14T

128

Dome
Mountain
7560'

Minor
Lake

317T

Weir
Peak
7270'

137T

137T

360T

135T

Sugarloaf
Mountain
7568'

Sky
Lakes

Treasure
Mountain
7694'

Libby
8 Miles

618

Gordon
Mountain
7395'

Doonan
Peak
6820'

136T

56

326T

Gus Brink
Mountain
7029'

Mt. Snowy
7618'

Crowell
Mountain
6994'

Houser
Peak
6438'

Granite
Lake

Bockman
Peak
8174'

Big Loaf
Mountain
7585'

↓ To MT 200

able campsites are close to fishable lakes, which show some adverse effects, such as compacted soil, defaced trees, and fire-blackened rocks. The most heavily used trails are in the northeast and southern portions. From north to south the highest use trails are 1) Cedar Creek Trail 141 to Cedar Lakes; 2) Trail 360 from Cedar Lakes south to Sky Lakes; 3) Flower Creek Trail 137 to Sky Lakes and Hanging Valley; 4) Granite Creek Trail 136 to Granite Lake; 5) the short Leigh Creek Trail 132 to Leigh Lake (largest in the wilderness and closed to overnight camping and stock use); 6) the Bramlet Creek Trail 658 to Bramlet Lake; 7) the Lake Creek Trail 656 to the Geiger Lakes (no open fires are permitted at Lower Geiger Lake) and south along the divide to the Baree Cabin; and 8) the Baree Creek Trail 489 to the Baree Cabin. Stock use is also prohibited on Trail 646 within the Saint Paul Lake basin, and Trail 924 from Upper Wanless Lake #4 to the main Wanless Lake.

If you're looking for solitude, you'd do well to avoid these trails when exploring the Cabinets. There are ample secluded locations, especially on the west side. The country along the east side from Carney Peak north to the Snowshoe Lakes divide is sensitive in terms of wildlife use and should be avoided if possible.

Winter recreation in the Cabinets is on the rise. The considerable snow depths and spectacular scenery offer terrific choices for snowshoeing and ski touring. Access routes in the southern third of the Wilderness are generally less prone to avalanches and are therefore more popular for winter travel and snow camping. Technical climbing in many areas of the Cabinets is unsafe because of unstable sedimentary rock formations. To protect wilderness, parties must limit their numbers to eight people and eight stock, at maximum. If you're planning a larger group trip be sure to obtain information and written permission at the local ranger station.

HOW TO GET THERE: West-central: From MT 56 about 23 miles south of Troy and 16 miles north of MT 200, turn east on the South Fork Bull River Road (FR 410) and drive 2.2 miles. Turn left (north) and go 0.5 mile on FR 2722 to the turnoff for the Middle Fork Bull River Trail 978. Turn right on this rough two-track and proceed another 0.4 mile to the trailhead at road's end for Trail 978. To reach the North Fork of Bull River Trail 972 continue up FR 2722 another 1.3 miles to the end-of-the-road trailhead.

Southwest: From MT 200, about 0.25 mile northwest of the Cabinet Ranger Station, take the Swamp Creek road due north for 2.2 miles where it joins FR 1119. Go another 2 miles to the end-of-the-road trailhead for the Swamp Creek Trail 912. If approaching from the north take the other end of the Swamp Creek Road loop, which takes off to the east from MT 200, 4 miles north of the Cabinet Ranger Station. After 2.5 miles turn left (north) on FR 1119 to the trailhead.

3B CABINET MOUNTAINS WILDERNESS COMPLEX

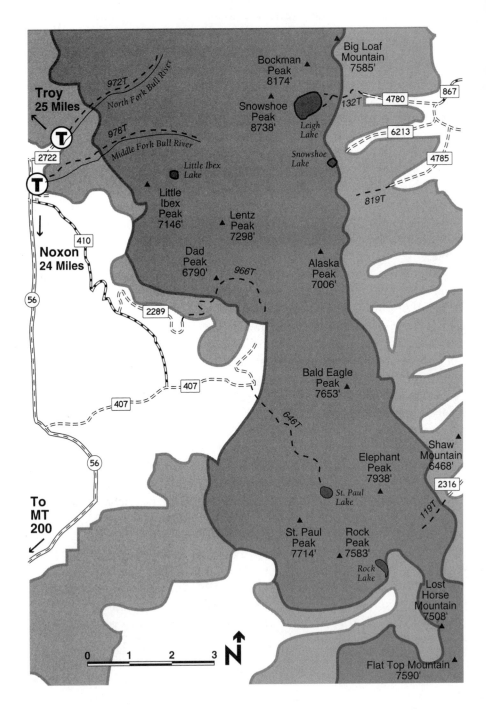

Day Hike

Southwest Portion: Goat Ridge-Swamp Creek Loop
Distance: 10 to 12 miles out-and-back; or 12-mile loop.
Difficulty: Moderate to strenuous.
Topo map: Goat Peak-MT.

Most drainages in the Cabinets are short, climbing steeply into glaciated, lake-filled cirques. A delightful exception is the 8- to 10-mile streamside trail up Swamp Creek in the extreme southwest corner of the complex. The relatively moderate stream gradient of the trail is unique in the Cabinets because of its length, but is noteworthy for other reasons as well. The rocky Swamp Creek Trail 912 provides a scenic stream, rockslide, and canyon out-and-back trip 5 miles up to the Wilderness line and beyond.

For a more strenuous and panoramic off-trail loop, cross the mouth of Goat Creek 0.5 mile up and begin climbing the prominent south-facing Goat Ridge that separates Goat Creek from Swamp Creek. The transmission line and old timber cuts east of Swamp Creek are more than compensated for by the sheer enjoyment of the climb, made even more so by a surprisingly good game path up the mostly open center of the ridge. With carpets of trillium underfoot and a Douglas-fir/lodgepole forest overhead, Goat Ridge offers ledge-top vistas of sheer cliffs and the high Cabinet divide beyond. Continue due north to reach the unmarked Wilderness boundary, after about 4 miles, on a level part of the ridge in a mountain hemlock forest at 5,600 feet, a 3,000-foot climb from the trailhead. If time and energy allow, you can continue another 2 miles, first on the trail then up the rocky ridge to 6,889-foot Goat Peak. To complete the loop drop steeply down the boundary ridge to the east, losing about 2,300 feet in 1 mile. Watch for Trail 912 just before reaching Swamp Creek. The first half of the descent is a moderate bushwhack through mixed forest and brush. Angle gradually to the right to intercept the rocky ridge. This steeper second half of the descent on loose layers of sedimentary rock and cliff can be safely negotiated with careful routefinding. Upon reaching the trail take it south 5 miles back to the trailhead.

Day hike or Overnighter

West-Central Portion:
Distance: 10 miles out-and-back.
Difficulty: Moderate.
Topo maps: Ibex Peak-MT; and Snowshoe Peak-MT.

Trail 978 starts out at 2,550 feet in a thick forest of Douglas-fir and pine, crosses the North Fork of the Bull River, and heads up the Middle Fork of the

3C CABINET MOUNTAINS WILDERNESS COMPLEX

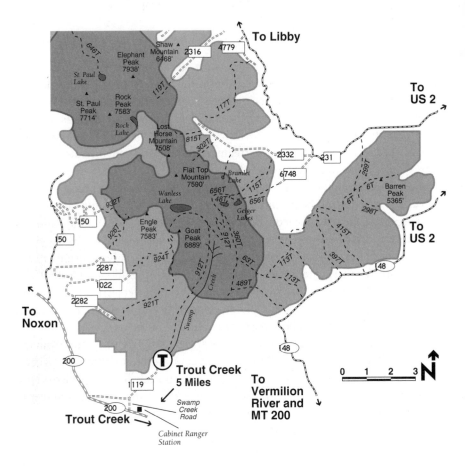

LOWER SWAMP CREEK ON THE SOUTH END OF THE CABINETS.

Bull River. Just before the Wilderness boundary, about 2 miles up, sits a level two-tent campsite, surrounded by cottonwoods with the rapid Middle Fork boiling only a few feet away. Another 3 miles will bring you to an open cedar-hemlock forest with a sign proclaiming "end of trail." And indeed it is. At this point you've traveled 5 miles on a good but lightly used trail, crossing rockslides and a few uncut logs, with fleeting glimpses of waterfalls, Ibex Peak, and the remote apex of the Cabinets—8,738-foot Snowshoe Peak.

This 10-mile round-trip follows the foaming cascades of the Middle Fork through a verdant ancient forest carpeted with mosses, ferns, and devil's club. The maintained trail ends at 4,100 feet, making for a 1,600-foot elevation gain from the trailhead. The map incorrectly shows the trail climbing up Ibex Creek another 2 to 3 miles. An old, abandoned trail sort of exists, off and on, for another 0.5 mile, but it is hard to follow, especially with a full pack. One option would be to set up camp at the 5-mile point then bushwhack into the upper Ibex Creek basin with a day pack.

With a full layover day and an early start, experienced and well-conditioned climbers could ascend an additional 4,600 feet to the summit of Snowshoe Peak—a strenuous 11- to 12-mile round-trip from base camp. First climb east to a nameless point at 7,718 feet and then gain the final 1,000 feet by way of the main southeast ridge. The views are spectacular into Blackwell Glacier and surrounding hanging valleys and glacial cirques with alpine lakes. Extremely rugged A Peak rises to 8,634 feet about 1.5 miles to the northwest with a rough, narrow ridge halfway between the two peaks. The sharp ridges and cliffs to the north of A Peak and Vimy Ridge are among the most dramatic in the range. Potentially dangerous snowfields along the east face of the main ridge above the glacier should be avoided by all except those well experienced and equipped for ice travel. Note: Trail 980 to Little Ibex Lake has been abandoned and is virtually nonexistent. Crossing the turbulent Middle Fork during the early season is impossible unless a log is used.

DAY HIKE

North Fork of Bull River
Distance: 8 miles round-trip.
Difficulty: Moderate.
Topo maps: Ibex Peak-MT and Snowshoe Peak-MT.

Head up the soft, moss-cushioned Trail 972, which parallels the North Fork; the trail is mellow and meandering at first, but becomes increasingly wild farther up. This 4-mile dead-end trip to Verdun Creek is magical, with an old-growth forest of cedar, hemlock, and white pine interspersed with tiny green glades and springs.

Cube Iron-Silcox 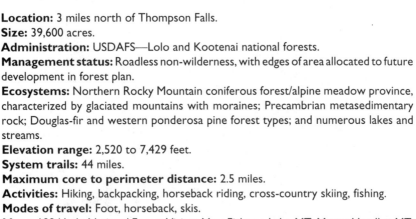 4

Location: 3 miles north of Thompson Falls.
Size: 39,600 acres.
Administration: USDAFS—Lolo and Kootenai national forests.
Management status: Roadless non-wilderness, with edges of area allocated to future development in forest plan.
Ecosystems: Northern Rocky Mountain coniferous forest/alpine meadow province, characterized by glaciated mountains with moraines; Precambrian metasedimentary rock; Douglas-fir and western ponderosa pine forest types; and numerous lakes and streams.
Elevation range: 2,520 to 7,429 feet.
System trails: 44 miles.
Maximum core to perimeter distance: 2.5 miles.
Activities: Hiking, backpacking, horseback riding, cross-country skiing, fishing.
Modes of travel: Foot, horseback, skis.
Maps: 1994 Lolo National Forest Visitor Map; Fishtrap Lake-MT; Mount Headley-MT; Priscilla Peak-MT; Thompson Falls-MT; and Eddy Mountain-MT (1:24,000 topo maps).

OVERVIEW: The high lake country of Cube Iron-Silcox is the centerpiece of the southern Cabinet Range. The area is bounded by 7,429-foot Mount Headley, 7,179-foot Cube Iron Mountain, and 4,500 feet of vertical relief from the Clark Fork Valley to Mount Silcox. Beyond the steep, open, Douglas-fir-clad hillsides visible from adjacent Thompson Falls lies an intricate array of glaciated peaks, lake-studded alpine basins, old-growth groves of ancient conifers, and clear, rushing streams. Few wild places in Montana present such a compact blend of landforms, forest types, and resulting wildlife, including grizzlies, mountain lions, lynx, and bobcats. Nearly two dozen drainages fan out like spokes on a wheel from the main divide. A few of these streams still harbor the combination of fine gravels and shady habitat needed to support a relict population of native cutthroat and bull trout.

RECREATIONAL USES: Local folks have long enjoyed good fishing at Arrowhead, Cabin, Duckhead, Stony, Terrace, Deer, and Lawn lakes. Fishing continues to be popular in this compact but rugged wildland, as does hiking, backpacking, horseback riding, berry picking, and, to a lesser extent, cross-country skiing. Steep, narrow drainages limit most of the skiing to ski moun-

4 CUBE IRON-SILCOX

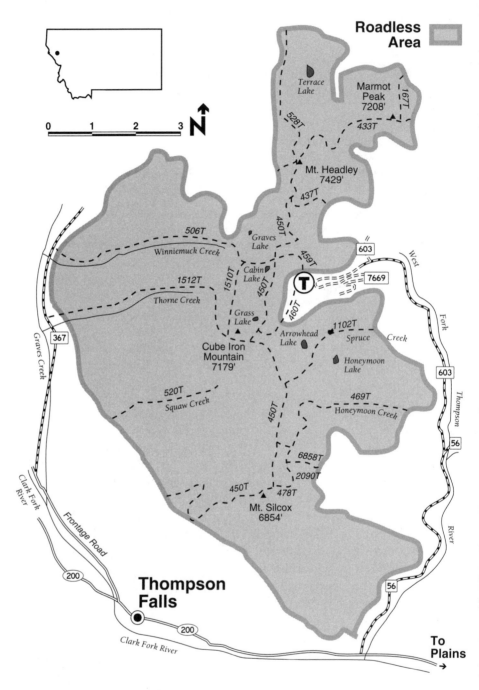

Roadless Area

0 1 2 3

N

Terrace Lake

Marmot Peak 7208'

167T

528T

433T

Mt. Headley 7429'

437T

506T
Winniemuck Creek

Graves Lake

450T

459T

603 West

Cabin Lake

1510T

450T

7669

460T

1512T
Thorne Creek

Grass Lake

Arrowhead Lake

1102T

Spruce Creek

Fork

367
Graves Creek

Cube Iron Mountain 7179'

Honeymoon Lake

603 Thompson

520T
Squaw Creek

450T

469T
Honeymoon Creek

56

6858T

2090T

Clark Fork River

450T 478T

Mt. Silcox 6854'

River

Frontage Road

56

200

Thompson Falls

200

Clark Fork River

To Plains

taineering, which should be attempted only when avalanche danger is low. At least half of the annual recreational use takes place during fall when hunters pursue deer and elk. An outfitter camp sits on Big Spring at the head of Squaw Creek, just below the top of the ridge.

Public access into the country is provided along the West Fork Thompson River Road on the east side as well as at the Winniemuck Creek trailhead on Graves Creek Road to the west. These two roads also reach the north end, with the lower end of the West Fork road providing the more reliable winter access for cross-country skiing. Ashley Creek at the area's south edge is the municipal water source for Thompson Falls and is thus closed to vehicular use.

The backcountry visitor can explore portions of twelve trails covering 44 miles within this roadless area. The most heavily used trails start from the east side up to the scenic high lakes. Cabin Lake is the single most popular destination. However, steep terrain and dense vegetation afford ample solitude, whether on or off the trail.

How to get there: From Thompson Falls drive 5 miles east on MT 200, then drive 8 miles north on FR 56 along the Thompson River (paved for 4 miles, then turning to gravel). Turn left and go about 7 miles up the West Fork of the Thompson River, then turn left up Four Lake Creek. Go about 3 miles to the Four Lakes trailhead for Cabin Lake Trail 459.

MULTI-DAY BACKPACK OR HORSE-PACKING TRIP

Cube Iron-Silcox Divide
Distance: 22 miles point to point (2 to 3 days).
Difficulty: Moderate.
Topo maps: Mount Headley-MT and Priscilla Peak-MT.

This route from the Cabin Creek trailhead to the Big Spruce Creek trailhead on Trail 1102, with options for several side trips to nearby peaks, provides a perfect overview of the southern Cabinet Mountains. Begin on Trail 459 to Cabin Lake, which climbs steeply some 1,500 feet over a long series of switchbacks to the lake. Cabin Lake sits in a 6,000-foot subalpine basin with dense spruce and fir, bounded on three sides by sharp, rocky peaks. From the main ridge above the lake, the highest summit—7,429-foot Mount Headley— is a worthwhile 4-mile side trip to the north. The trail crosses several steep, open, grassy slopes with rock overhangs—ideal for avalanches during winter and foraging grizzlies in the spring. The east face of Mount Headley displays a series of sheer 1,000-foot cliffs overlooking a lush, subalpine basin. The top of this and most of the other nearby high ridges and peaks are mostly open and grassy with little in the way of rock or broken talus.

Hiking the trail to Mount Headley in the Cube Iron-Silcox.

Backtrack to the south, past Cabin Lake, then go on for another 2 miles to lovely Four Lakes Basin. The "Four Lakes" pose a fascinating living study of the slow succession of lakes to ponds, then bogs, and finally meadows filled with mountain irises and glacier lilies. From Squaw Pass be sure to make the easy 600-foot walk to the top of Cube Iron Mountain in the heart of the roadless area. From here south, the trail makes a delightful 1.5-mile contour across the head of Squaw Creek to a junction above aptly named Duckhead Lake, where the upper end is defined by a perfectly square rock cliff with no visible inlet. Another worthwhile side trip from just above Duckhead Lake follows the fairly level Trail 450 2.5 miles south to Mount Silcox, which overlooks the Clark Fork River valley at Thompson Falls.

To complete this point-to-point exploration of the Cube Iron-Silcox area, double back to Duckhead Lake and make a steep 4-mile descent through the old-growth forests of Big Spruce Creek on Trail 1102. You'll end up on the West Fork Thompson River Road 3 to 4 miles below your point-of-origin at the Four Lakes trailhead.

Ten Lakes

5

Location: 5 to 7 miles east of Eureka.
Size: 45,150 acres.
Administration: USDAFS—Kootenai National Forest.
Management status: Congressional Wilderness Study Area and roadless recreation (41,040 acres); 4,110 acres allocated in forest plan to future development.
Ecosystems: Northern Rocky Mountain coniferous forest-alpine meadow province, characterized by steep, glaciated overthrust mountains; Precambrian and soft sedimentary rocks; Douglas-fir forest type; and numerous streams and higher elevation lakes.
Elevation range: 3,320 to 7,832 feet.
System trails: 63 miles.
Maximum core to perimeter distance: 2.5 miles.
Activities: Hiking, backpacking, horseback riding, cross-country skiing, fishing.
Modes of travel: Foot, skis, and horseback.
Maps: 1994 Kootenai National Forest Visitor Map; Ksanka Peak-MT; Stahl Peak-MT; and Mount Marston-MT (1:24,000 topo maps).

OVERVIEW: With British Columbia at its northern doorstep, the Ten Lakes Montana Wilderness Study Area resembles a giant starfish. Its roadless tentacles wrap around developed lands that were salvage logged after the 1950s spruce bark beetle epidemic. From glaciated Therriault Pass northward, an alpine core of sparkling lakes, lush mountain meadows, rocky peaks, talus slopes, gnarled subalpine larch and whitebark pine, and exposed ridges lends a distinctive alpine flavor to this last vestige of western Whitefish Range wild country. A variety of habitats from gentle, forested foothills to glacial hanging valleys beckons to a corresponding diversity of wildlife. Elk, moose, black bear, and deer are common. More rare is the transient grizzly bear, wolf, or woodland caribou that may be hiding in the security of old-growth forests. The remoteness of Ten Lakes is deepened by snow depths up to 12 feet in high, sheltered cirques. The steep west side of the roadless area, the "Burma Face," dominates the Tobacco Valley as viewed from nearby Eureka.

RECREATIONAL USES: The high core of Ten Lakes is a scenic area that was established in 1964 for hiking, nature study, camping, horseback riding, fishing, and hunting. With the exception of snowmobiles the backcountry is closed to off-road vehicles. There are developed campgrounds at the Therriault Lakes, which provide main jumping-off points into the high country. Small mountain

5   TEN LAKES

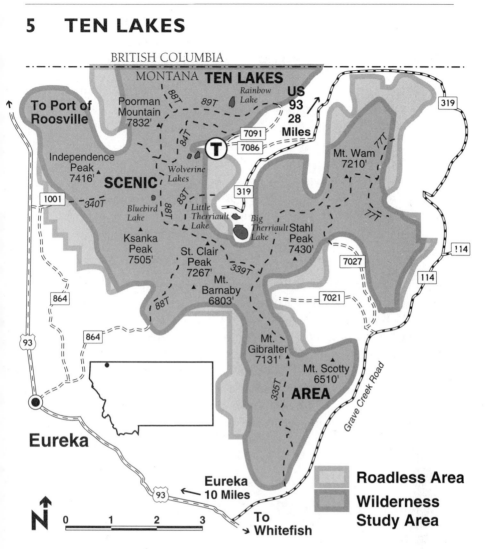

BRITISH COLUMBIA

MONTANA **TEN LAKES**

To Port of Roosville

Poorman Mountain 7832'

Rainbow Lake

US 93 28 Miles

319

Independence Peak 7416'

SCENIC

Wolverine Lakes

7091

7086

T

Mt. Wam 7210'

77T

77T

1001

340T

Bluebird Lake

Little Therriault Lake

319

Big Therriault Lake

Stahl Peak 7430'

!14

Ksanka Peak 7505'

St. Clair Peak 7267'

Mt. Barnaby 6803'

339T

7027

114

864

7021

Mt. Gibralter 7131'

AREA

Mt. Scotty 6510'

335T

Grave Creek Road

93

864

Eureka

Eureka 10 Miles

93

To Whitefish

N

0   1   2   3

Roadless Area

Wilderness Study Area

lakes and ponds dot this alpine landscape, with cutthroat trout in Bluebird, Rainbow, and Wolverine lakes. Therriault Pass is a prominent, glaciated saddle surrounded by rock outcroppings and avalanche chutes. Many of the trails follow lofty ridges with panoramic vistas into Glacier National Park. During summer the lush mountain meadows are ablaze with a dazzling display of wild-flowers. During winter reaching the upper Wigwam River basin requires a 25-mile snowmobile ride, but the western and southern edges of the Ten Lakes country are more accessible to ski mountaineers. For example, Gilbralter Ridge Trail 335 can be climbed on skis from Grave Creek Road only 1.5 miles inside the national forest boundary. Another possibility is to ascend the main divide Trail 88 from FR 7077 on the west-central boundary, climbing a fairly open ridge toward 7,267-foot Saint Clair Mountain. Skiers must keep a wary eye out for avalanches, which can be serious on steep slopes and along the edges of upper basins.

HOW TO GET THERE: From Eureka drive 8 miles south on US 93 and turn northwest on Grave Creek Road (FR 114). After about 13 miles (at Drip Creek) the road number changes to 319, which is also the main road continuing to the left (north). About 11 miles farther Wolverine Flats Road (FR 7086) goes to the right over a bridge on Wigwam Creek. After about a mile take the short spur left to the trailhead for the Wolverine Trail 84. The other option is to continue on past FR 7086 to the end of FR 319 (28 miles from the highway) to the campgrounds and trailheads at both Big and Little Therriault lakes for trips into Bluebird Basin or up to Stahl Peak.

DAY HIKE OR OVERNIGHTER

Poorman Mountain
Distance: 8- to 10-mile loop.
Difficulty: Moderate.
Topo maps: Ksanka Peak-MT and Stahl Peak-MT.

On Trail 84 climb steadily through a spruce-fir forest for about 2.5 miles to Wolverine Lake. Here sits a small cabin with a big stove, which is popular with snowmobilers during winter. If the basin is still snowbound, which is often the case well into July, it may be hard to find Trail 92 leading up to the pass on the main divide south of Poorman Mountain. If you're up for a vigorous climb, bushwhack around the upper lake and claw your way straight up a steep, grassy avalanche chute to the top of the ridge. You'll meet Trail 88 on the backside of the ridge. Continue north for the easy walk to the top of 7,832-foot Poorman Mountain, some 2,200 feet above the trailhead. Here you'll find

WOLVERINE LAKES, IN THE NORTH END OF THE TEN LAKES COUNTRY.

the interesting remains of an old fire lookout. The views far to the north into Canada and every other direction are overwhelming. Continue north another 0.5 mile to Trail 89, which takes off to the right (east) on a prominent ridge. The trail is easy to miss, so keep a watchful eye. Just to the north of the junction sits a two-lake basin. A secluded campsite can be had by dropping 400 feet from the ridge to the upper lake. Back on Trail 89, a sheer 1,000-foot cliff plunges just east of the lake basin. Soon the trail overlooks clear, deep Rainbow Lake 700 feet below. The ridge is adorned with subalpine larch, whitebark pine, and a profusion of red Indian paintbrush. Head east for a couple more miles, eventually joining up with an old logging road (FR 7091) that ends up at the trailhead after about 1.5 miles.

North Fork
Wildlands

6

Location: Immediately west of Glacier National Park; 15 miles east of Eureka.
Size: 117,380 acres.
Administration: USDAFS—Flathead and Kootenai national forests.
Management status: Roadless non-wilderness, with some area allocated to future development in the forest plan.
Ecosystems: Northern Rocky Mountain coniferous forest-alpine meadow province, characterized by steep, glaciated overthrust mountains; Precambrian and soft sedimentary rocks; Douglas-fir forest type; numerous streams and some lakes at higher elevations.
Elevation range: 4,160 to 8,086 feet.
System trails: 146 miles.
Maximum core to perimeter distance: 4 miles.
Activities: Hiking, backpacking, horseback riding, fishing, cross-country skiing, mountain biking.
Modes of travel: foot, skis, horse, mountain bike .
Maps: 1991 Flathead National Forest Visitor Map and 1994 Kootenai National Forest Visitor Map; Tuchuck-MT; Mount Hefty-MT; Trail Creek-MT; Mount Thompson-Seton-MT; Red Meadow Lake-MT; and Whale Buttes-MT (1:24,000 topo maps).

OVERVIEW: The security and lush productivity of the northern Whitefish Mountains provide some of the most densely occupied grizzly bear habitat in North America. With an abundant prey base of white-tailed deer, elk, moose, and perhaps even the rare woodland caribou, the North Fork Wildlands are also being colonized by descendants of the famed "Magic Pack" of wolves, now reproducing on the U.S. side of the border as the Camas Pack.

Starting with the 13,720-acre Mount Hefty area on the British Columbia border, this northern trio of undeveloped lands is commonly known as the North Fork Wildlands. From 7,585 feet the north face of glaciated Mount Hefty drops into Canada. Steep canyons riddled with caves cut through gently rolling moraines. Huge, intense fires during the early part of the twentieth century account for today's dense forests of lodgepole pine and western larch, with whitebark pine and subalpine fir dominating above 6,000 feet.

Telltale signs of past glaciation are even more evident in the remote 19,820-acre Tuchuck roadless area, where cirque headwalls rise sharply above narrow canyons. Cutthroat swim the frigid waters of one of six tiny lakes near the head of Thoma Creek. Elk summer in moist basins studded with fir and subalpine larch.

6   NORTH FORK WILDLANDS

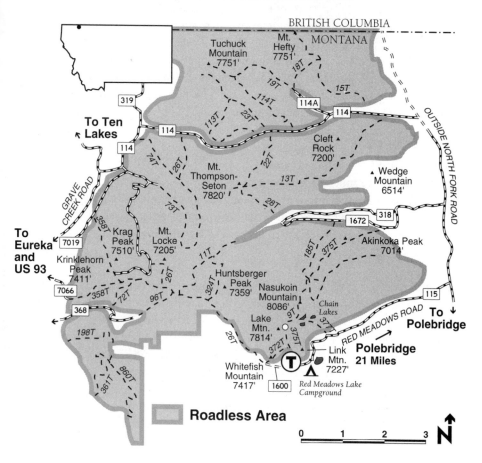

BRITISH COLUMBIA

MONTANA

Tuchuck Mountain ▲ 7751'

Mt. Hefty 7751'

18T

19T

15T

114T

231

113T

319

114A

114

To Ten Lakes

114

114

Cleft Rock ▲ 7200'

74T

26T

22T

▲ Wedge Mountain 6514'

Mt. Thompson-Seton 7820'

13T

28T

GRAVE CREEK ROAD

73T

1672

318

OUTSIDE NORTH FORK ROAD

To Eureka and US 93

358T

7019

Krag Peak 7510'

Mt. Locke 7205'

11T

185T

375T

Akinkoka Peak ▲ 7014'

Krinklehorn Peak 7411'

26T

Huntsberger Peak 7359'

324T

Nasukoin Mountain 8086'

7066

358T

72T

96T

Chain Lakes

115

368

26T

9T

3T

To Polebridge

198T

Lake Mtn. ▲ 7814'

375T

RED MEADOWS ROAD

860T

26T

372T

Link Mtn. ▲ 7227'

Polebridge 21 Miles

361T

Whitefish Mountain 7417'

1600

T

Red Meadows Lake Campground

Roadless Area

0   1   2   3   **N**

The Thompson-Seton wild country of some 83,840 acres is named for the famed turn-of-the-century naturalist. Jagged Krag and Krinklehorn peaks on the west side are dubbed for characters in Ernest Thompson-Seton's popular children's story, "Krag, the Kootenai Ram." The lobe of wild country south of heavily developed Whale Creek is dominated by the high point of the Whitefish Range, rounded 8,086-foot Nasukoin Mountain, which is encircled by fifteen sub-alpine lakes, including fish-filled Chain Lakes. The imposing east cliff face of 7,814-foot Lake Mountain towers above a sheltered lake still frozen in July. A prominent ridge to Nasukoin overlooks secret basins ideal for foraging grizzlies. Subalpine larch grows here in every form imaginable, from twisted and windblown to stately tall trees. Glacier lilies abound, as does another kind of lily—bear grass. Ridges and peaks possess the split personality of being rounded on one side and broken into cliff faces on the other. And, always, there is the profound presence of Glacier National Park to the east. The lower, more subdued crests of these wildlands are a pleasing contrast to their higher, more rugged neighbors across the North Fork of the Flathead River.

RECREATIONAL USES: The North Fork wildlands are extremely remote, particularly to the north, adjacent to British Columbia. The lower, less jagged North Fork country of the Whitefish Range is overshadowed by its well-known next door neighbor—Glacier National Park. As such, recreational use is light, consisting mostly of fall big-game hunting with some hiking and horseback day trips. On the north the Mount Hefty country has at least four known caves with some limited spelunking possibilities. To the southwest near Tuchuck Mountain lie six small lakes, only one of which contains trout. To the south the larger Thompson-Seton/Nasukoin roadless unit shows strong evidence of past glaciation with about fifteen high mountain lakes and tarns, including the Chain Lakes. Several of these lakes support a good trout fishery. Some of the streams, such as Whale Creek, are important for the endangered bull trout. A segment of the Whitefish Divide trail from Mount Young south to Meadow Creek Road has been designated a National Recreation Trail. During winter plowed road access to the higher reaches of the roadless area is nonexistent. However, the North Fork Road is kept open and can provide reasonable skier access to the Trail Creek Road on up into the Mount Hefty country, and other drainages to the south, such as Moose Creek, which lead into the higher unroaded basins.

HOW TO GET THERE: From Columbia Falls go north on the North Fork Road 486 about 36 miles (5 miles past Polebridge) to Red Meadow Lake Road (FR 115). Proceed some 15 miles up FR 115 to Red Meadow Lake Campground. Cross the main Whitefish Range divide just beyond the lake and either drive a rough 1-mile road to the right or hike the distance to the beginning of Trail 372. This climbs quickly to Trail 375. The Whitefish Divide National Recreation Trail 26 also takes off from this point.

LOOKING NORTH FROM LAKE MOUNTAIN TOWARD NASUKOIN MOUNTAIN IN
THE NORTH FORK WILDLANDS.

DAY HIKE

Nasukoin Mountain
Distance: 10 miles-out-and-back.
Difficulty: Moderately strenuous.
Topo map: Red Meadow Lake-MT.

Begin on Trail 372 switchbacking 600 feet up to the saddle-ridge above Link Lake. For a short side trip drop a couple of hundred feet to Link Lake at 6,436 fee and fish a while. On the way back take a right-hand turn on the junction to Trail 375 about 500 feet from the southwest end of the lake. If you stay on the ridge the trail north to Lake Mountain can be hard to find. Simply head up the bear grass ridge above the saddle overlooking Link Lake and you will soon come to Trail 375. Another 1.5 miles of switchbacks leads to the top of 7,814-foot Lake Mountain—a prominent open ridge of cliffs rising above a lake at 7,164 feet that is often still frozen into mid-July. This chain-of-lakes country is largely a series of high ridges surrounded by logging roads and old clearcuts. The roads are gated for grizzly bear security. An up-and-down (mostly up), 3-mile ridge walk from Lake Mountain north to 8,086-foot Nasukoin Mountain provides intimate views into several secluded basins. Cliffs adorn the west face of the ridge with snow cornices on the east side well into summer. The trail veers off the south summit of Nasukoin and drops along a narrow ridge to the remnants of an old lookout on the northeast summit. Below the north slope lies a hanging valley with a pure stand of subalpine larch. The profound presence of Glacier National Park's Livingston Range rises to the east. Nasukoin is a large, open mountain, almost bald, sitting by itself as the southern sentinel of the North Fork. Most of the surrounding ridges and peaks are rounded but they still possess a rough-hewn look. The total elevation gain of 2,074 feet from the trailhead to Nasukoin is well distributed throughout much of the 5-mile distance.

Glacier National Park
Wilderness
Complex

7

Location: 2 miles west of East Glacier; 22 miles northeast of Kalispell.
Size: 1,051,500 acres in four roadless units.
Administration: National Park Service—Glacier National Park; Blackfeet Indian Reservation.
Management status: National park and contiguous unclassified tribal lands.
Ecosystems: West side—Northern Rocky Mountain coniferous forest-alpine meadow province, characterized by steep, glaciated overthrust mountains with sharp alpine ridges and cirques at higher elevations; Precambrian metasedimentary and soft sedimentary rocks and glacial deposits; Douglas-fir forest type; deeply incised streams and numerous lakes.
East side—Middle Rocky Mountain steppe-coniferous forest-alpine meadow province, characterized by glaciated mountains with limestone scarps and ridges interspersed with intermountain basins; Douglas-fir and western spruce-fir forest types in association with aspen groves, limber pine, and foothills prairie; with numerous lakes and perennial streams.
Elevation range: 3,200 to 10,446 feet.
System trails: 750 miles.
Maximum core to perimeter distance: 12 miles.
Activities: Hiking, backpacking, mountaineering, horseback riding, cross-country skiing, floating (raft, canoe, kayak), fishing.
Modes of travel: Foot, horse, skis, boat.
Maps: 1968 USGS Glacier National Park 1:100,000 scale 80-foot contour map (See Appendix D for a listing of the 44 1:24,000 topo maps covering the complex.)

OVERVIEW: Glacier National Park is America's premier wilderness park, with 99.3 percent of its 1,013,100 acres still wild in four roadless units. The Continental Divide separates Glacier's spectacular backcountry into two nearly equal parts, and is itself bisected by a road in only one place, the Going-to-the-Sun Highway at Logan Pass. This "land of shining mountains" was molded by fire, torrential rains, internal pressures, and great continental ice sheets to produce a million wild acres dotted with more than two hundred gem-like tarns, elongated lakes, countless waterfalls, a startling vertical relief of more than 1 mile in some valleys, and broad U-shaped drainages. The grinding rivers of ice that melted some 10,000 years ago left an ongoing record of the forces of

7A GLACIER NATIONAL PARK WILDERNESS COMPLEX

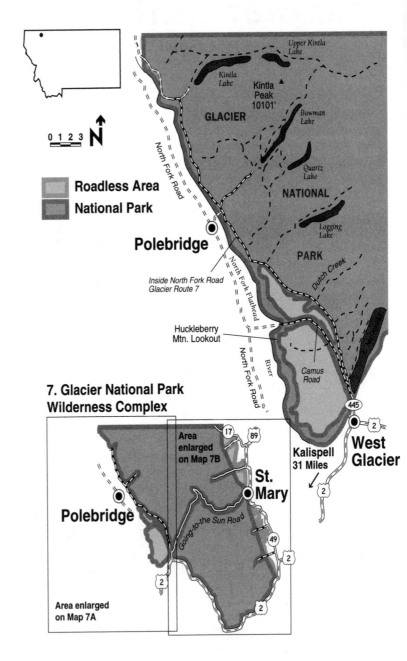

N

0 1 2 3

Roadless Area

National Park

Upper Kintla Lake

Kintla Lake

Kintla Peak 10101'

GLACIER

Bowman Lake

North Fork Road

Quartz Lake

NATIONAL

Logging Lake

Polebridge

PARK

Dutch Creek

North Fork Flathead

Inside North Fork Road
Glacier Route 7

Huckleberry
Mtn. Lookout

North Fork

River

Camus Road

North Fork Road

7. Glacier National Park
Wilderness Complex

Area
enlarged
on Map 7B

17

89

Kalispell
31 Miles

445

2

West
Glacier

Polebridge

St.
Mary

2

Going-to-the Sun Road

49

2

2

Area enlarged
on Map 7A

2

7B GLACIER NATIONAL PARK WILDERNESS COMPLEX

B.C.

ALBERTA
MONTANA

To Port of
Piegan

Waterton
Lake

Mt.
Cleveland
10438'

114

17

Mt.
Merritt
10004'

Babb

Lake
Sherburne

Many Glacier Road

89

Mt. Siyeh
10009'

St.
Mary
Lake

St. Mary

Cut Bank
Creek Road

Going-to-the-Sun Road

East
Glacier
21 Miles

CD Tr.

Red Eagle Lake Tr.

CD

Triple
Divide
Pass
Trail

T

Gunsight Pass Tr.

CD

Triple
Divide
Peak
7397'

Two
Medicine
Road

49

Mt. Jackson
10052'

West
Glacier

CD

Cut Bank
Creek
Trail

East
Glacier

Nyack Creek Tr.

445

L. McDonald

Dutch Creek

2

Kalispell
31 Miles

Mt. Stimson
10182'

2

To
Browning

Coal Creek Tr.

0 1 2 3 N

Fielding - Coal

Creek

2

Ole Creek Tr.

Marias
Pass

MISCHIEF AT TRIPLE DIVIDE PASS.

erosion and glaciation on sedimentary rock. These thick Precambrian formations appear as broad bands of greens and reds on the landscape.

Upon this jagged and varied land live some 1,200 plant species, at least 200
kinds of birds, and around 60 species of mammals. The grizzly and wolf require the security of Glacier's rugged terrain, dense vegetation, and remoteness.
From arctic ice and snow along the Great Divide backcountry travelers can
descend into alpine tundra, primeval coniferous forest, deciduous forest and,
finally, to grassland. These five undisturbed life zones account for the variety
of flora and fauna.

North Glacier is the largest of the four wild areas at 575,000 acres, which
includes about 30,000 acres along the eastern slopes of the Lewis Range on the
Blackfeet Reservation. This untamed region extends into Canada's Waterton
Lakes National Park as the most remote country in Glacier. The north end is
crowned by the park's highest point—10,448-foot Mount Cleveland. With a rise
of 6,700 feet in only 4 miles, the impressive north face of Cleveland has the steepest vertical ascent in all of Montana's wildlands. Some of the lightning-caused
1988 Red Bench fire in the North Fork of the Flathead burned intensely into the
Quartz-Logging Creek region of North Glacier, presenting an excellent opportunity to learn about the ecological effects of fire in a wilderness setting.

The 430,000-acre South Glacier roadless area includes about 15,000 acres
of foothill/aspen parklands on the Blackfeet Reservation. This 25-by-35-mile
expanse is a wonderland of alpine lakes and lofty peaks, including fabled Triple

Divide Peak, which gives birth to three ocean watersheds: the Pacific, the Atlantic, and Hudson Bay.

The Apgar Mountains contain some of Glacier's best grizzly habitat within a 33,000-acre roadless enclave between the North Fork of the Flathead and Camas Creek Road. Immediately north is the linear 13,500-acre Camas Creek roadless area, which stretches from Apgar to above Logging Creek.

It is ironic, but I think fortunate, that this million-acre wilderness is so formidable that more than 98 percent of park visitors are content to view it from a comfortable distance as they motor over Logan Pass.

RECREATIONAL USES: Glacier contains some of the most stunning and overpowering glaciated mountainscape on the continent. With all of this wild magnificence comes superlative opportunities for hiking, backpacking, mountaineering, camping, and fishing. But there is a price for paradise. To help protect this wild beauty—and the visitors themselves—anyone wishing to camp overnight must obtain a free backcountry permit from any of the visitor centers or ranger stations in the park. The permit must be obtained in person on a first-come basis no more than 24 hours in advance. It is good only for the designated campsites and dates specified with no changes in the itinerary allowed. When you get your permit, the ranger will let you know of any reported bear activity, trail conditions, and applicable regulations. Fires can be built but only in the fireplaces provided at the campsites. Be sure to review "The Backcountry Camping Guide," a digest of camping regulations.

Day hikers don't need a permit. However, if you plan off-trail hiking and mountaineering, it's advisable to register first at a visitor center or ranger station. Most of the climbing in Glacier involves scrambling. The exposed sedimentary rock is often loose and crumbling, so special care and skill are needed.

The use of stock is not allowed in some portions of the park. Indeed, some of the trails are physically impassable to stock. Grazing of stock is not permitted in Glacier, so stock users must pack in feed. Consult the free brochure, "Public Stock Use," then check the local situation at the closest visitor center or ranger station. Regularly scheduled, guided horseback day trips leave from Many Glacier, Lake McDonald Lodge, and Apgar.

Trails are normally open for travel by mid-June, but some of the higher passes may be snowbound into late July. From December through April backcountry travel requires skis or snowshoes. Find out about avalanche conditions and special camping regulations before setting out and be sure to check back in with the Park Service upon your return. Quality winter excursions abound. For example, enjoyable low-elevation skiing can be had along the North Fork of the Flathead around Polebridge, which is about 35 miles north of Columbia Falls on the North Fork Road. Listen for the haunting howls of the wolves that have colonized the North Fork during the past decade. Another

MEDICINE GRIZZLY LAKE FROM TRIPLE DIVIDE PEAK.

enjoyable day ski tour is along the Glacier National Park Autumn Creek Trail, which provides several out-and-back or loop possibilities between Marias Pass and the False Summit on US 2 bordering the south end of the park.

HOW TO GET THERE: Glacier's main entrances are accessible from US 2 about 15 miles northeast of Columbia Falls, or from US 89 between Browning and the Canadian border. For the hike described below, head north from US 2 at East Glacier on MT 49. Drive about 17 miles north then 4 miles west on Cutbank Creek Road, passing the Cutbank Ranger Station to the parking area/trailhead.

DAY HIKE OR OVERNIGHTER

Triple Divide Peak
Distance: 15 miles round-trip.
Difficulty: Moderately strenuous.
Topo maps: Mount Stimson-MT and Cutbank Pass-MT.

The Cutbank Creek valley is one of the more lightly visited drainages in Glacier National Park, but with waterfalls cascading down red argillite mountains and hanging lake-filled cirques it is truly one of the more scenic. After crossing meadows below 5,000 feet the trail gradually climbs through an open lodgepole pine/Douglas-fir forest. Watch for bighorn sheep near the northern cliff faces of 8,350-foot Bad Marriage Mountain. Four miles up take the Triple Divide Pass trail to the right. If you're planning to spend the night at the nearby Atlantic Creek campground hang your gear on the cache pole just east of the trail junction. The trail climbs steadily and easily to the west along the north wall of the Atlantic Creek drainage for about 3 miles to Triple Divide Pass. This rock-strewn notch sits beneath the imposing northeast ridge of 8,020-foot Triple Divide Peak. The summit can be reached by way of a rock scramble south across steep talus to the second couloir above the headwall of Atlantic Creek. Work your way up the couloir to a level saddle for the final easy walk up the south slope to the top, which rises 623 feet above the pass. Triple Divide Peak is one of only two points along the entire hemispheric Continental Divide that sheds water into three distant oceans. Treat yourself to a slow 360-degree turn. Hudson Bay Creek flows north to the Saskatchewan-Nelson River system and on to the Arctic Ocean. Atlantic Creek runs to the east where it eventually mixes with the Missouri en route to the Atlantic Ocean. To the southwest tiny Pacific Creek is part of the mighty Columbia River, which reaches the Pacific.

This 15-mile round-trip is a superb sample of South Glacier's Continental Divide country as well as a visit to what is arguably the most significant topographic feature in the park.

Bob Marshall
Wilderness
Complex

Location: Along the Continental Divide south of Glacier National Park, centrally located between Kalispell, Great Falls, Missoula, and Helena.

Size: 2,476,328 acres.

Administration: USDAFS—Flathead, Lewis & Clark, Lolo, and Helena national forests; BLM-Butte District; Montana Department of Fish, Wildlife & Parks; and private (The Nature Conservancy and Boone & Crockett Club).

Management status: Wilderness (1,535,352 acres); BLM Wilderness Study Areas; three MDFWP Wildlife Management Areas; two private nature preserves; roadless non-wilderness, some of which may be allocated to future resource development.

Ecosystems: West side—Northern Rocky Mountain coniferous forest-alpine meadow province, characterized by steep, glaciated overthrust mountains with sharp alpine ridges and cirques at higher elevations along with broad valleys along main watercourses; Precambrian metasedimentary and soft sedimentary rocks and glacial deposits; Douglas-fir forest type; and moderately incised streams with some lakes, mostly at higher elevations.

East side—Middle Rocky Mountain steppe-coniferous forest-alpine meadow province, characterized by glaciated mountains with limestone scarps and ridges interspersed with intermountain basins; Douglas fir and western spruce-fir forest types in association with aspen groves, limber pine, and foothills prairie; and numerous perennial streams.

Elevation range: 3,936 to 9,411 feet.

System trails: 3,200 miles plus.

Maximum core to perimeter distance: 38 miles.

Activities: Hiking, backpacking, mountaineering, horseback riding, cross-country skiing, fishing.

Modes of travel: Foot, skis, horseback.

Maps: 1990 Bob Marshall Complex Map-5/8"/mile contour; 1991 Flathead Forest Visitor Map; 1988 Lewis & Clark Forest Visitor Map; 1994 Lolo Forest Visitor Map; and 1991 Helena Forest Visitor Map. (Note: see overview map for topographic map titles and locations along with Appendix D for a complete listing of the 102 topo maps covering the complex).

OVERVIEW: The most widely accepted sacred ground in Montana is the revered Bob Marshall country, flagship of our nation's Wilderness "fleet." Affectionately dubbed "the Bob," this largest of Montana's wildlands is an unroaded expanse of nearly 2.5 million acres. The contiguous Great Bear, Bob Marshall,

8   BOB MARSHALL WILDERNESS COMPLEX

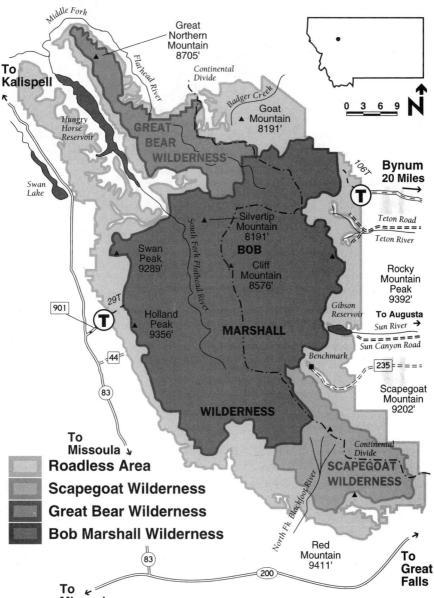

EAST TO PINE BUTTE ON THE NATURE CONSERVANCY'S PINE BUTTE
PRESERVE—SANCTUARY FOR THE LAST OF THE PLAINS GRIZZLY.

and Scapegoat Wilderness areas make up the 1.5 million-acre core of the complex that has been formally classified as Wilderness. The remaining 1 million acres encircle the core like a giant horseshoe. These peripheral wildlands along the west-side Swan Face and east-side Rocky Mountain Front contain the wildest and least visited country in the ecosystem. More than 140 miles without a road separate Marias Pass on the north from Rogers Pass on the south, making the center of the Bob by far the most remote location in Montana in terms of distance from the nearest road—nearly 40 miles.

Great Bear Wilderness: This 286,700-acre Wilderness encompasses the entire upper drainage of the Middle Fork Flathead River from the Continental Divide west to the rugged Flathead Range. Knife ridges along the divide give way to densely forested mountainsides, meadows, and open river-bottom parks. Glaciers created U-shaped valleys and cirques. As the surging lifeline of this wilderness watershed, the Middle Fork is Montana's wildest river. The stream changes moods continually, from placid pools so clear that the spots can be counted on the backs of native cutthroat to churning rushes of whitewater hellbent for the Pacific.

Bob Marshall Wilderness: The most remote reaches of this 1,009,356-acre wilderness lie along the serpentine spine of the Great Divide—the heart of which is the fabled Chinese Wall. This imposing limestone precipice, towering

1,000 feet for 13 miles, is the soaring backdrop for the annual fall pageant of bugling bull elk competing for their harems. Moist Pacific maritime weather on the west side—with lush, diverse forest—changes markedly to drier, more open country to the east. The vast east-side Sun River drainage includes a 200,000-acre Wilderness game preserve that the Montana legislature closed to hunting in 1913 to maintain the aboriginal Sun River elk herd of some 3,000 head. Here is the last great stronghold of the silvertip grizzly, that threatened symbol of true wilderness.

Although comprised mainly of alternating river valleys and north-south mountain ranges, the Bob also contains more than one hundred lakes, the largest of which is 4.5-mile-long Big Salmon. Other key features include the trailless Flathead Alps, the 20-mile long anticline of the remote White River, and the northern sentinel of 8,890-foot Silvertip Mountain—site of one of the deepest known cave systems.

Scapegoat Wilderness: The highest point on the Continental Divide within the Bob Marshall country is massive 9,202-foot Scapegoat Mountain, the majestic centerpiece of this 239,296-acre Wilderness. The awe-inspiring 1,000-foot limestone cliffs of Scapegoat, covering nearly 4 miles along the east face of the massif, are a southern extension of the Chinese Wall.

The Rocky Mountain Front: Here the dramatic transition from mountains to plains can be seen along an overpowering sweep of limestone scarps from Badger-Two Medicine south to Falls Creek-Silver King. On the north end, the Badger-Two Medicine is a vital biological corridor for wildlife between Glacier Park, the Great Bear and Bob Marshall Wilderness areas, and the high plains of the Blackfeet Indian Reservation. East-flowing Badger Creek is guarded by steep massifs of limestone dissected by narrow canyons. A resurgence in the practice of traditional Blackfeet religion depends on the pristine quality of the Badger-Two Medicine.

In the remote fens and foothills below the Teton River high peaks, the plains grizzly makes its last stand on the continent. The Teton Peaks are the loftiest pinnacles on the Front. Formed by thrust faults with steep east faces and gentle west slopes, these mountains are cut by a jumble of valleys and streams. Both grizzlies and mountain goats dwell on the rocky slopes of impressive 9,392-foot Rocky Mountain Peak.

To the south, the Deep Creek portion of the Front harbors the central winter range of the largest native herd of bighorn sheep in the Lower Forty-eight. Open south-facing gulches provide winter forage for migrating Sun River elk and mule deer. To the south of the Sun River, the Renshaw country consists of three major landforms. Patrick's Basin drains north through a wide, forested basin. Next, the high, grassy Fairview-Ford Creek plateau is a mix of winter and spring habitat for elk and bighorns. Third, the South Fork of the Sun is the

A LLAMA PARTY ENTERS "THE BOB" AT HEADQUARTERS PASS.

most popular east-side route to the Bob. The imposing east face of 8,246-foot Fairview Mountain is seen far out on the plains.

On the southern end of the Front the landscape rises in majesty to the alpine summits of Crown and Steamboat mountains. Falls Creek is the largest unprotected pristine watershed on the Front south of the Badger-Two Medicine. Born on Scapegoat Mountain, the wild Dearborn River cuts a steep-walled gorge through Devil's Glen. Rapids alternate with deep emerald pools before leveling out into a wide rocky valley.

Southern Reaches: The southern corner of the complex is dominated by the highest peak in the Bob Marshall Country—9,411-foot Red Mountain, which supports an unusual community of whitebark and limber pine growing together at 8,000 feet. Two major drainages flow south to the Big Blackfoot River through deep canyons and wide forested valleys—Monture Creek and the North Fork of the Blackfoot. The North Fork is where the 250,000-acre Canyon Creek fire of 1988 reached its greatest intensity. In contrast, the lengthy Monture Valley is carpeted with green forest from giant old-growth larch to gnarled whitebark pine at the head of alpine amphitheaters. This is the major elk migration corridor from the Bob to the Clearwater winter range.

Swan Front/Swan Crest: The Swan Range is the formidable western guardian of the Bob, extending 100 miles from the Blackfoot Valley north to 7,234-foot

Columbia Mountain near Glacier National Park's west entrance. A once-great inland sea left fossils along the top of the east-leaning Swans. From its treeless alpine crest to its foothold in the forested Swan Valley a vertical mile below, the Swan Face is an ecological whole with five major life zones: high peaks and alpine basins; intermediate and hanging valleys; canyon country; ridge-valley faces; and the main Lion Creek Canyon. Lion Creek is the longest undisturbed drainage in the Swan Range. Wide hanging valleys are separated by cascades plummeting over great rock barriers. The largest hanging valleys are adorned with cathedral-like stands of ancient giant cedars. Two great waterfalls with spellbinding power and height are closed in by cliffs.

The spectacular Alpine Trail winds along the unbroken crest of the Swan. En route, it passes through Jewel Basin. The Jewel is a treasure of twenty-eight sparkling high lakes encircled by low rocky mountains with bubbly streams, lush meadows, and open subalpine forest.

RECREATIONAL USES: Summer is the major season of use in the Bob Marshall Country, with July being the peak month. From the September 15 early rifle season on, big-game hunting becomes the most popular recreational activity west of the Continental Divide. About 30 percent of the hunters go with one of the fifty-five professional outfitters who operate in the complex. Elk is by far the most popular big-game species. Hunting is not allowed in the 200,000-acre Sun River Game Preserve, which extends from the North Fork of the Sun River, west to the Continental Divide. The South and Middle forks of the Flathead River, along with the main forks of the Sun River and their major stream and lake tributaries, offer excellent fishing for native cutthroat trout.

The Bob is classic horse country because of its vastness, relatively gentle terrain, and wide mid-elevation river valleys with abundant forage for grazing. It is probably one of the few Wildernesses where horse users still outnumber hikers and backpackers. The Forest Service has imposed only the minimum amount of regulations to safeguard wilderness values. These include a maximum party size of fifteen people with no more than thirty-five head of stock and a fourteen-day limit on camping in any one location within any forty-five-day period. Heavily used campsites are sometimes closed for natural restoration. For example, the heads of Moose and Rock creeks below the Chinese Wall are closed to camping and grazing to rehabilitate fragile alpine meadows. Camping with stock and grazing is prohibited within 500 feet of Bear Lake, My Lake, and Lake Levale.

Following is a summation of the more heavily visited areas and trails by subregion within the Bob Marshall complex:

Bob Marshall West of the Divide—Use is heaviest east of Holland Lake. A 1982 Wilderness user survey at forty-eight trailheads revealed that the seven most used trailheads had half of all the use. About 90 percent of the visits began at the most used half of the trailheads and many of the entry points received no recorded use from the 750 parties sampled in the study. Ironically, the most lightly used areas are often close to trailheads, whereas some of the most heavily visited locations are among the most remote, such as Big Prairie on the South Fork of the Flathead.

The most heavily used trails and locations are:
Gordon Creek Trail 35 down to the South Fork Flathead River Trail 80, and from there all the way down to the northern wilderness boundary at Meadow Creek;
Big Salmon Creek Trail 110 to its junction with the South Fork Trail 80;
Gorge Creek Trail 218;
Sunburst Lake Trail 693;
Black Bear area;
Salmon Forks;
Pendant Creek Trail 457;
Big Prairie;
Youngs Creek Trail 141;
Danaher Trail 126;
White River Trail 112;
Bowl Creek Trail 324;
Gateway Creek Trail 322;
and Strawberry Creek Trail 161.

Bob Marshall East of the Divide—From north to south, the more heavily used trails and locations are:
South Fork Birch Creek Trail 105;
West Fork Teton Trail 114;
North Fork Sun River Trail 201 from Gibson Reservoir upstream to Sun River Pass;
Headquarters Pass Trail 165 from the South Fork of the Teton River to Gates Park;
Trail 130 from Gates Park to the Chinese Wall and then north along Trail 175 to Open Creek;
Rock Creek Trail 111 to the Chinese Wall and then south to Moose Creek;
Moose Creek Trail 131;
West Fork Sun River Trail 203 from Moose Creek down to the South Fork of the Sun;
White River Pass Trail 211;
Bear Creek Trail 222;
and the entire length of the South Fork Sun River Trail 202 from Medicine Springs south to Benchmark.

The greatest visitation is below the Chinese Wall and along the South Fork of the Sun River. The most heavily used trailheads into the east side of the Bob are the West Fork Teton; South Fork Teton and Gibson Reservoir; with the most use of all fanning out from the major jumping off point of Benchmark, where two large end-of-the-road campgrounds and stock facilities accommodate large numbers of visitors.

Great Bear—Here the most heavily used trails and areas are:
Morrison Creek Trail 154;
Schafer Creek Trail 327;
The extremely high-use Schafer Meadows, which contains a backcountry landing strip;
Big River Trail 155 (especially below Schafer);
Spruce Park on the Middle Fork;
Granite Creek Trail 156;
and Flotilla Lake.

Rafting the wild Middle Fork of the Flathead is best from mid-July to mid-August, when good weather coincides with adequate flows. By late summer, low water may dictate portaging some stretches. Only the skilled expert should attempt to float the Middle Fork during peak runoff in June. The wildest whitewater boils in the canyon below Spruce Park, where it drops an average of 41 feet per mile. Most of the float parties put in at Schafer, after either flying or packing in. Schafer is the only historic aircraft landing field within the complex open to the public.

One of the more challenging climbs is an ascent of the rooftop of the Great Bear—8,705-foot Great Northern Mountain in the northwest panhandle of the Wilderness. The most popular route takes off from the Hungry Horse Road (FR 38) and FR 1048 between Lost Mare and Hungry Horse creeks on a ridge leading up to the northwest summit ridge. Every year a few intrepid souls attempt an extended ski tour over the Continental Divide and all the way down the Middle Fork to US 2. In places avalanche danger is extreme, particularly on the south-facing slopes of Mount Bradley. A party of no less than four experienced, well-equipped backcountry skiers is strongly recommended for such an expedition.

Scapegoat—The most heavily used trails leading out from Benchmark are the Hoadley Reef Trail 226 and Straight Creek Trail 212. To the south the scenic Dearborn River Trail 206 is gaining in popularity. Little wonder. The Lower Dearborn contains a good trout population, and the deep emerald pools in Devil's Glen 3 miles up are spellbinding. On the southeast corner the mainline trails are:

MOUNT FIELD IN THE BIRCH CREEK COUNTRY, NORTHEAST CORNER OF THE BOB MARSHALL WILDERNESS.

Heart Lake/East Fork Trail 481;
Landers Fork Trail 479;
Bighorn Creek Trail 438;
and Arrastra Creek Trail 482.

Hitching rails, stock loading ramps, and limited parking exist at the Indian Meadows, Arrastra Creek, Dry Creek, and Wildcat trailheads. Heart Lake, Parker Lake, and Twin Lakes receive heavy visitation. These lakes are not recommended for overnight horse use due to a lack of available forage. Bighorn, Webb, and Meadow lakes receive somewhat less use, but of these, only Webb and Meadow lakes have limited forage for grazing.

On the southwest end the heaviest use by far takes place on the Hobnail Tom Trail 32 up the North Fork of the Blackfoot River. More moderately used trails include Trail 481 from the North Fork cabin east to the East Fork of the Blackfoot and the Dry Fork Trail 31 up to the almost unnoticeable Dry Fork/Flathead Divide, the easiest pass in the complex. Heavily used campsites that should be avoided include Carmichael Cabin, a meadow near the mouth of Canyon Creek (close to where a bolt of lightning started the monumental 1988 Canyon Creek fire); a meadow on the Dry Fork near the mouth of Cabin Creek; the North Fork cabin; and where the East Fork joins the North Fork of the Blackfoot River.

Despite restoration closures, restrictions, and heavy-use areas, this vast expanse of wild country contains abundant places in which to enjoy secluded, high-quality wilderness outings, sometimes even within the heavily used sites and trails mentioned above. The key is to go gently on the land, remaining sensitive to wildlife and to other wilderness visitors.

Rocky Mountain Front (east side)—If you can handle the ever-present wind, the Front offers a wide variety of early season hikes and overnighters during a time when the higher snowbound country remains mostly inaccessible. May and June are perfect for wildflower hikes, birding, wildlife viewing, and rambling through a vast, uncluttered landscape. Two nationally significant trail systems wind through the Badger-Two Medicine portion of the Front just south of Glacier National Park. The Two Medicine-Elk Calf Mountain National Recreation trail is a loop starting and ending at Summit Campground. The other is the Continental Divide National Scenic Trail, which is shown on the Bob Marshall complex map. Other popular though lightly used trails in the Badger include:

Whiterock Trail 102;
North Badger Trail 103;
South Badger Trail 104;
North Fork Birch Creek Trail 121;
Elbow Creek Trail 145;
and Muskrat Creek Trail 147.

Much of the Front is wilder and less used than a lot of the adjacent designated Wilderness. An exception is Our Lake in the South Fork Teton drainage. Because of its classic alpine beauty, abundance of mountain goats, and accessibility (only 3 miles from the South Fork trailhead), the lake is the most popular day-use destination on the entire Front. Nearby Rocky Mountain Peak at 9,392 feet is the apex of the Front Range and the second highest point in the complex. The summit is well worth a rock scramble up its northeast ridge, leaving South Fork Teton Trail 165 above the waterfalls about 2 miles above the trailhead.

To the south, the gravel road to Sun River Canyon, paved from the Forest Service boundary, is kept open year-round, providing access for ski touring, showshoeing, hiking, and horseback riding. Trails venture north from the Sun River up Hannan, Blacktail, and Mortimer gulches. Both Hannan and Blacktail have gently sloping valleys in their lower reaches with steeper gradients in the upper 2 miles. Mortimer and Big George drop more sharply to Gibson Reservoir. Other than the hard-to-find Big George Trail 251, the trails are generally well maintained. Some have gut-busting ascents, such as the final 0.25-mile, 800-foot climb up Blacktail Gulch Trail 220 to 7,600-foot Cabin Creek Pass on the Bob Marshall Wilderness boundary.

EAR MOUNTAIN RISES ABOVE THE PLAINS ON THE EAST SIDE OF THE BOB
MARSHALL WILDERNESS COMPLEX.

The Swan Face (west side)—Most of the recreational use of the Swan Face
occurs during fall when hunting parties take packstrings up the steep trails to
hunting camps in the Bob. Summer day tripping and overnight camping are
also popular at a half dozen high lake basins, which have been stocked with
cutthroat trout. The Swan Range gets lots of moisture, even during summer,
and thunderstorms are common. Steep, rugged terrain, combined with rapid
changes in the weather, can lead to challenging and sometimes hazardous
mountaineering. In places the climbing rock is rotten and unstable, adding yet
another dimension of danger. Swan Peak at 9,289 feet and Holland Peak at
9,356 feet are adorned with small glaciers. Strenuous non-technical routes are
available on each of these sentinels of the Swan. Although tricky in spots, most
of the Swan Crest can be hiked without difficulty. The views from anywhere
along the divide into the Bob and across the Swan Valley to the Missions are
breathtaking. The easiest entry to the crest is from the Napa Point Trail 31
where some 3,000 feet are gained by automobile on the 12-mile FR 10505. A
3-mile, up-and-down ridgetop trail leads to Inspiration Pass on the main divide,
about 6 miles north of glaciated Swan Peak.

HOW TO GET THERE: *Blackleaf-Dupuyer*—From Bynum on US 89 (15 miles north
of Choteau) go 20 miles west on Blackleaf Road to the trailhead at road's end just
inside the national forest boundary at the outer edge of Blackleaf Canyon.

Smith Creek—From Condon, on MT 83, take FR 901, which heads north-west. Continue on FR 901 about 3 miles to FR 9762. Turn right on FR 9762 and go 1.5 miles to the Smith Creek trailhead for Trail 29.

EAST-SIDE DAY HIKE OR OVERNIGHTER

Blackleaf Canyon - Volcano Reef
Distance: 4 to 5 miles out-and-back or a 7-mile loop.
Difficulty: Easy to moderate.
Topo map: Volcano Reef-MT.

From the trailhead take Blackleaf Trail 106 west through the narrow lime-stone mouth of formidable Blackleaf Canyon. Hold onto your hat. This is one of the windiest places along the entire 110-mile sweep of the Front! As you enter the broad valley of the Blackleaf you'll be overwhelmed by the imposing sheer escarpments of Mounts Frazier and Werner, which define the crest of the Rocky Mountain Front Range. After about 1.5 miles look carefully for the faint Dupuyer Trail 153, which heads north up an open slope. Another 1.5 miles and 900-foot gain in elevation brings you to an open saddle between Blackleaf and Dupuyer creeks. To reach Volcano Reef head east, first up a small hill and then down to a flat that climbs gradually to a wide plateau over-looking the reef and, beyond, the northern plains. Hike in either direction along the rolling, gently rising plateau above limestone cliffs and forests of Douglas-fir and limber pine.

To complete the 7-mile loop back to the trailhead go south to the 6,892-foot high point of Volcano Reef. From there angle downslope for the next mile, losing about 1,200 feet, to the bottom of Blackleaf just above the canyon en-trance. Even during winter it is often possible to drive the windswept Blackleaf Road within 1 or 2 miles of the trailhead. However, the adjacent State of Montana Blackleaf Wildlife Management Area is closed to off-road travel from December 1 to May 15 to protect wintering wildlife.

Having explored the options for an enjoyable out-and-back hike into the canyon or a loop climb to Volcano Reef, a third choice would be to continue north on Trail 153 to the South Fork of Dupuyer Creek where the lightly used trail intercepts a scenic campsite. This is classic "Front of the Front" country with thick patches of limber pine and Douglas-fir interspersed with aspen-grass parklands. As you drive to the trailhead look for evidence of past natural gas drilling. Despite world-class wildlife and wilderness values, the Bureau of Land Management has long advocated full-field gas development in Blackleaf, and a final decision is pending.

WEST-SIDE OVERNIGHTER

Smith Creek Pass

Distance: 10 miles out-and-back.
Difficulty: Moderate.
Topo map: Holland Peak-MT.

Trail 29 is a well-graded switchback trail designed for the horses and packstock that frequent this route in the fall. A total of 3,600 feet is gained over a distance of 5 miles to Smith Creek Pass, which straddles the Swan Crest. About 2 miles of the lower trail switchback up through old, private-land timber cuts before reaching the forest primeval. Just below the pass the trail enters an alpine hanging valley surrounded by the rocky pinnacles of the Swan divide. There are several good camping spots here and some just over the pass at a small lake within the Bob Marshall Wilderness.

Either location would make an ideal base from which to explore this segment of the Swan Range. For starters, climb to the pass and then go southward off trail along the crest, gaining about 750 feet to the summit of 8,709-foot Cooney Mountain. The peak is a walk-up, but watch for loose, crumbly rock in the final 100 feet to the top. Another enjoyable excursion is to scramble along the divide north for 1 mile or so and then take a prominent ridge another mile west to the old lookout site of 8,456-foot Condon Mountain.

Mission Mountains
Wilderness Complex

9

Location: 4 miles east of Ronan and 12 miles west/northwest of Seeley Lake.
Size: 174,377 acres.
Administration: Confederated Salish & Kootenai tribes (west) and USDAFS-Flathead National Forest (east).
Management status: Tribal and national forest Wilderness with some contiguous non-wilderness roadless land.
Ecosystems: Northern Rocky Mountain coniferous forest-alpine meadow province, characterized by steep, glaciated overthrust mountains with sharp alpine ridges and cirques at higher elevations; Precambrian metasedimentary and soft sedimentary rocks and glacial deposits; Douglas-fir forest type; many moderately to deeply incised streams and high lakes.
Elevation range: 3,500 to 9,820 feet.
System trails: 90 miles.
Maximum core to perimeter distance: 5.5 miles.
Activities: Hiking, backpacking, horseback riding, mountaineering, cross-country skiing, fishing.
Modes of travel: Foot, skis, and horse.
Maps: 1992 Mission Mountains Wilderness map-1-1/4"/mile contour; 1991 Flathead National Forest Visitor Map; Cedar Lake-MT; Piper-Crow Pass-MT; Peck Lake-MT; Mount Harding-MT; Hemlock Lake-MT; Saint Marys Lake-MT; and Gray Wolf Lake-MT (1:24,000 topo maps).

OVERVIEW: The steeper slopes of a jagged 40-mile sweep of the Mission Mountains are a single interdependent Wilderness despite the split administration between the Flathead Indian Reservation and the Forest Service. The Missions were formed from ancient Precambrian sedimentary rocks, which were then uplifted and tilted to the east. More recently, the upper layers of the Belt rock were washed away by the large-scale erosion of Ice Age glaciers, leaving today's striking mountainscape of rocky crags, sheer cliffs, knife ridges, cirques, horns, arêtes, U-shaped valleys, and hundreds of tarns. Sparkling streams tumble over bedrock to the Swan Valley thousands of feet below. The most rugged terrain is in the southern Missions with vertical relief up to 5,000 feet.

Popularly known as the American Alps, the overpowering western face of the Missions pierces the sky almost 7,000 feet above the valley floor. In 1979 the Confederated Salish and Kootenai tribes designated 89,500 acres of privately owned tribal lands along the western slopes as Wilderness—the first such dedication by any tribe on its own.

9 MISSION MOUNTAINS WILDERNESS COMPLEX

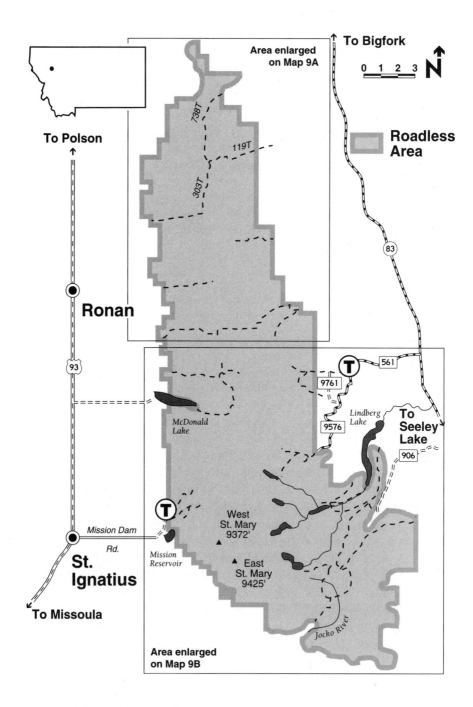

The apex of the range is glacier-studded 9,820-foot McDonald Peak in the rugged south, where a dozen other summits rise above 9,000 feet. Permanent snowfields feed hundreds of gem-like tarns in one of the highest densities of alpine lakes in the northern Rockies. Waterfalls are abundant, with the best known being the 1,000-foot plunges of Elizabeth and Mission falls.

The west side Tribal Wilderness is managed with a priority for wildlife. Each summer grizzlies gather on the snowfields of McDonald Peak to feast on swarms of cutworm moths and ladybugs. In order to avoid displacing these great bears, the tribe closes about 12,000 acres to all public use from mid-July to October. The closed area is part of a larger trailless region that serves to discourage humans from entering the grizzly's home during a critical time.

RECREATIONAL USES: *West side Tribal Wilderness:* Most people go into the Wilderness on day trips in average party sizes of three or four. About 95 percent of the visitors on both sides of the Mission Divide travel on foot with the remainder being horse users. The Missions are not good horse country due to short trail distances, poor-quality trails, steep, rocky terrain, and lack of suitable forage. In fact, the entire Tribal Wilderness is closed to all livestock use between March 1 and June 30. Tribal regulations limit groups in the Wilderness to eight people and eight head of livestock, with a time limit of three days in any one campsite.

The Grizzly Bear Conservation Zone consists of 12,000 acres from Post Creek south to the divide from Glacier Peaks west to the Wilderness boundary. The zone is closed to all recreational use from July 15 to October 1. The Ashley Lakes area and trail, located within the closure, is limited to day use only from October 2 to July 14. The tribal management plan states flatly that no new trails will be built in the Wilderness. However, trailheads are rerouted wherever landowner problems exist. The Eagle Pass trail was relocated to about 0.5 mile north of the Cheff Ranch with signs, a footbridge, and about 1.5 miles of new trail that provide a much more enjoyable hike than did the previous road. The trail system is well distributed with all the major drainages having trail access from the valley floor. Six trails enter the east side from the Mission Divide. The only maintained trails are Mud Lakes, North Crow, Terrance, Mollman, Eagle Pass, Post Creek, and Buck Lake. The Ashley Lake and Cliff Lake trails are being allowed to return to nature and have become grown over in places. The tribes are managing much of the southern end of the Wilderness, from McDonald Lake south to Saint Marys Lake, as a trailless area. Although much of this 14-mile-wide expanse of country lies above timberline and can be traversed without trails, there is also much of it in stream bottoms that are clogged by avalanche debris, downfall, spruce-fir jungles, and *Menziesia*—enough to discourage the most intrepid bushwhacker.

If you are not a tribal member, and are between the ages of 18 and 64, you

9A MISSION MOUNTAINS COMPLEX

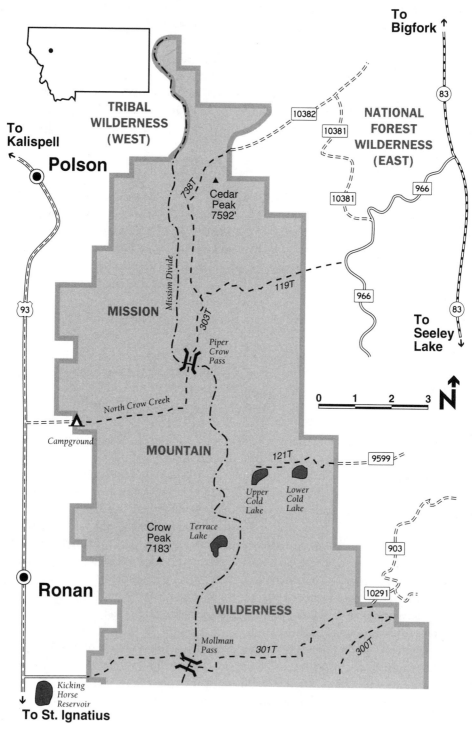

To Bigfork ↑

TRIBAL WILDERNESS (WEST)

To Kalispell

NATIONAL FOREST WILDERNESS (EAST)

Polson

10382
10381

83

966

10381

Cedar Peak 7592'

738T

Mission Divide

MISSION

119T

966

303T

Piper Crow Pass

To Seeley Lake

83

0   1   2   3   N↑

North Crow Creek

Campground

MOUNTAIN

121T

9599

Upper Cold Lake

Lower Cold Lake

Crow Peak 7183'

Terrace Lake

903

10291

Ronan

WILDERNESS

Mollman Pass

301T

300T

Kicking Horse Reservoir

↓ To St. Ignatius

93

must obtain and carry a tribal recreation permit, which entitles you to hike, fish, camp, and enjoy the Wilderness as well as other Flathead Reservation lands that are open to recreation. The permits are available at a number of stores within and near the reservation in communities such as Missoula, Kalispell, Seeley Lake, and Thompson Falls. Despite the permits, tribal managers downplay regulations in favor of education. If people understand the need for no-trace camping and grizzly bear closures around McDonald Peak, enforcement problems will be minimal. We should also appreciate why the Missions were set aside in 1979 as the only Tribal Wilderness in the nation established by the actual tribe. In the words of the Mission Mountains Committee: "These mountains belong to our children, and when our children grow old they will belong to their children. In this way and for this reason these mountains are sacred."

East side National Forest Wilderness: An astounding 75 percent of wilderness users here take day hikes and/or fishing trips to Glacier Lake, Cold Lake, or Crystal Lake—thereby concentrating the use and impacts. As a result, Glacier Lake and Upper and Lower Cold Lake are closed to overnight camping to rehabilitate the shorelines. At the other end of the spectrum, some of the more remote trailless basins rarely have a human visitor. However, despite the formidable terrain and dense undergrowth, off-trail travel is on the rise. Formerly

LUCIFER LAKE ON THE SOUTH END OF THE MISSION MOUNTAINS TRIBAL WILDERNESS.

9B MISSION MOUNTAINS COMPLEX

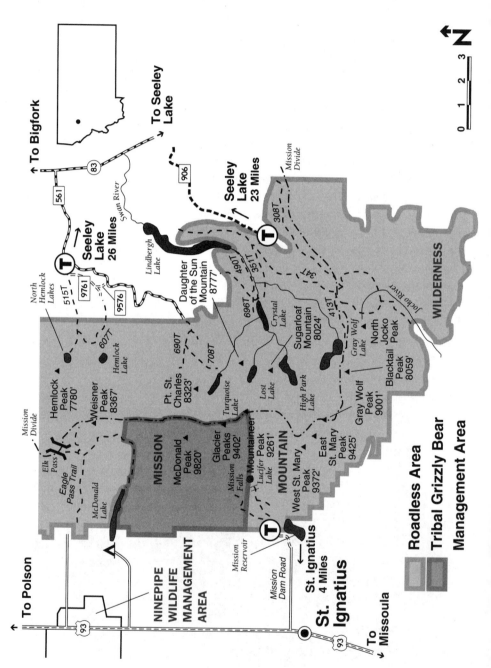

remote areas are now approachable by the informal way trails created by bush-whackers. These are evident around the southeast shore of Gray Wolf Lake, from Island Lake to Post Creek Saddle, and in the Jim Lakes Basin.

Horse use accounts for only 5 percent of the visitors. Most of the pack and saddle stock enter the Wilderness from tribal lands via Post, Crow, Mollman, and Hell Roaring creeks, or the Jocko trails on the south end. There are 71 miles of trails within the east side Wilderness: 40 miles are maintained by the Forest Service and 5 miles have been abandoned. The Forest Service has a policy of no new trails in the rugged but fragile southern corner of the Wilderness. The agency encourages party size of eight or fewer to avoid the impacts of concentrated use. Educational efforts are designed to disperse recreation away from the more heavily used areas. The following major trailheads are presented in order of heaviest to lightest use: Glacier, Cold, Crystal, Cedar, Piper, Jim Lakes, Beaver Creek to Gray Wolf, Hemlock, and Elk Creek. The Missions offer easy walks, like the level 1-mile jaunt to Glacier Lake, or tough trekking, like the primitive Indian trail up Elk Creek that can be done as either a difficult day hike or overnighter.

During summer, the best time is generally the drier season of late July to mid-September. Keep in mind that this is wet country and the mosquitoes are often abundant until the end of August. Some of the greatest discoveries can be found on non-technical, cross-country scrambles to the top of almost every pinnacle in the Missions: Gray Wolf, Weisner, and Sunset Crag, all three of which have summit registers. Winter can best be enjoyed in March-April when temperatures moderate and the snowpack is consolidated enough for cross-country skis or snowshoes. The steep Mission canyons and sideslopes are prime for avalanches, so keep a wary eye out for such conditions during the avalanche season, which can extend from late fall to late spring.

HOW TO GET THERE: *Tribal west side:* From US 93 turn east on the Mission Reservoir road at the north edge of Saint Ignatius. Go east 3 miles, turn right (south) 1 mile, then turn left and drive the remaining 0.5 mile to the Mission Dam, campground, and trailhead.

National Forest east side: From MT 83 (the Swan Highway), 19 miles north of Seeley Lake, drive about 7 miles west on the Kraft Creek Road (FR 561). Turn right on FR 9576 about 0.5 mile up Red Butte Creek to the trailhead for Hemlock Lake Trail 607.

DAY HIKE OR BACKPACK ON THE TRIBAL WEST SIDE

Lucifer Lake
Distance: 10 miles out-and-back.
Difficulty: Strenuous.
Topo maps: Saint Marys Lake-MT.

The first 3 miles of this primitive trail are fairly easygoing, but the trail definitely deteriorates with its rather startling increase in gradient up to, above, and then beyond spectacular Mission Falls. A lightly used way trail continues to climb another 1,000 vertical feet in 1.5 miles to Lucifer Lake, which is about 2,800 feet above the trailhead. In places you'll literally be pulling yourself up by grabbing onto branches. There is a good campsite at the outlet, along with an angler's trail around the south side. It is then possible to hike up the open alpine country along the Middle Fork of Mission Creek, climbing steeply to Lake of the Stars, which is usually under ice into July. An easy side trip to Picture Lake yields a stunning view of the sheer Garden Wall along the main divide. Be extremely cautious about cliff scrambling on the unstable sedimentary rock on or near the divide.

DAY HIKE OR OVERNIGHTER ON THE NATIONAL FOREST EAST SIDE

Hemlock Peak
Distance: 10-mile loop.
Difficulty: Moderate.
Topo maps: Hemlock Lake-MT.

The well-maintained but brushy Hemlock Lake Trail 607 winds northwest across several small drainages in heavy forest to where it intersects with the North Fork Hemlock Creek Trail 515. Climb the ridge trail for almost 1 mile to lovely little North Hemlock Lake where the country opens up into slab rock and subalpine forest. The fishless lake has several good camping spots. Climb the old lookout trail 900 vertical feet to the top of 7,780-foot Hemlock Peak—about 2,800 feet above the trailhead. Superb vistas of the Mission Divide, Elk Lake, Mount Harding, and McDonald Peak can be enjoyed to the south. Then work south cross-country on the open main ridge for about 1 mile and drop to the southeast another mile into Hemlock Lake, which offers fishing and overnight camping. The outlet trail will quickly lead you back to Trail 607, on which you began the trip, less than 3 miles above the trailhead.

Anaconda Hill

10

Location: 15 miles northeast of Lincoln.
Size: 17,709 acres.
Administration: USDAFS-Helena National Forest.
Management status: Roadless non-wilderness (wildlife/custodial).
Ecosystems: Middle Rocky Mountain coniferous forest province, characterized by moderately glaciated mountains with limestone scarps and ridges; Precambrian and Paleozoic limestone rocks; Douglas-fir forest type; dendritic drainage pattern.
Elevation range: 4,800 to 7,153 feet.
System trails: 15 miles.
Maximum core to perimeter distance: 1.5 miles.
Activities: Hiking, backpacking, horseback riding, cross-country skiing.
Modes of travel: Foot, horse, skis.
Maps: 1991 Helena National Forest Visitors Map; Rogers Pass-MT and Wilborn-MT.

OVERVIEW: The Anaconda Hill roadless area stretches north at Flesher Pass, overlapping the slopes of the Continental Divide for 13 miles to Rogers Pass on MT 200. Both sides of the Great Divide are characterized by sparse clumps of Douglas-fir and lodgepole pine, with steep, open, grassy sidehills and fingers of small, splintered rock. The high, windy divide is a mosaic of fescue grassland and limber pine, lending itself to cross-country travel. In places the east side is abrupt, with sheer rock faces rising hundreds of feet. In the north end, near Midnight Hill, a visitor can look eastward and savor the dramatic change from mountains to prairies as well as the vast expanse of the Scapegoat Wilderness to the north. Of some historic note, the coldest temperature on record for the Lower Forty-eight—minus 70 degrees Fahrenheit—was recorded on January 20, 1954, at a mining camp just west of Rogers Pass on the northwestern edge of the roadless area.

RECREATIONAL USES: The Continental Divide National Scenic Trail winds for 13 miles through the Anaconda Hill roadless area, along the divide from Rogers Pass (5,609 feet) south to Flesher Pass (6,131 feet). By far the major recreational activities are hunting grouse and big game. A couple of four-wheel-drive roads penetrate the south end of the roadless area, intersecting at a couple of places on the CDNST, but the roads are closed yearlong for wildlife secu-

10 ANACONDA HILL

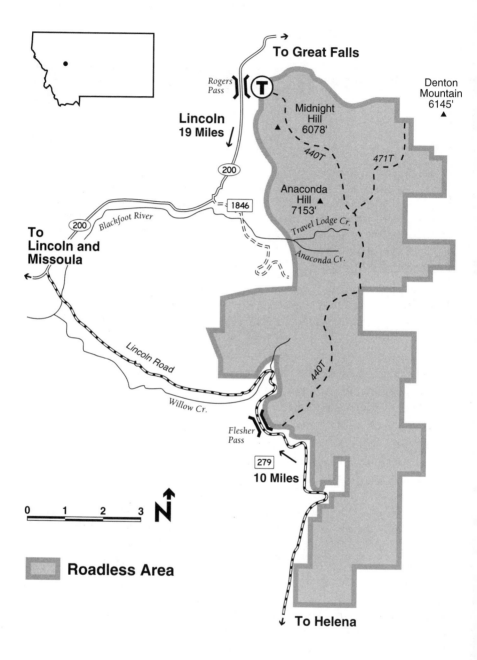

To Great Falls

Rogers Pass

Denton Mountain 6145'

Midnight Hill 6078'

Lincoln 19 Miles

440T

471T

200

Anaconda Hill 7153'

1846

Blackfoot River

Travel Lodge Cr.

To Lincoln and Missoula

Anaconda Cr.

Lincoln Road

440T

Willow Cr.

Flesher Pass

279
10 Miles

0 1 2 3 N

Roadless Area

To Helena

LOOKING SOUTH ALONG THE CONTINENTAL DIVIDE INTO THE NORTH END OF
ANACONDA HILL ROADLESS AREA NEAR ROGERS PASS.

rity. Access for skiing, hiking, or horseback riding is provided throughout the
year from paved highway routes at both passes. Trail 440 takes off steeply
from both passes but is a little less steep at Flesher Pass, which is therefore
better suited for horseback riding. This is rolling high divide country with a mix
of grassy ridges, rocky points, and dense forests of lodgepole and Douglas-fir.

HOW TO GET THERE: Rogers Pass is 19 miles east of Lincoln on MT 200.
Flesher Pass is on Route 279 between Helena and Lincoln.

DAY TRIP

Continental Divide Trail
Distance: 13 miles point-to-point.
Difficulty: Moderate.
Topo maps: Rogers Pass-MT and Wilborn-MT.

From Rogers Pass hike straight up from the south side of the highway,
climbing along the Continental Divide ridge through sparse clumps of Douglas-
fir and lodgepole pine, broad, grassy slopes, and fingers of splintered, loose
shale and limestone rock. After a steep 1,200- to 1,500-foot climb the din of
the highway will be only a memory. Midnight Hill rises from the divide after
about 2 miles. The western slopes are gradual with grassy parks and stringers
of conifers dropping into narrow gulches. In contrast, the eastern face of the

divide is abrupt, dramatic, with sheer outcroppings of reddish rock rising several hundred vertical feet in places. To the south the roadless headwaters of side drainages become more heavily forested. For the most part, the trail is nonexistent. No problem. This high, windy, open landscape lends itself to easy cross-country travel. This stretch of the Great Divide runs close to the Great Plains. As a result, one can savor the transition between mountains and prairie by looking northeast from almost anywhere along the divide. The highest point in the roadless area, 7,153-foot Anaconda Hill, sits just west of the divide.

With a car shuttle, a 14-mile point-to-point day trip can be arranged between the two passes, or exchange keys halfway with an oncoming party. The direction of travel makes little difference. Over the years I've made it a practice to stop at Rogers Pass, whenever possible, to scramble up the divide toward Midnight Hill. Sometimes I have only an hour, maybe two, but always I've found the hike to be exhilarating, a wonderful way to break up the long drive from one side of the divide to the other. And never, during all these years, have I seen anyone else bother to stop and stretch their legs along this wonderfully accessible stretch of the Great Divide.

The incessant wind keeps the divide mostly snow-free during winter. Avalanche danger is generally low along the divide itself, increasing in steeper side drainages. Only once during several dozen times have I stopped when snow conditions were such that I was able to climb with skins on my skis, going as high as I had time and stamina for, followed by a crude attempt at telemarking back down through scattered clumps of trees to the bottom of the first small drainage just west of the pass.

Nevada Mountain ██ 11

Location: 25 miles northwest of Helena or 5 miles southeast of Lincoln.
Size: 49,934 acres.
Administration: USDAFS-Helena National Forest.
Management status: Roadless non-wilderness core with wildlife emphasis and some peripheral lands allocated to future development in the forest plan.
Ecosystems: Middle Rocky Mountain coniferous forest province, characterized by moderately glaciated mountains with limestone scarps and ridges; Precambrian and Paleozoic limestone rocks; Douglas-fir and western spruce-fir forest types; dendritic drainage pattern.
Elevation range: 4,880 to 8,338 feet.
System trails: 33 miles.
Maximum core to perimeter distance: 2.5 miles.
Activities: Hiking, backpacking, horseback riding, cross-country skiing, mountain biking.
Modes of travel: Foot, skis, horse, mountain bike.
Maps: 1991 Helena National Forest Visitor Map; Lincoln-MT; Swede Gulch-MT; Finn-MT; Nevada Mountain-MT; and Granite Butte-MT (1:24,000 topo maps).

OVERVIEW: The Nevada Mountain roadless area straddles the Continental Divide for 15 miles. The more prominent pinnacles are Nevada Mountain and Black Mountain—each rising above 8,000 feet. The heads of drainages along the divide are characterized by picturesque rocky cirques, especially on the east side. On the west slope, steep, thickly forested finger ridges are dotted with grassy parks on the south-facing aspects. This habitat mix is ready made for some 1,500 elk and nearly as many deer. Heavy roading and logging on all sides make the remaining dense stands of lodgepole pine crucial for elk security cover during hunting season. Because of deep snowpack and the many streams that head up along the divide, Nevada Mountain is an important producer of pure water for downstream users in the Little Prickly Pear Creek and Blackfoot River drainages.

RECREATIONAL USES: Although lacking what some regard as key attractions—such as jagged pinnacles and trout-filled lakes—Nevada Mountain offers sublime beauty and an abundance of uncluttered space in a huge expanse of wild Continental Divide country which, outside of hunting season, is lightly visited. Actually, there are notable landmarks, such as Nevada and Black mountains,

11 NEVADA MOUNTAIN

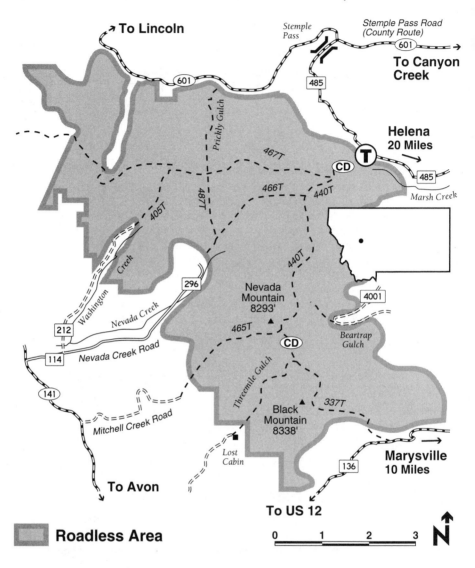

Roadless Area

the Continental Divide National Scenic Trail, and the historic Helmville-Gould Trail. Backpackers are rare, which is another reason to explore this area.

In winter, both the Continental Divide National Scenic Trail (440) and the Helmville-Gould Trail (467) are well suited to serious backcountry skiers. Instead of heading north from Stemple Pass on CR 601, as most skiers do, ski 3 miles south past Granite Butte. From there, ski to either trail—they intersect about 1 mile southwest of the closure. An out-and-back route (rather than a loop trip) is more feasible given the steepness of the forested slopes dropping from both sides of these high ridge trails.

How to get there: Take MT 279 northwest out of Helena 14 miles to Canyon Creek. Then head west on Prickly Pear Road 707 about 5.5 miles. Turn right (north) up Marsh Creek on FR 485 and drive 7 or 8 miles to the Continental Divide. Go south about 0.5 mile to the road closure, which is near the start of Trail 467 leading to the west as well as Trail 440 along the divide to the south.

LOOKING SOUTH TO NEVADA MOUNTAIN ALONG THE CONTINENTAL DIVIDE.

DAY TRIP OR BACKPACK

Continental Divide Trail
Distance: 12 miles out-and-back
Difficulty: Moderate.
Topo maps: Nevada Mountain-MT and Granite Butte-MT.

From the closure described above, backpack south along the Continental Divide Trail 440 about 6 miles to the head of Gleason Creek. For the most part the divide is open, up and down, and all-in-all a subalpine delight for trekking. There is an excellent camping spot in the forested head of Gleason Creek that requires a steep 700-foot drop from a saddle on the crest of the divide.

Or head west, where the east-west Helmville-Gould Ridge Trail 467 is a great choice for an out-and-back day trip, suitable in most places for foot, mountain bike, or horse travel. This trail is open to ATVs, motorbikes, and snowmobiles, so stay alert to avoid any potential user conflict.

Ranging between 7,000 feet and 7,600 feet, the ridge runs west for 10 miles. The country alternates between dense subalpine forest, open rolling parks, and rock face cliffs. Backcountry skiers can access the Helmville-Gould ridge by parking at Stemple Pass on the all-weather Stemple Pass Road 601 and then skiing south on unplowed FR 485, passing Granite Butte to the start of the ridge—a distance of 5 to 6 miles.

Electric Peak- Little Blackfoot Meadows

Location: 20 miles southwest of Helena.
Size: 47,005 acres.
Administration: USDAFS-Helena and Deerlodge national forests.
Management status: Roadless non-wilderness, with some peripheral lands allocated to future development in the forest plans.
Ecosystems: Middle Rocky Mountain coniferous forest-alpine meadow province, characterized by moderately glaciated mountains; Precambrian and Paleozoic limestone rocks; Douglas-fir and western spruce-fir forest types interspersed with wet meadows and numerous perennial streams.
Elevation range: 5,700 to 8,597 feet.
System trails: 46 miles.
Maximum core to perimeter distance: 3.5 miles.
Activities: Hiking, backpacking, horseback riding, fishing, mountain biking, cross-country skiing.
Modes of travel: Foot, skis, mountain bike, and horse.
Maps: 1991 Helena National Forest Visitor Map and 1990 Deerlodge National Forest Visitor Map; Baggs Creek-MT; Bison Mountain-MT; Sugarloaf Mountain-MT; and Thunderbolt Creek-MT (1:24,000 topo maps).

OVERVIEW: The Great Divide twists for 13 miles through the southern reaches of the wildlife-rich Electric Peak/Little Blackfoot Meadows roadless area reaching its apex at 8,597-foot Thunderbolt Mountain. To the immediate south a lush, mile-long meadow and thick lodgepole pine/spruce forest encircle Cottonwood Lake—a favored watering hole for summering elk, deer, and moose. Across the divide an elaborate network of beaver ponds in Blackfoot Meadows occupies most of a wide basin near the head of the Little Blackfoot River. This "land of a thousand springs" is perfectly suited for family outings, a place where kids might see a moose feeding in one pond while catching pan-sized cutthroat and brookies from another.

RECREATIONAL USES: The overwhelming majority of recreational use occurs during the summer and fall hunting seasons. The most popular activities are hiking, backpacking, horseback riding, hunting, fishing, and mountain biking. An outfitter maintains a hunting camp at Blackfoot Meadows, which is also used once in a while during summer. Another outfitter runs a hunting camp on

12 ELECTRIC PEAK-LITTLE BLACKFOOT MEADOWS

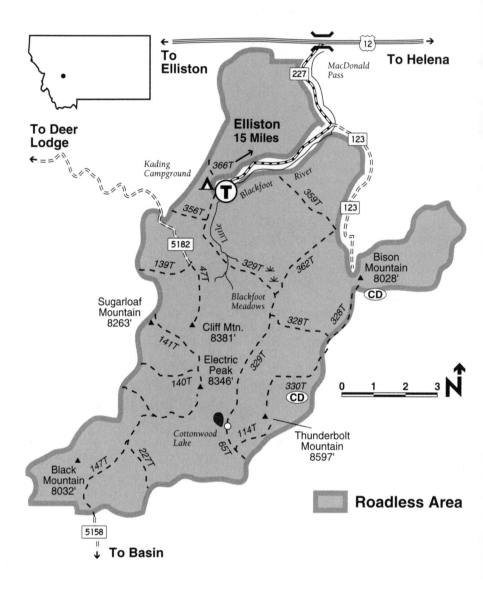

the divide near Sugarloaf Mountain, taking occasional day hunting trips into the Little Blackfoot drainage. The most popular recreation access to the roadless area is by way of the Little Blackfoot River road. The country is traversed by a section of the Continental Divide National Scenic Trail. The trail winds from Bison to Thunderbolt mountains, where it drops to Cottonwood Lake by way of Thunderbolt Creek, and then climbs back up to the divide at Electric Peak.

The Helena Ranger District rents the Kading Cabin yearlong, except from April 15 to June 1. The cabin is popular with cross-country skiers who then ski into Blackfoot Meadows. In a good Montana winter, cabin visitors have to ski about 6 miles of unplowed road to Kading and another 5 miles into the meadows on day trips. About 2 miles east of Kading, Larabee Gulch also offers an enjoyable ski tour. Although the core meadows area is closed to most forms of motorized recreation, it is open to snowmobiling after November 30.

HOW TO GET THERE: From Helena drive 20 miles west on US 12, over MacDonald Pass to the Little Blackfoot River Road, on the left. (The turnoff is 1 mile east of Elliston on US 12.) Head south about 15 miles to the USDAFS Kading Guard Station and campground. The road becomes FR 227 upon entering the national forest boundary. From Kading the road turns into a jeep track and is open during summer for another mile to the trailhead for Trail 329 to Blackfoot Meadows.

LOOKING SOUTHEAST FROM ATOP CLIFF MOUNTAIN, IN THE CENTRAL REACHES OF THE ELECTRIC PEAK-LITTLE BLACKFOOT MEADOWS ROADLESS AREA.

DAY HIKE OR OVERNIGHTER

Blackfoot Meadows

Distance: 10 miles out-and-back.
Difficulty: Easy.
Topo map: Bison Mountain-MT.

Most of those who hike the relatively gentle 5-mile Blackfoot Meadows Trail 329 to the meadows are day users, either anglers or backcountry explorers. Unfortunately, the popularity of this area for backpacking and hunting is evident from the badly overused campsites scattered along the edges of the meadows.

Centrally located Blackfoot Meadows is an excellent jumping-off point for side trips if you make a base camp there for one or more nights. A cross-country/trail loop would be to bushwhack southwest through a lodgepole/Douglas-fir forest to the broad, open summit of Cliff Mountain, then go south 2 miles to Electric Peak on the Continental Divide. Drop to the saddle above Cottonwood Lake and Trail 329 leading 4 miles north back to the meadows—a 10- to 12-mile loop through the heart of this Great Divide country.

An 8- to 9-mile loop on trails 362 and 328 to 8,028-foot Bison Mountain also provides an excellent panorama of this and surrounding wildlands.

LITTLE BLACKFOOT MEADOWS, A POPULAR DAY TRIP DESTINATION IN THE HEART OF THE "LAND OF A THOUSAND SPRINGS."

OVERNIGHT SKI TOUR

Cottonwood Lake
Distance: 15 miles.
Difficulty: Strenuous.
Topo maps: Bison Mountain-MT; and Thunderbolt Creek-MT.

March is a good time to take a challenging and somewhat strenuous overnight, point-to-point ski tour from Kading to the Boulder River Road. Head south to Blackfoot Meadows, then over the densely forested Continental Divide to Cottonwood Lake. From here the steep grade of Thunderbolt Creek leads to FR 1572, which ends up on the Boulder River Road about 8 miles west of I-15, a few miles southwest of Basin. The distance from Kading south to the Boulder River is about 15 miles. All the better if you can time your trip during a full moon when moonlight skiing across Blackfoot Meadows or the frozen expanse of Cottonwood Lake is an unforgettable experience.

Black Mountain-
Mount Helena

Location: 5 miles southwest of Helena.
Size: 22,600 acres (includes Jericho Mountain roadless area along the Continental Divide plus the 13,300-acre Black Mountain roadless area to the immediate east; separated from each other by the Rimini Road).
Administration: USDAFS—Helena National Forest.
Management status: Roadless non-wilderness/wildlife, with some peripheral lands allocated to future development in the forest plan.
Ecosystems: Middle Rocky Mountain coniferous forest province, characterized by granite and basalts; Douglas-fir forest type; and with a dendritic drainage pattern of widely spaced perennial streams.
Elevation range: 4,815 to 7,217 feet.
System trails: 3 miles.
Maximum core to perimeter distance: 1.5 miles.
Activities: Hiking, cross-country skiing, horseback riding, and mountain biking.
Modes of travel: Foot, skis, horse, mountain bike.
Maps: 1991 Helena National Forest Visitor Map; MacDonald Pass-MT; Black Mountain-MT; Helena-MT; Three Brothers-MT; and Chessman Reservoir-MT (1:24,000 topo maps).

OVERVIEW: There is an astonishing amount of wildlife and natural diversity packed within this compact wildland. Dense forests, wet springs, and grassy parks combine as year-round habitat for up to 400 elk as well as moose, mule deer, cougar, bobcat, marten, fox, and black bear.

The open top of 7,217-foot Colorado Mountain connects to a saddle ridge through mature lodgepole pine to Black Mountain, which is crowned with a rock pile graced by a delicate little aspen tree. Just below the summit another rock outcrop offers a more open view, especially to the south toward the large Blackhall Meadows and the head of Colorado Gulch. This feature also provides a perfect sitting rock with a comfortable backrest!

To the immediate west the Jericho Mountain roadless area is split by the Continental Divide. Here the Continental Divide National Scenic Trail traverses rolling lodgepole pine/subalpine fir forests for about 7 miles at elevations above 6,500 feet. Wildlife use is year-round, but the streams are only seasonal.

13 BLACK MOUNTAIN-MOUNT HELENA

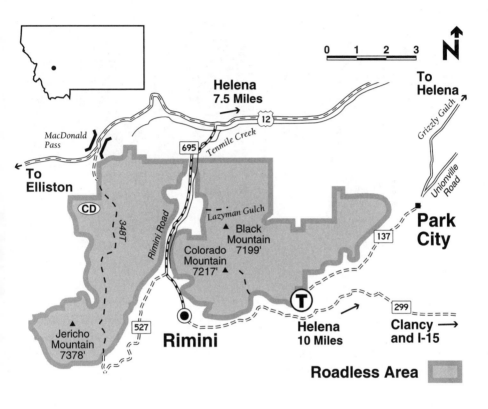

RECREATIONAL USES: Just as the Rattlesnake area is to Missoula, Black Mountain is Helena's backyard wilderness and, as such, has significant value to the community for hiking, wildlife viewing, horseback riding, and hunting. Despite its proximity to a major highway (US 12) and the capital city of Montana, Black Mountain's diverse topography and dense forests allow for a deep sense of solitude. The major landmarks are Colorado Mountain, Black Mountain, and Blackhall Meadows, all of which are favored destinations for mostly day trips. Although snow cover is often unreliable during winter, Lazyman Gulch, Moose Creek, and Blackhall Meadows are sometimes skiable. It is possible to hike south from the city limits of Montana's capital city along the Mount Helena-Skyline National Recreation Trail into the Black Mountain roadless area. To do so requires a 6- to 7-mile off-trail traverse along the main ridge from Park City to Blackhall Meadows.

LOOKING NORTH TO BLACK MOUNTAIN FROM COLORADO MOUNTAIN.

HOW TO GET THERE: From Helena head south up Park Avenue (upper Last Chance Gulch) 3 miles to Unionville and the end of the pavement. Continue south, following signs for Park Lake, another 3 to 4 winding, uphill miles. Shortly after topping a ridge, turn right on FR 137 and drive another meandering 2.6 miles to a "dead end" sign with a fence and road closure across a set of wheel tracks on the right. A pass gate allows easy access for hikers.

DAY HIKE

Black Mountain-Blackhall Meadows
Distance: 8-mile loop.
Difficulty: Moderate.
Topo Maps: Black Mountain-MT, Chessman Reservoir-MT

From the road closure on FR 137 climb 1.5 miles along the wheel track through open lodgepole and scattered small openings to Blackhall Meadows. Expect to see cattle grazing during the summer. From the meadows there is a great view of prominent Red Mountain to the southwest and of both Colorado and Black mountains to the north. A short hike up through grassy parks and scattered conifers will take you to the summit of 7,217-foot Colorado Mountain where an old fire lookout once stood. A rock-lined path circles around the broad top where grand views can be enjoyed in all directions. Heading north cross-country to Black Mountain entails a 440-foot drop into a saddle with occasional granite rock outcroppings that overlook both sides of this compact wild area. The top of 7,149-foot Black Mountain is reached after a steep 400-foot ascent from the second saddle. An enjoyable pastime on this closed-in summit is to read the notes contained in a small plastic bottle left by folks from as early as 1960. To complete the loop, angle downhill to the southeast toward Blackhall Meadows on a series of game trails winding through a lodgepole/Douglas-fir/spruce forest where numerous tiny wet springs and meadows show ample evidence of elk, moose, and other wildlife. By maintaining your contour around the head of Colorado Gulch and continuing south through a series of larger grassy openings, Blackhall Meadows will be reached after about 2 miles. The intimate, hidden discoveries of wildlife use make this short off-trail leg of the loop more than worthwhile. Plan 5 to 6 hours for this exploratory circuit, which involves about 8 miles of hiking and roughly 1,200 vertical feet of up-and-down, most of which occurs on the ridge between Colorado and Black mountains.

Flint Creek
Range

14

Location: 4 miles east of Philipsburg and 10 miles west of Deer Lodge.
Size: 60,297 acres.
Administration: USFS—Deerlodge National Forest.
Management status: Roadless non-wilderness, with about 5 percent of the roadless area along the edges allocated to future development in the forest plan.
Ecosystems: Middle Rocky Mountain coniferous forest-alpine meadow province, characterized by high, steep, glaciated mountains with glacial and lake basins leading up to alpine ridges and cirques; Precambrian granite and metasedimentary rock; Douglas-fir and western ponderosa forest types; many perennial streams and high mountain lakes.
Elevation range: 5,820 to 10,164 feet.
System trails: 50 miles.
Maximum core to perimeter distance: 3.5 miles.
Activities: Hiking, backpacking, horseback riding, cross-country skiing, mountain biking, fishing.
Modes of travel: Foot, skis, mountain bike, and horse.
Maps: 1990 Deerlodge National Forest Visitor Map; Pikes Peak-MT; Rock Creek Lake-MT; Fred Burr Lake-MT; Pozega Lakes-MT; and Mount Powell-MT (1:24,000 topo maps).

OVERVIEW: All of the major peaks of the Flint Creek Range are within the roadless core of the range, including Mount Powell, the loftiest point at 10,164 feet. Once cut off by the low-standard Rock Creek Road, the Dolus Lakes basin to the north is now joined with the country to the south by the closure of a jeep trail. In general, the mountains here are lower, most between 8,000 and 9,000 feet, and more gently rounded than in nearby ranges. Dozens of dark-colored lakes beckon walk-in anglers.

Close to the perimeter, rolling hills covered with dense lodgepole pine and mixed conifers lead upward to steep slopes with an array of trees, grass, and rock talus. Upslope, the glaciated U-shaped canyons end in large cirques with cliff faces crowned by blunt summits. Wind-sculpted subalpine fir and whitebark pine cling to the upper timberline. The highest ridges are dotted with house-size boulders, often cloaked in black, yellow, and orange lichens. Long, rounded, grassy ridges radiate from the peaks, their sides falling sharply into narrow avalanche chutes. From the Deer Lodge Valley, the long bare ridge connecting Deer Lodge Mountain and Mount Powell looks deceptively level and rounded, but the entire back side is a sheer, curving cliff called The Crater.

14 FLINT CREEK RANGE

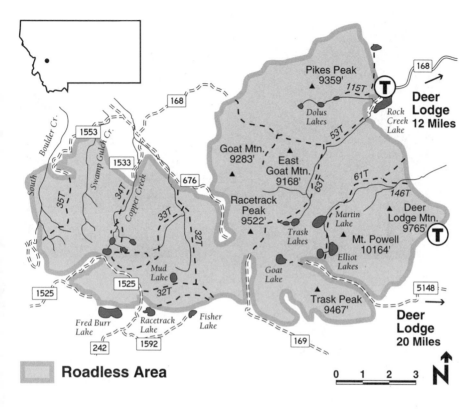

Roadless Area

0   1   2   3   **N**

RECREATIONAL USES: From challenging cross-country climbs to gentle trail hikes the Flints have it all. Backcountry recreational use in this previously little-known range is rising enough to impact campsites and to make it a little harder to find solitude. Still, classic alpine scenery here makes these mountains well worth getting to know. Hunting is popular in the fall for blue grouse on the ridges, deer in the parks, elk in the forests and high basins, and, for the four lucky permit holders, goats on the peaks. Three outfitters offer fall hunts into the backcountry.

The Flints are large and rugged enough for challenging excursions for those willing to make the effort. Nonetheless, the more accessible fishing lakes are ideal for family day hikes and exploration.

In response to growing backcountry use, the Forest Service is emphasizing semi-primitive non-motorized recreation, especially in the Copper Creek/Boulder Lakes basins, Dolus Lakes, Trask Lakes, and in the North Fork of Dempsey

TRASK LAKE BASIN IN THE CENTRAL FLINT CREEK RANGE.

Creek southeast of Mount Powell. Yet even these more primitive and remote reaches of the Flints are open to snowmobiling after December 1, although steep terrain limits the area suitable for snowmobiling. Five low-standard jeep tracks penetrate a little way into the exterior boundary of the roadless area. The Deer Lodge Ranger District rents the six-person capacity Doney Lake Cabin year-round. The cabin can be reached by way of the somewhat rough FR 645 on the northeast corner of the range. During normal winter snow conditions it's possible to drive within 5 miles of the cabin. From the cabin, Trail 138 can be skied south to Rock Creek Lake, where Trail 115 can be picked up into the Dolus Lakes basin. The trail is steep at first but, thanks to a mostly forested route, the avalanche hazard is usually low.

HOW TO GET THERE: From I-90 at Deer Lodge drive 5.5 miles south on the frontage road. Head west on the Prison Ranch road and go north past the Prison Ranch headquarters on FR 8507, angling west-northwest for another 5 miles to the North Fork of Dempsey Creek just before the national forest boundary and Long Park. Find a place to pull off the road for the cross-country ascent of Mount Powell.

To reach trailheads for several lake basins, including Dolus and Trask Lakes drive northwest on the main road past the prison (Road 006) for 7 miles toward Rock Creek Lake. Turn left on FR 168 and drive 5 miles to Rock Creek Lake, where Trail 115 to Dolus Lakes and Trail 53 to Trask Lakes begin.

DAY HIKE

Mount Powell Cross-Country Climb
Distance: 14-mile loop.
Difficulty: Strenuous.
Topo map: Mount Powell-MT.

From just before the national forest boundary below Long Park hike northwest up a steep, open grassy park to the main southeast summit ridge of 9,765-foot Deer Lodge Mountain. The first part of the route used to be a gunnery range, so stay clear of any old live rounds you may happen across. Fortunately, these grasslands are now used by elk during winter. Ascend 1,400 feet to enter a lodgepole pine forest followed by a rocky ridge. Another 1,000 feet and you'll be on the open, rock-strewn mound of an nameless 8,266-foot point with a grand view of the peaks and valleys of the southwestern Flints. Climb again and leave the upper timberline of whitebark pine at around 9,000 feet, where an alpine carpet of tundra takes over all the way to Deer Lodge Mountain and beyond. Mid-June to mid-July is a wonderful time to enjoy the colorful array of dozens of tiny alpine flowers in full bloom. The easy 2-mile walk from Deer Lodge Mountain to the apex of the range—10,168-foot Mount Powell—is directly above The Crater—the most impressive topographic feature in the entire mountain uplift. Giant granite ribs resembling the backbone of a dinosaur flank its sheer cliff faces. After reveling in the view from the peak, take the south ridge of Mount Powell, angling to the east, down to a lush subalpine meadow at 8,600 feet which, in turn, leads to the main ridge south of the North Fork of Dempsey Creek. Loop eastward for several miles through a pine forest interspersed with small openings, descending Long Park to your starting point.

DAY HIKE OR OVERNIGHTER

Dolus Lakes and Pikes Peak
Distance: 6 miles.
Difficulty: Moderate.
Topo maps: Pikes Peak-MT and Rock Creek Lake-MT.

Three miles on Trail 115 along with a 1,400-foot climb will get you to lower Dolus Lake from Rock Creek Lake in the northeast edge of the roadless area. The Dolus Lakes offer fishing and a vigorous 2,000-foot climb to 9,167-foot Pikes Peak to the immediate north. The pristine upper Dolus Lakes basin opens up to a fairly easy route to the top of Pikes Peak ridge.

Stony Mountain   15

Location: 10 miles east of Hamilton and 17 miles west of Philipsburg.
Size: 103,172 acres.
Administration: USDAFS—Lolo, Deerlodge, and Bitterroot national forests.
Management status: Roadless non-wilderness, with some peripheral lands allocated to development in the forest plans.
Ecosystems: Middle Rocky Mountain coniferous forest-alpine meadow province, characterized by high, steep, moderately-glaciated mountains with glacial basins leading up to alpine ridges; Precambrian granite and metasedimentary rock; Douglas-fir and western ponderosa forest types; and numerous perennial streams.
Elevation range: 4,320 to 8,656 feet.
System trails: 73 miles.
Maximum core to perimeter distance: 3 miles.
Activities: Hiking, backpacking, cross-country skiing, horseback riding, fishing.
Modes of travel: Foot, skis, and horseback.
Maps: 1990 Deerlodge National Forest Visitor Map; 1994 Lolo National Forest Visitor Map; and 1989 Bitterroot National Forest Visitor Map; Sawmill Saddle-MT; Quigg Peak-MT; Willow Mountain-MT; Burnt Fork Lake-MT; Stony Creek-MT; and Skalkaho Pass-MT (1:24,000 topo maps).

OVERVIEW: Ironically, there is no "Stony Mountain" within or anywhere near this large roadless chunk of the northern Sapphire Range. Angular rock piles and gnarled whitebark pine highlight the 18 miles of Sapphire crest, which bisects the heart of this country. The divide rises to aptly named 8,656-foot Dome Shaped Mountain, where small cirques tell the story of past glaciation. The geology is complex with granitic intrusions, limestone, numerous faults, and glacial deposits in the Upper Burnt Fork.

An extensive Douglas-fir/lodgepole pine forest opens with several large natural meadows, five small lakes, and countless potholes in the Skalkaho Basin near the south boundary. Most of the northern half is rocky, especially where breaks plunge to the larger streams. The exception is some 10,000 acres of gently rolling lodgepole pine forest in the drainages that flow northeast into Rock Creek.

On the western Bitterroot side of the divide, the Stony Mountain area contains the 25,000-acre Skalkaho Game Preserve where visitors can observe and photograph elk, goats, and other wildlife in the best summer/fall habitat in the entire Sapphire Range. The Palisade Mountain and Easthouse national recre-

15 STONY MOUNTAIN

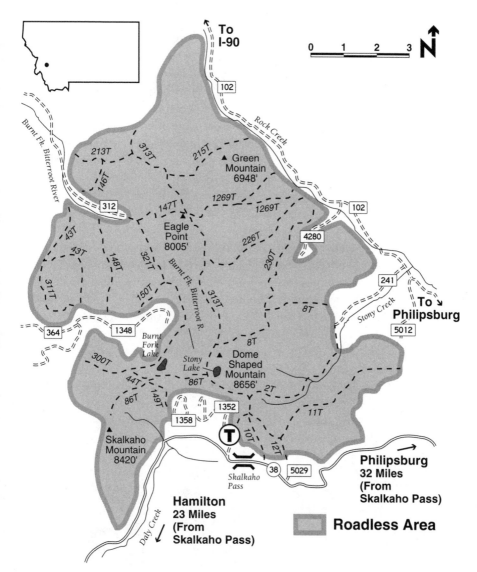

To
I-90

0   1   2   3   N

102

Rock Creek

Burnt Fk. Bitterroot River

213T   313T   215T   ▲ Green
                                        Mountain
                                        6948'

146T   147T   1269T
312   1269T   102

43T   226T   4280

43T   148T   321T   230T   241

311T   150T   To
                                        Philipsburg

313T   8T   5012

364   1348   Burnt
                    Fork
                    Lake   8T

300T   Stony   ▲ Dome
            Lake   Shaped
44T   Mountain   2T
86T   149T   86T   8656'   11T

▲ Skalkaho   1352
Mountain   1358
8420'   T   10T   12T

Stony Creek

Skalkaho   38   5029   Philipsburg
Pass   32 Miles
                                        (From
Hamilton   Skalkaho Pass)
23 Miles
(From
Skalkaho Pass)   Daly Creek

Burnt Fk. Bitterroot R.

Roadless Area

ation trails lead to several fishable lakes. Another trail serves Fuse Lake, located about 2 miles east of Skalkaho Pass, which contains arctic grayling.

RECREATIONAL USES: This large northern Sapphires roadless area receives moderate use for big game and grouse hunting, horseback riding, hiking, backpacking, and fishing. The core of the country—Hutsinpilar, Eagel, and Wyman creeks—plus the upper reaches of Stony, Willow, and Daly creeks, and the Burnt Fork, are well-protected by high, steep terrain with good opportunities for deep solitude. The blend of accessible drainage bottoms, gentle ridges, and open grassy parks allows for cross-country travel. Of the five tiny tarns in the south, Stony Lake provides spotty fishing for cutthroat. Winter access for cross-country skiing is difficult because of distances from plowed roads. A few skiers snowmobile or catch a ride to the top of Skalkaho Pass and then climb to the crest for a day of ski mountaineering.

How TO GET THERE: From Hamilton drive 3 miles south on US 93 and turn left (east) up the Skalkaho Road (MT 38). Drive 26 miles to Skalkaho Pass. Or from the east, drive 6 miles south from Philipsburg on MT 1 and turn right (west) on MT 38. Drive about 25 miles up to the pass. The trailhead for the Easthouse/Sapphire Crest Trail 313 is on the north side of the pass.

LOOKING EASTWARD FROM DOME SHAPED MOUNTAIN IN THE STONY MOUNTAIN COUNTRY.

STONEY LAKE BASIN VIEWED FROM THE SAPPHIRE CREST.

DAY HIKE OR OVERNIGHTER

Stony Lake - Dome Shaped Mountain
Distance: 14 miles out-and-back; optional 8-mile out-and-back side trip.
Difficulty: Moderately strenuous.
Topo maps: Burnt Fork Lake-MT; Stony Creek-MT; and Skalkaho Pass-MT.

On the north side of Skalkaho Pass look for an old wooden sign marked simply, "trail." This well-blazed but lightly used trail switchbacks steadily upward about 800 vertical feet in about 2 miles, then drops into a saddle where it intersects with the wider, more heavily used Crystal Lake Trail 10. After another mile through a mixed conifer forest the trail to Stony Lake splits off to the right, dropping 800 feet in less than 1 mile. There is a good campsite at the outlet. Dome Shaped Mountain could then be accessed by way of an 8-mile round-trip from this lakeside camp. The Sapphire crest is marked by sheer buff-colored cliffs, which rise from the deep southwest edge of the lake. The apex of the area—8,656-foot Dome Shaped Mountain—is another 4 miles north along the crest on Trail 313.

The hike to Dome Shaped Mountain is on good trail with a 1,400-foot elevation gain, most of which occurs in the first 2 miles as the trail climbs from the pass to the main divide. This high-country hike is entirely above 7,000 feet with no water along the ridge, so be sure to carry enough with you.

Continuing north whitebark pine becomes more prevalent, interspersed with subalpine larch. The country opens up from a rocky ridge 1 mile south of Dome Shaped Mountain. The top of the mountain is a large level plateau presenting magnificent mountain vistas in every direction. The ridge to the immediate north displays a brilliant reddish orange soil not found elsewhere in the vicinity. A metal sign denotes the "Easthouse Memorial Recreation Trail." Look for elk around the potholes at the head of Little Stony Creek and for more rarely seen mountain goats.

Quigg

16

Location: 26 miles southeast of Missoula.
Size: 77,000 acres.
Administration: USDAFS-Lolo and Deerlodge national forests; BLM-Garnet Resource Area.
Management status: Roadless non-wilderness, with some lands on the eastside Deerlodge Forest portion allocated to development in the forest plan.
Ecosystems: Middle Rocky Mountain coniferous forest province, characterized by high, steep, moderately glaciated mountains with glacial basins leading up to partially developed cirques; Precambrian granite and metasedimentary rock; Douglas-fir and western ponderosa forest types; and medium density of perennial streams.
Elevation range: 3,780 to 8,480 feet.
System trails: 50 miles.
Maximum core to perimeter distance: 5.5 miles.
Activities: Hiking, backpacking, cross-country skiing, horseback riding.
Modes of travel: Foot, skis, and horseback.
Maps: 1994 Lolo National Forest Visitor Map and 1990 Deerlodge National Forest Visitor Map; Grizzly Point-MT; Spink-MT; Quigg Peak-MT; and Alder Gulch-MT (1:24,000 topo maps).

OVERVIEW: Sliderock. Tens of thousands of acres of it are spread across half of the large oval-shaped Quigg roadless area in the northern Sapphires. Immediately east of the Stony Mountain country, talus slopes and Douglas-fir/lodgepole pine forests rise 4,500 feet from the bottom of Rock Creek to a series of high, open ridges and glacial moraines. The country is a study in contrasts: rugged enough for bighorn sheep and a few mountain goats, yet gentle enough for nursing and summering elk.

RECREATIONAL USES: Quigg contains five system trails totaling about 50 miles—a density light enough to allow sizeable chunks of trailless country. The five trailheads from north to south are Grizzly Creek, Ranch Creek, Butte Cabin Creek, Hogback, and Sandstone Ridge. All of the trails head out from the famous blue-ribbon trout stream, Rock Creek. Use is light, increasing to moderate during hunting season. A small amount of outfitted hunting occurs in Ranch Creek and along Sandstone Ridge.

A lack of pointed peaks, alpine lakes, and fishable streams explains the low number of summer and early fall visitors. So if you're looking for solitude, an exhilarating ridgetop hike, and a wild forested mountainscape in every direction, then give Quigg a second look.

16 QUIGG

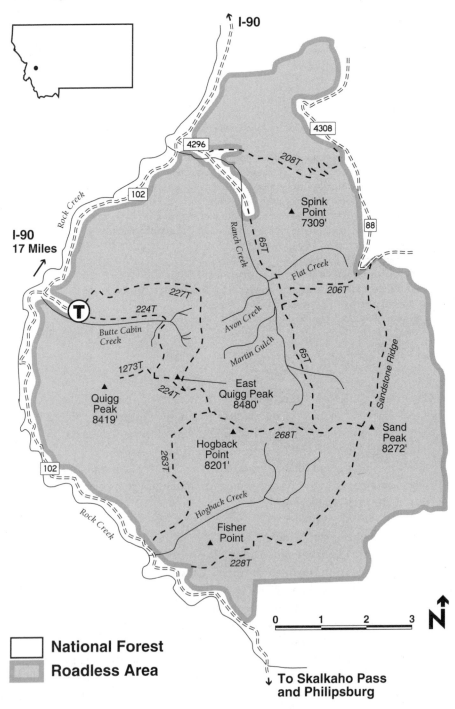

National Forest

Roadless Area

LOOKING NORTHWEST FROM QUIGG PEAK.

HOW TO GET THERE: Take the Rock Creek exit off I-90 about 25 miles east of Missoula and head south up Rock Creek on FR 102 for about 17 miles. Turn left onto a fairly rough road that winds 0.5 mile east to the trailhead for Butte Cabin Creek Trail 224.

DAY TRIP

Quigg Peak
Distance: 12-mile climb to and from Quigg Peak, or 16-mile loop trip to and from Quigg Peak.
Difficulty: Moderately strenuous.
Topo maps: Grizzly Point-MT and Quigg Peak-MT.

Butte Cabin Creek Trail 224 begins on the north side of the creek and can be easily located with a bit of searching. Sliderock is continuous for miles along the bottom. The trail climbs steadily for 2,000 feet in a forest that changes constantly from old ponderosa pine and Douglas-fir to spruce and subalpine fir, and finally to open lodgepole pine forest above the forks where the trail veers south toward Quigg Peak. Upon reaching the main ridge at 7,700 feet the trail angles to a saddle and then onto the top of 8,419-foot Quigg Peak. The remains of an old fire lookout are scattered across the rounded, grassy summit. The trip back down to the trailhead is a delight—a classic 4,000-foot descent from the grassy, rock-strewn peak to a high, narrow ridge of whitebark pine above a steep headwall, to a lateral moraine paralleling the creek, and, finally, along a tight stream bottom with moss-covered rocks and a soft dirt trail. This is a moderately strenuous 12-mile round-trip.

A variation on the return would be to hike 2 miles east to the highest point in the roadless area (8,480-foot East Quigg Peak) and then 3 miles north on Trail 227 to where it turns west on the north ridge above Butte Cabin Creek. This would add about 4 miles to the route, with the advantage of a loop. Both of these lightly used trails are suitable for hiking or horseback riding. Be sure to carry plenty of water when exploring this high, dry ridge country.

Welcome Creek
Wilderness

17

Location: 27 miles southeast of Missoula.
Size: 29,235 acres.
Administration: USDAFS—Lolo National Forest.
Management status: 28,135-acre Wilderness (1978); 1,100 acres of contiguous non-wilderness roadless land.
Ecosystems: Middle Rocky Mountain coniferous forest province, characterized by steep, moderately glaciated mountains; Douglas-fir forest type with lodgepole pine and spruce-fir in the general forest zone and ponderosa pine at lower elevations; deeply cut streams.
Elevation range: 3,750 to 7,723 feet.
System trails: 30 miles.
Maximum core to perimeter distance: 2.5 miles.
Activities: Hiking, backpacking, horseback riding, cross-country skiing.
Modes of travel: Foot, skis, and horse.
Maps: 1991 Lolo National Forest Visitors Map; Elk Mountain-MT; Iris Point-MT; Cleveland Mountain-MT; and Grizzly Point-MT (1:24,000 topo maps).

OVERVIEW: The 28,135-acre Welcome Creek Wilderness, along with 1,100 acres of contiguous roadless land on the south, borders the west side of Rock Creek, a famed trout stream. The densely forested slopes, exposed ridges, and deep canyons of this heart-shaped Wilderness contribute an all-too-rare example of relatively low-elevation general forest to the National Wilderness System. The land rises gently from the main Sapphire Range Divide and then drops abruptly to form breaks that are surprisingly steep and rough. Old-growth stands of lodgepole pine interspersed with sylvan groves of spruce and Douglas-fir provide homes for elk, deer, mountain lion, bobcat, pine marten, mink, and weasel. Some of the lower slopes near Rock Creek are parklike, with stately stands of large, yellow-plated ponderosa pine.

The wildness of Welcome Creek is captured by an excerpt from the October 14, 1974 journal of noted Montana conservationist Bud Moore: "

> Except for [Welcome] Creek's energetic music, I hiked alone in silence deepened by the mountain's shadow. Each intimate twist in the trail—there are many—opened sudden new vistas, mini worlds they were, each different from the last, expanding ahead then closing behind a giant rock point or spruce tree as I ambled on through the spell of evening hush.

17 WELCOME CREEK WILDERNESS

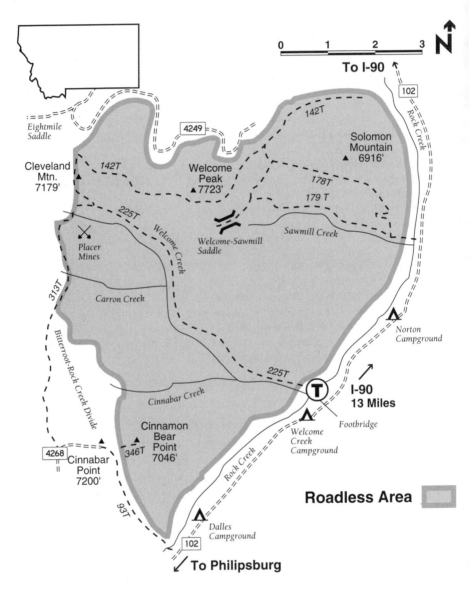

0   1   2   3

N

To I-90

102

Rock Creek

Eightmile
Saddle

4249

142T

Solomon
Mountain
▲ 6916'

Cleveland
Mtn.
7179'

142T

Welcome
Peak
▲ 7723'

178T

179 T

225T

Welcome Creek

Sawmill Creek

Placer
Mines

Welcome-Sawmill
Saddle

313T

Carron Creek

Bitterroot-Rock Creek Divide

Norton
Campground

225T

T

**I-90
13 Miles**

Cinnabar Creek

Footbridge

Cinnamon
Bear
Point
7046'

Welcome
Creek
Campground

4268

346T

Cinnabar
Point
7200'

93T

Rock Creek

Roadless Area

Dalles
Campground

102

To Philipsburg

Welcome Creek has a past as colorful as the gold that lured outlaws, cabin-builders, and miners here more than a century ago. Gold was first discovered in Welcome Creek in 1888; most of the paydirt was extracted from placer claims. During its fleeting mining era Welcome Creek yielded one of the largest gold nuggets ever found in Montana—tipping the scales at 1.5 pounds. When the mines were abandoned, the steep mountains of Welcome Creek became a hideout for fugitives. One of the more infamous of these was Frank Brady, who met his end in a 1904 Thanksgiving Day shootout at a Welcome Creek cabin. Today, slowly decomposing cabins are very much a part of Welcome Creek's history and mystique. The crumbling remains of at least a dozen old cabins can be found, often in places where you least expect them. Of these, only two are in fair condition, one at the mouth of Cinnabar Creek, and the Carron Cabin.

Welcome Creek was designated Wilderness in 1978 as part of the Endangered American Wilderness Act largely through the good efforts of the late Senator Lee Metcalf (D-MT) and of Montana conservationists who recognized the relationship between protecting the headwaters of Rock Creek and maintaining its superb water quality and fishery.

RECREATIONAL USES: There are about 30 miles of trails, most of which lie on steep ridges and in the narrow stream bottoms. Most of the use occurs during the fall hunting season, and most of this is confined to the lower several miles of the stream-bottom trails. Summer day hiking is increasing in popularity; the most popular route is across the Welcome Creek swinging bridge over Rock Creek. Because forage for stock is scarce, less than 10 percent of the use involves horses for riding or packing.

Steep terrain and dense vegetation limit the number of suitable campsites near the larger streams, and only a few of these are adequate for larger parties. For this reason the maximum party size for both day use and overnight stays is ten people. The number of riding or pack animals is also limited to ten per party.

Cross-country skiing can be excellent in the high basins near or just below the Sapphire Divide in the western portion of the Wilderness. Ideal terrain and good late-season snow conditions compensate for the difficult access to the higher country. Avalanche hazard is generally moderate due to the mostly moderate mid-to-low-elevation terrain throughout most of the wilderness. Snowslide danger tends to be higher in narrow chutes on steep slopes just above the main drainages. Be sure to check local avalanche reports before venturing into the backcountry during ski season.

HOW TO GET THERE: Welcome Creek Wilderness sits in the northern Sapphire Range with I-90 to the north and the Sapphire Divide as its western backbone.

SPRINGTIME IN THE MAIN WELCOME CREEK DRAINAGE.

Welcome Creek can be visited on trails originating from FR 102 on the east (Rock Creek), FR 640 on the west (Three Mile), and FR 4249 on the north (Upper Gilbert). By far the best access is provided from Rock Creek as described in the following suggested trip. Take the Rock Creek exit on I-90 25 miles east of Missoula and follow the good gravel Rock Creek Road (FR 102) upstream. As you proceed up Rock Creek the Welcome Creek Wilderness is across the creek on the right from about mile 7 to mile 18.

DAY HIKE OR BACKPACK

Welcome Creek to Cleveland Mountain
Distance: 10 to 25 miles.
Difficulty: Moderate to strenuous.
Topo maps: Elk Mountain-MT; Cleveland Mountain-MT; and Grizzly Point-MT.

From I-90 drive about 13 miles south on Rock Creek Road (FR 102) to a sturdy suspension bridge across Rock Creek which leads directly to the Wilderness boundary and Welcome Creek Trail 225. Although once heavily used, the Welcome Creek trail today is little more than a game path in places. Dark forests, boiling streams, varied wildlife, and canyon solitude make up the hidden wilderness treasures of Welcome Creek. The trail climbs gradually at first through dense forest. As the gradient of the trail increases, so do its lack of maintenance and primitive nature. Some segments are nearly overgrown with gooseberry, nettles, and dogwood. This can be a demanding out-and-back day trip or a more relaxed overnighter. Intimate campsites can be found at the mouths of Cinnabar and Carron creeks and about 7 miles up near Spartan Creek. Canyons, cabins, and a climb to the Sapphire Divide are among the highlights.

An extension of this trip would be to climb Cleveland Mountain and then proceed north along the Sapphire Divide to Trail 142, which climbs several miles east to the apex of the Wilderness—7,723-foot Welcome Point. In the 1960s the Forest Service built a logging road for a marginal timber sale for which there were no bidders. If you're up for adventure take a trail about 2 miles south to the Welcome-Sawmill Saddle and then bushwhack down a series of steep ridges 1.5 miles to Welcome Creek where you'll end up just upstream from the Carron Cabin some 5 miles above the Rock Creek Road. This extended loop is almost 25 miles in length. Traversing it, you will have experienced the heart of this small but ecologically significant Wilderness.

Rattlesnake
Wilderness
Complex

18

Location: 4.5 miles north of Missoula.

Size: About 101,000 acres.

Administration: USDAFS-Lolo National Forest; Confederated Salish & Kootenai tribes.

Management status: A 61,000-acre National Recreation Area, which includes 32,844 acres of Wilderness in the higher country plus the North Fork Jocko Tribal Primitive Area on the Flathead Indian Reservation to the north.

Ecosystems: Northern Rocky Mountain coniferous forest-alpine meadow province, characterized by steep, glaciated overthrust mountains with sharp alpine ridges and cirques; Precambrian metasedimentary and soft sedimentary rocks along with glacial deposits; Douglas-fir and western ponderosa forest types; abundant perennial streams and higher elevation lakes.

Elevation range: 3,600 to 8,620 feet.

System trails: 56 miles.

Maximum core to perimeter distance: 5 miles.

Activities: Hiking, mountain biking, backpacking, cross-country skiing, fishing, horseback riding.

Modes of travel: Foot, skis, horse, mountain bike.

Maps: 1994 Lolo National Forest Visitor Map; Belmore Sloughs-MT; Upper Jocko Lake-MT; Stuart Peak-MT; Wapiti Lake-MT; Gold Creek Peak-MT; Northeast Missoula-MT; and Blue Point-MT (1:24,000 topo maps).

OVERVIEW: With the major trailhead only 4.5 miles north of Missoula, the 61,000 acres of glaciated topography in the Rattlesnake Wilderness and National Recreation Area (RWNRA) form Montana's premier urban wilderness, blending the best of both wilderness and civilization. The U-shaped Rattlesnake basin is fed by more than fifty small creeks that begin as seeps from springs and melting snowbanks in the upper Wilderness portion of the NRA. Resting in the more than thirty high mountain lakes, crystal clear water then plunges down waterfalls to hanging valleys separated by sheer headwalls and carpets of sub-alpine fir, lodgepole pine, and spruce sloping down to open Douglas-fir and ponderosa pine parklands.

The non-wilderness (yet still wild) part of the NRA, devoted to wildlife and recreation, is guarded by the southern flanks of Stuart Peak. From this

18 RATTLESNAKE WILDERNESS COMPLEX

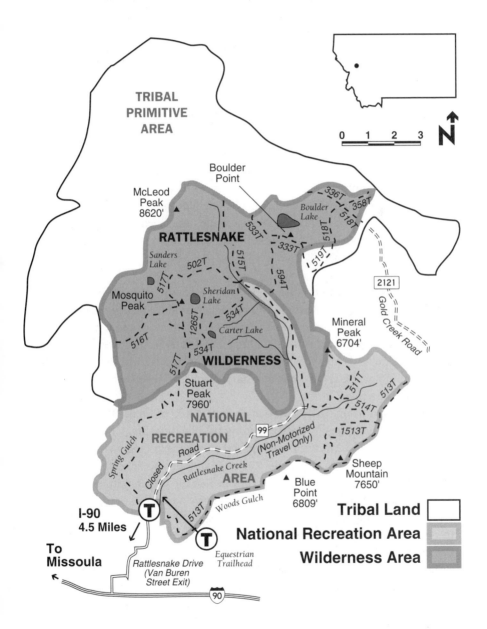

TRIBAL PRIMITIVE AREA

Boulder Point

McLeod Peak 8620'

RATTLESNAKE

Boulder Lake

336T
358T
518T
519T

533T

333T

Sanders Lake

502T

515T

594T

517T

Mosquito Peak

Sheridan Lake

1265T

534T

Carter Lake

516T

534T

WILDERNESS

Mineral Peak 6704'

2121

Gold Creek Road

517T

Stuart Peak 7960'

NATIONAL

511T

513T

514T

RECREATION

99

1513T

Spring Gulch

Road

(Non-Motorized Travel Only)

Closed

Rattlesnake Creek

AREA

Sheep Mountain 7650'

Blue Point 6809'

I-90
4.5 Miles

513T   Woods Gulch

To Missoula

Rattlesnake Drive (Van Buren Street Exit)

Equestrian Trailhead

90

0 1 2 3   N

Tribal Land

National Recreation Area

Wilderness Area

prominent point north a knife ridge climbs still higher to the sentinel of the Rattlesnake—remote 8,620-foot McLeod Peak. The east side of the ridge is marked by cliffs, cirques, and rolling basins of intermittent subalpine forest where transplanted mountain goats are thriving in the security of protected wildlands. The gentler western slopes lead down to the open bowl-like basin of upper Grant Creek. Although uncommon, occasional grizzly bears roam here, and every so often the haunting howl of a lone wolf deepens the feeling of wildness.

The adjacent wildlands north of McLeod Peak and the rugged Rattlesnake Divide were once vision-quest sites for the Salish Indians. Today, the Flathead Indian Reservation protects this land—the South Fork Jocko Tribal Primitive Area—as a sacred place open only to tribal members.

The wild core of the Rattlesnake Mountains stands as an enduring model of citizen determination to reclaim wildness from past logging, water development, and intermingled private land. The late University of Montana forestry dean and noted conservationist, Arnold Bolle, described this place as " . . . a pearl full of intimate little surprises . . . full of memories of happy kids, beautiful scenes, and special discoveries."

RECREATIONAL USES: Day use is by far the dominant form of recreation, largely due to a rapid increase in use by joggers and mountain bikers up both the main Rattlesnake Creek and Spring Gulch. With more and more mountain bikers penetrating the entire 16-mile-long non-wilderness Rattlesnake corridor as well as side trails and tributaries, restrictions on bike use for public safety are becoming necessary. Potentially dangerous are steep, narrow trails with blind curves, such as Spring Gulch.

Hunting and fishing are traditional uses of the Rattlesnake Wilderness. The main Rattlesnake Creek is open to catch-and-release fishing above the mouth of Beeskove Creek. Many of the high lakes are periodically stocked. When snow conditions permit, the main Rattlesnake and side drainages are readily accessible to cross-country skiers. For much of the upper Rattlesnake, recreation levels are much lower than in the "bigger name" wildernesses that are more distant from population centers. This is partly due to difficulty of access. Just to get to the wilderness boundary visitors must climb nearly 4,000 feet and cover 8 to 9 miles by horse or foot. The most popular access is from the main entrance (FR 99) and Stuart Peak Trail 517, which heads up Spring Gulch to the north just beyond the main entrance. As much as 95 percent of the overall use begins at the main entrance parking lot and more than two-thirds of those visitors continue up the main Rattlesnake drainage. Other popular routes include Sheep Mountain Trail 516 and Triangle Peak Trail 533.

The maximum party size is ten people along with a maximum of ten head of pack or saddle stock per party. Outfitter services are not available within the

Winter sets into Upper Grant Creek, on the west end of the
Rattlesnake Wilderness.

Wilderness portion of the National Recreation Area. Overnight camping is prohibited within 3 miles of the main Rattlesnake trailhead to protect water quality. Shooting is not allowed within the same 3-mile zone for public safety.

The South Fork Jocko Tribal Primitive Area, to the north of the main Rattlesnake Divide, is open only to members of the Salish and Kootenai tribes on the Flathead Indian Reservation.

HOW TO GET THERE: Take the Van Buren Street exit off I-90 on the east end of Missoula and go 4.5 miles north on Rattlesnake Drive to the main parking area and jumping-off point on the west side of Rattlesnake Creek. The road takes off up the old Rattlesnake FR 99, now closed to all motorized recreational travel. If you're visiting the Rattlesnake on horseback, park at the recently completed trailhead for equestrians on the east side of Rattlesnake Creek. The new horse trail leads to a horses-only bridge across the Rattlesnake just above the Stuart Peak/Spring Gulch trail.

DAY TRIP

Rattlesnake Creek
Distance: 4 to 6 miles out-and-back.
Difficulty: Easy.
Topo map: Northwest Missoula, MT.

A delightful trip, for an hour, a day, or longer, is to stroll, ski, bike, or horseback ride along scenic Rattlesnake Creek from the main entrance at Sawmill Gulch. Numerous short side trails drop down along the creek and eventually rejoin the main road (which is closed to motorized use). After about 3 miles you'll come to picturesque abandoned homesteads, a good turnaround point.

BACKPACK

Upper Rattlesnake Loop
Distance: 35-mile loop (3 to 4 days).
Difficulty: Strenuous.
Topo maps: Stuart Peak-MT; Wapiti Lake-MT; Northeast Missoula-MT; and Blue Point-MT.

The day hike described above is just the beginning. If you go farther and climb more steeply, you will encounter fewer and fewer people. After the first 5 miles there are lots of good camping spots. At mile 13 the trail forks toward the head of Rattlesnake, Lake, and Wrangle creeks. Take Trail 502 for about 3 miles to Little Lake and then on another mile to alpine Glacier Lake, from where both mountain sheep and goats are sometimes seen. From the lake it is a steep climb to the crest of Rattlesnake ridge. Continue south on the high ridge Trail 517 about 3 miles to Stuart Peak, then down Spring Gulch to the main entrance for a three- or four-day 35-mile loop.

DAY HIKE, SKI, OR SNOWSHOE

Stuart Peak
Distance: 19 miles.
Difficulty: Strenuous.
Topo maps: Stuart Peak-MT and Northeast Missoula-MT.

The climb to the summit of 7,960-foot Stuart Peak by way of Spring Gulch is a tough but rewarding 19-mile round-trip day hike or snowshoe/ski trip that will take you 4,100 feet above the trailhead. This summit offers one of the finest 360-degree vistas of any in the Rattlesnake. For solitude and a little more adventure, head up the main drainage about 3.5 miles, and then climb cross country up one of the several north-south ridges that intersect toward the top of Stuart Peak. Don't forget to take along plenty of drinking water because it is scarce on any of the ridge climbs. The cross-country midsection of this loop route is best completed on the uphill leg followed by the Stuart Peak Trail 517 down Spring Gulch—not only to make a loop out of the trip but because you'll probably be slogging this segment after dark and appreciate being on a trail.

Reservation Divide 19

Location: 20 miles northwest of Missoula.
Size: About 31,000 acres, 15,962 acres of which are on Lolo National Forest.
Administration: USDAFS-Lolo National Forest; and Confederated Salish and Kootenai tribes.
Management status: Roadless non-wilderness, with some lands allocated to future development on both sides of the divide.
Ecosystems: Northern Rocky Mountain coniferous forest province, characterized by steep, dissected mountains, narrow valleys; Precambrian and metasedimentary rocks; Douglas-fir and western ponderosa forest types; steep, deeply cut perennial streams.
Elevation range: 5,400 to 7,996 feet.
System trails: 34 miles.
Maximum core to perimeter distance: 1.5 miles.
Activities: Hiking, backpacking, cross-country skiing, and horseback riding.
Modes of travel: Foot, skis, and horse.
Maps: 1994 Lolo National Forest Visitor Map; Reservation Divide Trails pamphlet by the Lolo NF; Knowles-MT; Perma-MT; Stark North-MT; McCormick Peak-MT; and Hewolf Mountain-MT (1:24,000 topo maps).

OVERVIEW: The Reservation Divide forms the rugged backbone between the Ninemile Valley and the Flathead Indian Reservation. Along its crest a linear northwest-trending roadless area drapes both sides to about midslope. From the distinctive cone-shaped summit of 7,996-foot Squaw Peak—highest point on the divide—this wildland twists along the mountain crest for 30 up-and-down miles.

Scree slopes along the divide plummet to the more gradual headwall basins of major streams. On the reservation side below secluded Three Lakes Peak, minor glaciation has formed hanging valleys and carved partial cirques into the north faces of several peaks where tiny, deep lakes are nestled. Although close to the populated Ninemile Valley, the country is still wild enough for a resident wolf pack, attracted by a large white-tailed deer prey base. Giant western red cedar and devil's club understory in Kennedy Creek are among the many surprises in this narrow band of ridgetop wild country.

RECREATIONAL USES: The Forest Service considers Reservation Divide to be a backcountry "alternative" to designated wilderness—a sort of in-between set-

19 RESERVATION DIVIDE

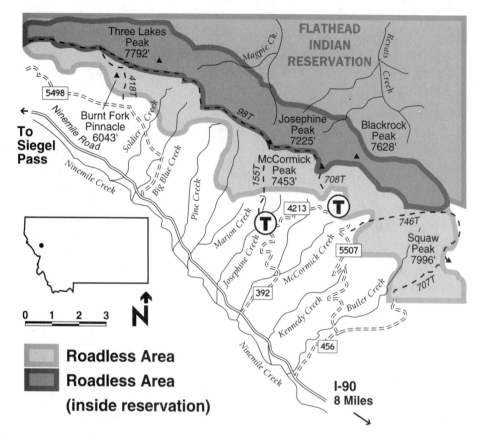

ting unsuitable for either primitive or highly developed recreation. Ironically, because of light use, visitors can enjoy more wilderness solitude here than in many of our better-known wilderness areas. Logging and mining roads in Rock, Stony, Butler, Kennedy, McCormick, Josephine, Marion, and Pine creeks reach upslope to the roadless boundary. The country is bounded by Edith Peak Road 476 on the southeast and the electronic site just above the foothills road (FR 5498) at Siegel Pass on the northwest.

Fall hunting accounts for most of the use, but summer hikes and horseback trips have gained in popularity. The only permitted outfitter in the area uses llamas on summer trips along the divide. Parts of six trails totaling 34 miles wind up to, along, and near the twisting divide, each offering pleasurable excursions. Please remember that you'll need a tribal recreation permit when traveling on the Flathead Indian Reservation side of the divide.

NEAR MCCORMICK PEAK LOOKING BACK TO BLACKROCK PEAK ALONG THE MAIN
RESERVATION DIVIDE.

HOW TO GET THERE: From Missoula drive 23 miles west on I-90 and take the
Ninemile exit. Drive 1.7 miles on the frontage road and turn right (northwest)
up the main Ninemile Road, past the historic Ninemile Ranger Station. Drive 11
miles to McCormick Creek Road (FR 392). Turn north (right) and go 2.3 miles
to the FR 4213 after crossing Little McCormick Creek. Continue on FR 4213
another 8 miles to the road closure, which serves as the trailhead for McCormick
Peak Trail 708. To reach Josephine Peak Trail 155 take FR 4213 for 3 miles to
FR 890, turn left, and drive 2.5 miles to the road closure. Another 3 miles by
foot, horse, skis, or mountain bike will bring you to the beginning of Trail 155.

DAY HIKE OR SKI ASCENT

McCormick Peak
Distance: 8 miles out-and-back; 10 to 12 miles on skis.
Difficulty: Moderate.
Topo maps: McCormick Peak-MT.

Although its narrow, linear shape and relatively small size limit the Reservation Divide to mostly day use, it offers many variations of loop and point-
to-point trips. Trail 708 begins at 6,000 feet in heavily-logged upper
McCormick Creek, then climbs 1,400 feet in 2 miles through lodgepole-grouse
whortleberry and talus rock, curving around the west side of 7,453-foot

McCormick Peak. The summit affords a spectacular view, from the Missions to the Bitterroots. Head north down the peak to intercept the unmaintained Trail 708 for the 2-mile journey to 7,223-foot Josephine Peak. The trail loses 1,000 feet as it drops into the saddle between the two rock-strewn summits.

If you want to vary this excursion with a point-to-point hike from McCormick Peak to Josephine Creek post a car at the road closure 2.5 miles up FR 890, which takes off from FR 4213 about 5 miles below the McCormick Peak trailhead. The other possibility is to talk your hiking partner into doubling back to the car and meeting you at the FR 890 road closure. The southward descent is delightful from Josephine Peak on Trail 155, which is actually an old jeep track slowly reverting to a primitive trail. After 2.5 miles and a 1,050-foot drop, Trail 155 joins FR 890. Turn left and take this grassy logging road 3 easy miles through clearcuts to the road closure just after crossing Josephine Creek. This roadbed is well suited for mountain biking to the start of the Josephine Peak Trail 155. It can also be skied during winter for an ascent of Josephine Peak by way of Trail 155, although an additional couple of miles of road skiing might be necessary, depending on road conditions. The forested, high ridge route to the centrally located 7,223-foot peak involves a steady, moderate climb with an overall 2,400-foot gain to the summit. Once on Josephine there is good access along the divide in both directions for high ridge side trips. Avalanche danger is minimal with these ridge and forest routes.

BACKPACK

Reservation Divide
Distance: 30 miles point-to-point.
Difficulty: Strenuous.
Topo maps: Knowles-MT; Perma-MT; Stark North-MT; McCormick Peak-MT; and Hewolf Mountain-MT.

Perhaps the ultimate Reservation Divide exploration is a traverse of the entire 30-mile divide from Siegel Pass southeast to Edith Peak Road (FR 476). The Reservation Divide West Trail 98.1 begins at an electronic site 1 mile above Siegel Pass on FR 5572, following the crest for 15 miles to McCormick Peak. The trailhead is 27 miles from the Ninemile Ranger Station by way of Ninemile Road, Foothills Road (FR 5498), and FR 5572. From McCormick Peak the next 8 miles to Squaw Peak require slow, trailless, but not difficult, hiking (or skiing in good snow conditions) across talus, scree, and bear grass-mantled ridges. You'll then intercept Kennedy Creek Trail 746, which climbs from the end of FR 5507 for 6 miles into the head of Butler Creek, reaching the divide about 2 miles north of 7,996-foot Squaw Peak. This apex of the roadless area provides a commanding view of much of western Montana—

from Glacier National Park south to the Continental Divide crest of the Anaconda-Pintlers. Continue southeast along the divide, picking up Trail 98.3 for the final 3.5 mile, 1,800-foot drop to Edith Peak Road 476. This trip deserves three days, a car shuttle, and at least two camps along the divide. Water is scarce late in the season. Good (but dry) camps can be found within 0.25 mile of springs near Burnt Fork Pinnacle and just south of majestic 7,792-foot Three Lakes Peak, which overlooks a trio of sparkling glacial tarns.

Mount Bushnell

Location: 5 miles south of Thompson Falls.
Size: 41,168 acres.
Administration: USFS—Lolo National Forest.
Management status: Roadless non-wilderness; portions allocated to development in the forest plan.
Ecosystems: Northern Rocky Mountain coniferous forest province, characterized by Precambrian and metasedimentary rocks; Douglas-fir and western ponderosa forest types with open parks, talus, and brushy, south-facing slopes scattered throughout; and with numerous perennial streams.
Elevation range: 2,800 to 6,081 feet.
Miles of system trails: 55 miles.
Maximum core to perimeter distance: 4 miles.
Activities: Hiking, backpacking, cross-country skiing, horseback riding, fishing, mountain biking.
Modes of travel: Foot, ski, horse, and mountain bike.
Maps: 1994 Lolo National Forest Visitor Map; Driveway Peak-MT; Table Top Mountain-MT; Thompson Falls-MT; Saltese-MT; Haugan-MT; and De Borgia North-MT (1:24,000 topo maps).

OVERVIEW: The east-west trending Cabinet-Coeur d'Alene (CC) Divide winds through the center of the Mount Bushnell roadless area, crossing the area's namesake 5,980-foot summit. Densely forested with lodgepole pine from the monumental 1910 fire, Mount Bushnell displays an inviting mix of mountain parks, talus and scree sideslopes, and warm, south-facing brushfields. Boggy springs in creek bottoms are favored by summering elk, and sizeable deer herds attract stalking mountain lions. Although lacking high, jagged peaks, Mount Bushnell is one of the last and best unroaded places for elk security in this part of western Montana. Lush riparian areas provide habitat for the tailed frog and Coeur d'Alene salamander. An extensive, well-distributed trail system resembles the branching pattern of area streams. The high CC Divide affords commanding views of this mountainous region of western Montana.

RECREATIONAL USES: On the surface and from a distance the country appears nondescript, a lightly used blank spot on the map. When things quiet down after hunting season a few cross-country skiers venture up toward the CC

20 MOUNT BUSHNELL

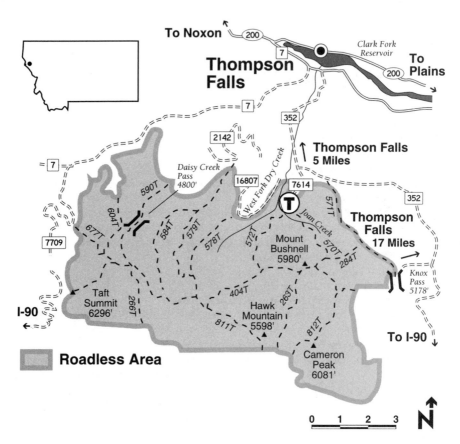

Roadless Area

Divide. Fishing, hiking, and horseback riding are popular on the well-distributed trail system as the season progresses. Visitors are attracted to the vista points of Mount Bushnell, Table Top Mountain, Taft Summit, and Hill 7. The more popular travel routes are the higher reaches of the 12 system trails and the CC Divide. An occasional mountain biker rides from 5,178-foot Knox Pass west on FR 378 and then along the divide 2 to 3 miles on a more primitive jeep track to 5,980-foot Mount Bushnell.

A June hike along the summit ridge of Mount Bushnell—east end of the roadless area.

How to get there: From just west of Thompson Falls on MT 200 turn south on FR 7. Drive about 1.5 miles, take a left toward the Gaging Station, then drive 5 miles south up Dry Creek Road 352. Turn right (south) on FR 7614 and go about 1 mile to the trailhead at road's end on the West Fork of Dry Creek for Trails 570 and 572.

Day Hike or Horseback Loop

Mount Bushnell Summit

Distance: 10 to 12 miles.
Difficulty: Moderate.
Topo map: Table Top Mountain-MT; Thompson Falls-MT; Haugan-MT; and De Borgia North-MT.

Climb steadily up Joan Creek on Trail 570 through an alternately thick then open forest with occasional views of adjacent sliderock and forested hillsides. After about 2 miles the trail drops to cross Joan Creek, a good place to fill up your water bottle. Another mile brings you to Trail 284. Take a right for the final uphill walk to the CC Divide. Head west up the gentle, forested slope to Mount Bushnell on Trail 404, which is actually an unobtrusive jeep trail from Knox Pass. The 2,800-foot elevation gain from the trailhead on the West Fork of Dry Creek to 5,980-foot Mount Bushnell is evenly spread over 4 miles. The rock-strewn summit is ringed by dense forest but still provides an open, all-encompassing vista of the Cabinets and other nearby mountain ranges. Continue west on the divide another 2 miles and then take a right on Trail 572. The trail descends a ridge through doghair lodgepole pine into the West Fork and back to the trailhead, thereby completing a varied loop through the center of one of the last large, unroaded, midelevation forests in the region.

Sheep Mountain–
State Line

Location: 2 miles west of Superior.
Size: 64,608 acres; 37,629 acres of which are in Montana.
Administration: USDAFS—Lolo and Saint Joe national forests.
Management status: Roadless non-wilderness in the higher country with some peripheral lands allocated to development in the forest plan.
Ecosystems: Northern Rocky Mountain coniferous forest-alpine meadow province, characterized by steep, dissected mountains, narrow valleys; Precambrian and metasedimentary rocks; Douglas-fir forest type and some alpine vegetation; steep, deeply cut perennial streams along with some lakes in high, glaciated basins.
Elevation range: 3,100 to 7,543 feet.
System trails: 36 miles.
Maximum core to perimeter distance: 2 miles.
Activities: Hiking, backpacking, horseback riding, cross-country skiing, mountain biking.
Modes of travel: Foot, skis, horse, mountain bike.
Maps: 1994 Lolo National Forest Visitor Map; Torino Peak-MT; Wilson Gulch-MT; Sherlock Peak-MT; and Illinois Peak-MT (1:24,000 topo maps).

OVERVIEW: Prehistoric Indians used the Bitterroot Divide within the Sheep Mountain roadless area for hunting as long ago as 6,000 years. Grinding tools found along the crest tell of the existence of widespread whitebark pine forests prior to the 1910 fire. Snow cornices up to 6 feet thick hang over the divide through early summer, giving rise to major streams flowing east to the Clark Fork River.

Raking in almost 70 inches of annual precipitation, the high Bitterroot crest is a true maritime habitat of mountain hemlock and subalpine fir. The State Line Trail contours through open clumps of stunted whitebark pine, products of past fires. The influence of these burns is especially striking at the head of Dry Creek, with its graveyards of white snags sticking up through fields of *Menziesia*, ninebark, and bear grass. An increasing number of moose along with mountain lion, lynx, and wolverine roam these forested highlands, as do summering elk in secluded hanging valleys where nine cirque lakes are nestled along the foot of the divide.

RECREATIONAL USES: Big-game hunting in the fall attracts most of the visitors. A few hunters pack in, including the area's single permitted outfitter, but most hunters head out on day trips from the major forest roads encircling the

21 SHEEP MOUNTAIN–STATE LINE

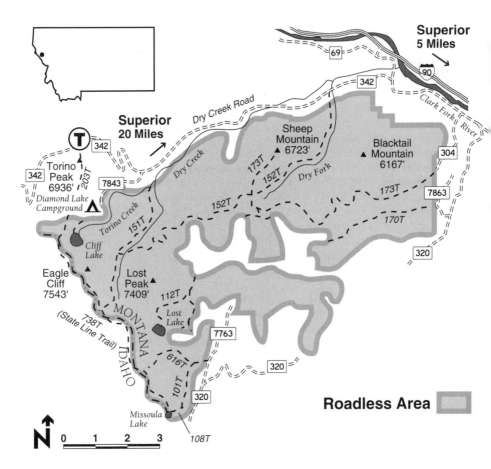

roadless area. Day-use fishing is also popular in Diamond Lake and at Cliff Lake, which is nestled in a cirque 500 feet above and 1 mile beyond the end-of-the road access to Diamond Lake. The sheer rock walls and permanent snowfield on the west end of Cliff Lake make the climb well worthwhile.

Hiking along the State Line National Recreation Trail is gaining in popularity although it would be a rare day, even during summer, to encounter more than one other party. Trails to several of the lake basins, such as the Bonanza Lakes, drop off the State Line Trail, providing fairly easy access. The snow usually clears off the divide and sheltered high places by the first or second week of July. At any time the weather along the exposed divide can be extreme, so be prepared with foul-weather clothing and survival gear, even on day trips.

The Sheep Mountain country has a strange blend of accessibility and remoteness, caused by good primary access from I-90 to an unknown region where solitude is deepened by steep terrain and heavy vegetation. From Superior, the Dry Creek Road (FR 342) on the north and the Cedar Creek Road (FR 320) to the south provide access to side roads and trailheads. About 8.5 miles of twisting high divide separate the two roads—an excellent day horseback ride or hike if cars are shuttled at both trailheads.

Winter use is almost nonexistent in this country. However, experienced backcountry skiers would enjoy ski touring up Thompson Creek Trail 173 with its moderate grade and lack of avalanche hazard. A bit of searching will be required at times to find the trail. The trail takes off from the end of FR 304 about 3 miles southwest of Superior and it climbs in and out of gullies above Thompson Creek to its intersection with the Dry Fork Trail about 9 miles up. Another good winter ski or snowshoe trip is to climb 6,723-foot Sheep Mountain by way of Dry Fork Trail 152, which takes off from Dry Creek Road (FR 342) about 2 miles above the interstate. This strenuous but rewarding 12- to 13-mile round-trip should be attempted only in stable snow conditions. In an avalanche chute about 1 mile up the Dry Fork, snowslides have snapped large trees like matchsticks 20 feet above the ground.

MID-JUNE AT HEART LAKE, BELOW THE STATE LINE-BITTERROOT DIVIDE.

WEST FROM EAGLE CLIFF PEAK, ALONG THE STATE LINE-BITTERROOT DIVIDE.

A variation of a Sheep Mountain trip during summer would be to mountain bike 3.5 miles up gated FR 7865 to Trail 152 and then hike the 4 or 5 miles to Sheep Mountain, where the remains of an old lookout add interest to the best vantage point of any of the peaks off the State Line Divide. FR 7865 takes off from the Cedar Creek Road about 6 miles southwest of Superior. With the exception of the short Cliff Lake Trail 100, most of the trails are suitable for horses. Native forage is scarce, so horse feed should be packed in.

HOW TO GET THERE: From Superior drive 5 miles west on I-90 and head southwest on Dry Creek Road (FR 342). After about 9 miles the road begins climbing along a series of switchbacks for another 5 or 6 miles to the trailhead for Trail 203 just north of 6,936-foot Torino Peak. FR 342 continues on past the trailhead to the stateline and on into Idaho.

OVERNIGHTER

State Line Divide
Distance: 12 miles point-to-point.
Difficulty: Moderate.
Topo map: Torino Peak-MT.

Because of persistent snowfields along the divide the lower Torino Peak trailhead for Trail 203 can usually be reached by car a week or two earlier, by early to mid-June. This scenic ridgeline trail provides a superb view of the Cliff Lake basin and the rocky buttress of 7,543-foot Eagle Cliff Mountain rising from the State Line Divide. Upon reaching the divide head south for 3 to 4 miles, picking up Trail 151, which drops steeply through bear grass slopes into the head of Dry Creek to aptly named Heart Lake—fishless but well suited for high-country camping.

Dry Creek is a pristine, U-shaped, glacier-carved valley where wildflowers explode in a flurry of color by July. Heading down Dry Creek, the trail drops off a steep headwall with a stunning waterfall just below the first crossing. The 2 miles down to Hidden Creek require three stream crossings, but then the trail stays cooperatively along the west side of the tumbling creek for the remaining 4 miles to the trailhead. With a drop of 2,300 feet in the 6 miles from Heart Lakes to Dry Creek Road the well-maintained trail is painfully steep in places. This is more than compensated for by expansive views of the entire Dry Creek drainage with its blend of meadows, avalanche chutes, and mountain parks breaking up an otherwise dense forest. A large meadow marks the halfway point with a panorama back toward the rugged rock cliffs of the divide.

The car shuttle for this point-to-point excursion can easily be accomplished by leaving a vehicle at the Dry Fork trailhead for Trail 151, which is along the road on the way up to the Torino Peak trailhead.

Burdette Creek

22

Location: 25 miles west of Missoula.
Size: 16,360 acres.
Administration: USDAFS—Lolo National Forest.
Management status: Roadless non-wilderness with wildlife emphasis, small amount of peripheral land allocated to future development in the forest plan.
Ecosystems: Northern Rocky Mountain coniferous forest province, characterized by steep, dissected mountains with rounded upper ridges; Precambrian and metasedimentary rocks; Douglas-fir and western ponderosa forest types; mostly steep, moderately cut drainages.
Elevation range: 3,380 to 6,302 feet.
System trails: 4 miles.
Maximum core to perimeter distance: 2.5 miles.
Activities: Hiking, backpacking, cross-country skiing, horseback riding.
Modes of travel: Foot, skis, and horse.
Maps: 1994 Lolo National Forest Visitor Map; Lupine Creek-MT (1:24,000 topo map).

OVERVIEW: Past forest fires have transformed almost all of the Burdette Creek roadless area into superb wildlife winter range where some 400 elk feed on the succulent new growth of serviceberry, ceanothus, and upland willow. In an enlightened reversal of its usual fire suppression policy, the Forest Service is deliberately burning nearly 500 acres in Burdette Creek per year during this decade. The goal is to establish a mosaic of verdant shrubs for forage along with a dense tree canopy for hiding cover.

A trail cushioned with larch needles hugs bubbling Burdette Creek, bending around gigantic old-growth larches. Every so often the forest opens to a grand view of the drainage with its sharp ridges and extensive brushfields interspersed with dense stringers of Douglas-fir in the protected draws and north-facing slopes. Steep grassy ridges separating Burdette and Lupine creeks support ponderosa pine parks with some of the fire-resistant veterans towering more than 100 feet.

RECREATIONAL USES: Little-known Burdette Creek is no secret to hunters seeking a special kind of day-use roadless elk hunt, and to a handful of off-season hikers looking for solitude is a landscape surrounded by both wilderness and heavy logging. Burdette seems remote, but only because it is unknown and overlooked. In fact, it is readily accessible from the west and south along the

22 BURDETTE CREEK

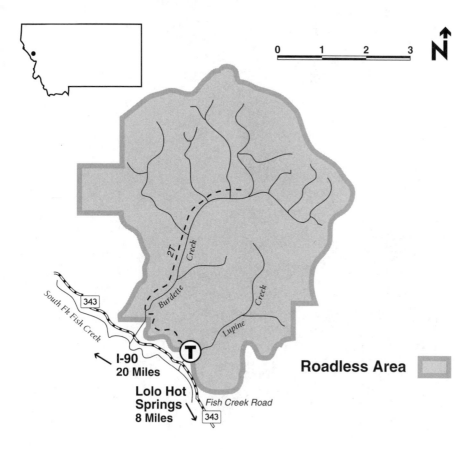

Roadless Area

Fish Creek Road, which can be reached from I-90 west of Alberton or from US 12 near Lolo Hot Springs. The only Forest Service trail in the roadless area is a 4-mile path up Burdette Creek, cushioned with mats of yellow larch needles in the fall. A prime time to visit Burdette is in early fall when these handsome monarchs display a golden mantle of needles. Before winter this uniquely deciduous conifer will have shed its needles. The Fish Creek Road to the trailhead is usually open from mid-April through Thanksgiving. During winter the unplowed road is packed down by heavy snowmobile use. Late-season cross-country skiing would be best on the open-forested ridges at the head of Burdette Creek if access weren't so troublesome. Either ride in on snowmobile or ski in 10 to 15 miles on unplowed roads from Graves Creek onto the Garden Point Road (FR 22) north of US 12.

OLD GROWTH PONDEROSA PINE TOWER ABOVE LUPINE CREEK.

HOW TO GET THERE: From the north on I-90 take the Fish Creek exit, 8 miles west of Alberton. Drive 22.5 miles south on the main Fish Creek Road (FR 343) to the Burdette Creek trailhead for Trail 2. From the south, drive 0.5 mile south from Lolo Hot Springs on US 12 and turn north onto FR 343. Drive about 8 miles north to the trailhead.

DAY HIKE

Burdette Creek
Distance: 8 miles out-and-back, or a 12-mile loop.
Difficulty: Moderately strenuous (cross-country).
Topo map: Lupine Creek-MT.

The spacious meadows near the mouth of Burdette Creek where it meets Fish Creek Road are privately owned and posted against trespassing. The actual trailhead for Burdette Trail 2 is about 0.5 mile south of the meadows. The trail starts up a draw above a mining claim, sidehills around the toe of the ridge, and drops into Burdette about 0.5 mile above Fish Creek Road. The small stream is lined with willows and dogwoods. Watch for cutthroat darting into the shadows of logs and overhangs. Beaver ponds become more common after the first 3 miles. A feeling of intimacy deepens as steep slopes of rock talus meet the trail where the canyon narrows. The trail becomes faint to nonexistent about 4 miles up, just past a large beaver pond. In this vicinity there are several good campsites on the south side of the creek that are used by private hunting parties in the fall. If you're feeling ambitious, head off-trail straight up a north-facing slope south of the creek to an open ridge summit of about 6,200 feet—a 1,800-foot ascent in 1 mile. Angle southeast across the slope to the prominent south-trending ridge that drops into Lupine Creek. During late winter and early spring these grass and ceanothus-covered midslopes are heavily used by elk at the 5,000- to 5,500-foot level. Between 4,800 feet down to the 4,300-foot bottom of Lupine you'll pass through open parks of stately ponderosa pine. Lupine Creek is smaller but more lush than Burdette, with fewer vistas of the surrounding country. However, the big old larch trees are even more impressive than in Burdette. An informal hunter's trail turns into an old jeep track about 0.75 mile above the Burdette Creek trailhead. This moderately strenuous loop is a 12-mile day hike, full of broad vistas, low-elevation native forests, and varied terrain.

Great Burn

23

Location: 30 miles west of Missoula.

Size: 251,892 acres 98,680 acres of which are in Montana.

Administration: USDAFS—Lolo and Clearwater national forests.

Management status: Primarily roadless with a small amount of peripheral land allocated to future development in the forest plan.

Ecosystems: Northern Rocky Mountain coniferous forest-alpine meadow province, characterized by glaciated mountains; granitic in the south, with argillite pinnacles on ridges to the north; Douglas-fir and western ponderosa pine forest types containing ponderosa pine at lower, drier elevations along with cedar, larch, and hemlock in stream bottoms (large areas of spruce-fir occur with some lodgepole pine in burns), and subalpine tundra along open slopes and high ridges; and abundant perennial streams, wet meadows, and mountain lakes at higher elevations.

Elevation range: 3,200 to 7,663 feet.

System trails: 140 miles.

Maximum core to perimeter distance: 8 miles.

Activities: Hiking, backpacking, horseback riding, cross-country skiing, fishing.

Modes of travel: Foot, ski, and horse.

Maps: 1994 Lolo National Forest Visitor Map; Hoodoo Pass-ID/MT; Straight Peak-MT/ID; St. Patrick Peak-MT; Bruin Hill-ID/MT; Schley Mountain-MT/ID; White Mountain-MT; Rhodes Peak-ID/MT; and Granite Pass-ID/MT (1:24,000 topo maps).

OVERVIEW: In 1910, raging flames stormed over the Bitterroot Divide only 30 miles west of Missoula, consuming the forest and illuminating the darkness like northern lights from hell. Today, charred snags, barren slopes, and expanses of subalpine tundra lend a distinctive character to a vast interstate wildland, nearly 100,000 acres of which drain into Montana's Fish Creek. This primeval land, known as the Great Burn, runs along both sides of the Bitterroot Divide for 40 miles. Induced by the 1910 fire, the tundra of the Great Burn lies at a much lower elevation than one would expect at this latitude. In striking contrast, ancient western red cedar grow in cathedral-like settings along shaded pools meandering through verdant, mossy beds of sword and maidenhair ferns.

The Great Burn consists of steep, rugged slopes, narrow, forested valleys, and dozens of crystal-clear lakes and streams. Avalanche chutes abound, and in many places impenetrable thickets of tag alder make bushwhacking nearly impossible. Although lower and less rugged than the main crest of the Bitter-

23   GREAT BURN

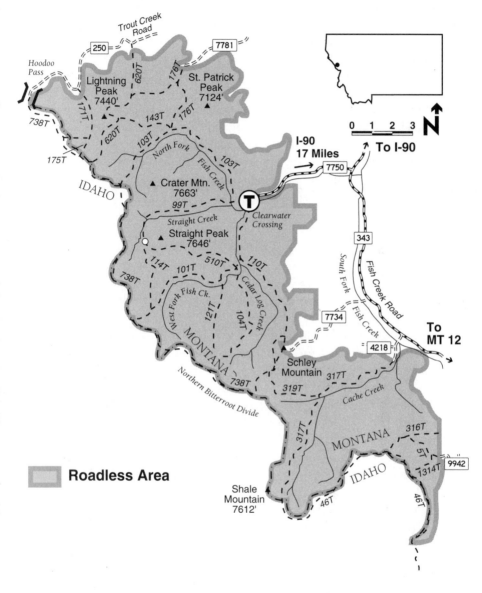

Roadless Area

roots farther south, the Great Burn did experience glaciation, as evidenced by its many cirque basins and U-shaped valleys. The geologic formations at the heads of Cache Creek, Pebble Creek, and White Creek are granitic, whereas the Great Burn to the north is mostly argillite. Some of the higher ridges are defined by rock pinnacles, especially from Williams Peak to Shale Mountain. These thin, irregular fins are called "dinosaur rocks" because they resemble the backs of these prehistoric creatures.

Elk are the big-game animals most commonly associated with the Great Burn. Here is found important summer and fall range for an interstate elk herd of national significance. Black bears are common also. And as many as fifty mountain goats dwell along the more rugged cliff faces of the divide and higher peaks. Moose live in every drainage, from the lowest elevations to the boggy meadows surrounding high mountain lakes.

RECREATIONAL USES: Most of the recreational use is big-game hunting in the fall, and elk are the star attraction. Pack trips with horses and mules, both out-fitted and private, have been popular for generations. Aside from hunting, the thirty-three scenic subalpine lakes along the divide draw most of the visitors. Most of the lakes and larger streams support fishable populations of cutthroat and rainbow trout, and golden trout live in at least one of the lakes. Recreational use is well distributed throughout the Great Burn because of a good trail system of more than 200 miles of which 140 are in Montana and along the State Line-Bitterroot Divide.

The vast and varied Great Burn is truly a four-season recreation paradise with good cross-country ski access to the high country from December to March at Hoodoo Pass on the north and connecting up to Granite Pass to the south. Snow permitting, low-elevation skiing can be excellent in the West Fork of Fish Creek with a plowed road all the way to the Hole in the Wall Lodge, only 1 mile from Clearwater Crossing. Lower country hiking can begin by early April with the hiking, backpacking, and fishing season extending into the fall. Of course by October day-use and backcountry hunters are heading to the hills.

You would be wise to avoid the disappointment and added impacts of camping at the heavily used Lower Siamese Lake, French Lake, Heart Lake, and Crater Lake. Crater Lake is a particular problem in that there is only one good campsite, which contains only one tent space, and this is degraded from overuse.

In addition to Hoodoo Pass, the Schley Mountain trailhead on the Surveyor Creek Road provides easy access to the Bitterroot Divide. The Forest Service has developed a dual trailhead here. The original trailhead at the end of the Surveyor Creek Road (FR 7734), some 3 miles past the Schley Mountain saddle, is open to hikers and backpackers during the summer and then is closed September 1. Stock use of this trail is discouraged. The newer lower trailhead

NEAR CHILCOOT PASS, AT THE HEAD OF STRAIGHT CREEK IN THE HEART OF THE GREAT BURN.

at Schley saddle accommodates all use after September 1 and is the main trailhead during the Idaho and Montana hunting seasons. During summer the upper trailhead allows folks of all ages and abilities to enjoy the alpine lakes and vistas of the high divide.

HOW TO GET THERE: To reach the Clearwater Crossing trailheads in the north-central region of the Great Burn drive 40 miles west of Missoula on I-90 and take the Fish Creek exit. Drive 10 miles south on Fish Creek Road 343 and turn right up the West Fork of Fish Creek on FR 7750, Drive 7 miles to the end of the road at Clearwater Crossing, passing the historic Hole in the Wall Lodge after 6 miles.

HORSE OR BACKPACKING LOOPS

Upper Fish Creek
Distance: 40-mile loop (4 to 6 days).
Difficulty: Moderate.
Topo maps: Straight Peak-MT/ID; St. Patrick Peak-MT; Bruin Hill-ID/MT; and Schley Mountain-MT/ID.

Perhaps the best overall access point into the Great Burn is from the Clearwater Crossing in the north-central region. This is a major end-of-the-road trailhead with stock unloading facilities 7 miles up the West Fork from the main Fish Creek Road. From here you can explore three main drainages—the West Fork, the North Fork, and Straight Creek. A number of loop trips are possible depending on time available. If you have close to a week, take the long loop up the North Fork Trail 103 for about 12 miles to Goose Lake, a shallow pond just over the divide in Idaho. Then head south for another dozen miles along the scenic Bitterroot Divide on State Line Trail 738, past Admiral Peak to Mud Lake, then down the Middle Fork of Indian Creek on Trail 121. Join the West Fork of Fish Creek on Trail 101, ending up at your point of origin at Clearwater Crossing. This varied 40-mile loop samples a bit of everything the Great Burn has to offer.

A shorter four- or five-day loop is to climb up the more open Straight Creek drainage on Trail 99 with its stairstep series of stunning waterfalls to Chilcoot Pass. Then drop to Siamese Lakes on Trail 114 and continue down through the giant cedars in the West Fork on Trail 101 to your starting point.

Selway-Bitterroot
Wilderness
Complex

24

Location: 12 miles southwest of Missoula and 4 miles west of Hamilton.
Size: 383,421 acres, of which 251,343 acres are included within the Montana portion of the 1,337,681-acre Selway-Bitterroot Wilderness.
Administration: USDAFS—Bitterroot, Lolo, Clearwater, and Nezperce national forests.
Management status: Wilderness (251,343 acres) and roadless management of 132,078 acres of contiguous national forest.
Ecosystems: Middle Rocky Mountain coniferous forest-alpine meadow province, Idaho Batholith section, characterized by strongly glaciated mountains with cirques and large U-shaped valleys; Lower Tertiary and mesozoic granite; grand fir-Douglas-fir, western spruce-fir, and western ponderosa forest types; and with many perennial streams and higher elevation lakes.
Elevation range: 4,265 to 10,157 feet.
System trails: 170 miles.
Maximum core to perimeter distance: 8.5 miles.
Activities: Hiking, backpacking, horseback riding, cross-country skiing, mountaineering, fishing.
Modes of travel: Foot, horse, skis, climbing gear.
Maps: 1980 Selway-Bitterroot Wilderness Map-5/8"/mile contour; 1989 Bitterroot National Forest Visitor Map. (See appendix for a listing of the 18 topographic maps covering the area.)

OVERVIEW: Hundreds of peaks separate more than thirty rugged drainages for nearly 90 miles along a dramatic mountain front stretching from the South Fork of Lolo Creek south to where rocky ridges break abruptly into the West Fork of the Bitterroot River. From the lofty vantage point of any of the 9,000-to 10,000-foot peaks the impression is one of barren rock—granite, gneiss, and schist—from the jagged crest of the Bitterroots to the valley floor. A closer look reveals sheer walls, cliffs, tumbling waterfalls, hanging valleys, subalpine lake basins, and a glaciated terrain so rough that, in comparison, most other Montana mountains seem like gently rolling hills.

The major glaciers probably receded less than 10,000 years ago, leaving deep, steep-walled, east-west canyons, each with a classic U-shape from Pleistocene Valley glaciation. With more than a mile of vertical relief, the variety of vegetation is equally impressive. From creeks to crest there is old-growth western redcedar ranging up to tenacious, slow-growing subalpine larch.

24 SELWAY-BITTERROOT WILDERNESS

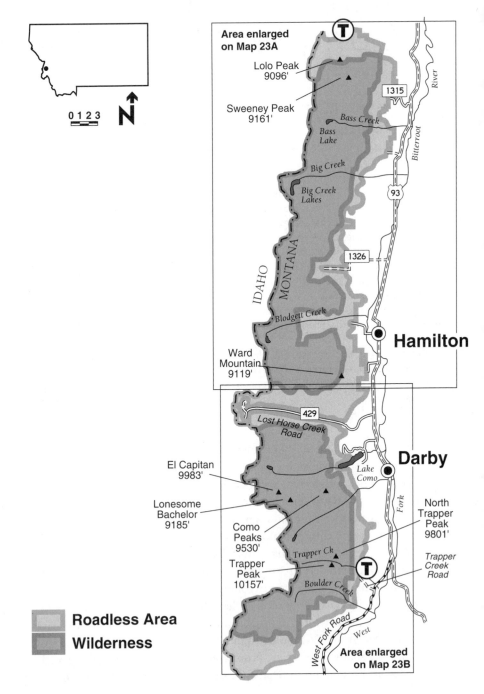

0 1 2 3 **N**

Area enlarged
on Map 23A

Lolo Peak
9096'

Sweeney Peak
9161'

1315

River

Bass Creek

Bass
Lake

Bitterroot

Big Creek

Big Creek
Lakes

93

IDAHO

MONTANA

1326

Blodgett Creek

Ward
Mountain
9119'

Hamilton

429

Lost Horse Creek
Road

Darby

El Capitan
9983'

Lake
Como

Lonesome
Bachelor
9185'

Como
Peaks
9530'

Fork

North
Trapper
Peak
9801'

Trapper Ck

Trapper
Creek
Road

Trapper
Peak
10157'

Boulder Creek

West Fork Road

West

Area enlarged
on Map 23B

Roadless Area

Wilderness

Although much of this primeval landscape is austere and treeless, there are surprising pockets of wildlife. Elk summer in lush basins along the divide and hide in heavily forested canyons during the fall hunting season. The native bighorn sheep herd in Sheephead and Watchtower creeks at the southern end is genetically pure. The sheep have a unique learned migration pattern between winter and summer range.

The east-facing Montana side of the Wilderness is so rugged that most visitors are confined to the shorelines of the numerous lakes and to the bottoms of canyons. Each of these glaciated canyons holds its own special discoveries—from the natural arch in Blodgett to a massive landslide across Nelson Creek that backed up Nelson Lake.

RECREATIONAL USES: During the past decade there has been a modest increase in recreational use within the Wilderness. The exception has been day use which appears to have risen markedly, particularly in the northern canyons west of Stevensville. Hikers only slightly outnumber horse users except during the fall when the vast majority of visitors are hunters with riding and packstock.

Vast portions of these mountains remain pristine due to severity of terrain and access. User impacts such as bare, hard-packed ground are concentrated in the canyon bottoms and around lakes that are served by trails. Some of the more

EL CAPITAN AS SEEN FROM THE COMO PEAKS IN THE RUGGED BITTERROOT RANGE.

24A SELWAY-BITTERROOT WILDERNESS

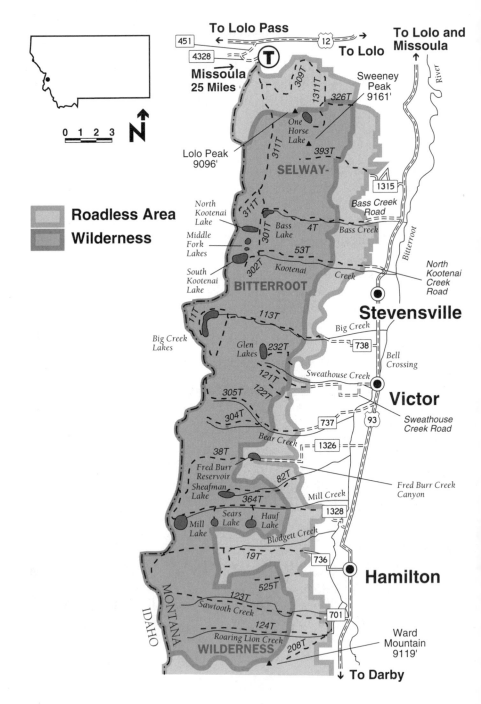

Roadless Area

Wilderness

heavily used sites are Peterson Lake and Bass Lake, where human waste and litter are problems. Areas with some of the heaviest stock use include South Kootenai Lake, Big Creek Lake, Elk Lake/Rock Creek, Tincup Lake, and the chain of lakes at the head of Boulder Creek: Boulder, Dollar, Turbid, and Crystal.

During the days of the Civilian Conservation Corps an extensive trail system was developed for fire control. Some of the trail grades exceed 40 percent, indicating that the trail builders didn't anticipate the advent of today's wilderness recreationist. Trails are well-distributed throughout the wilderness, perhaps almost to a fault; almost every place that can be accessed by a trail is. Still, eleven pristine areas without trails have been identified within the wilderness, comprising about 10 percent of the Selway-Bitterroot. The largest is some 26,000 acres of alpine splendor along the jagged Bitterroot Divide surrounding the Heavenly Twins, which offer several mountaineering routes and wilderness solitude.

If you avoid the heavy use areas, especially during weekends and holidays, you won't be disappointed in any of the more than twenty major drainages flowing east from the Bitterroot Mountains. Typically, the access trail begins at about 3,400 feet, close to the mouth of a deep, rocky canyon. It then parallels a rushing stream for 6 to 8 miles. Soon this prototypical trail climbs a steep moraine to a high lake basin just below the crest of the Bitterroot Range.

There are many winter ski mountaineering possibilities such as 9,096-foot Lolo Peak on the north end, 8,886-foot Gash Point west of Victor from FR 737, and the apex of the wilderness—10,157-foot Trapper Peak on the southeastern edge. Trapper can be accessed during each of the four seasons, but skiers should be experienced enough to negotiate steep descents. During the summer Trapper is a 5-mile walk up Trail 133 from a switchback on Lavene Creek Road (FR 5630A). To reach the trailhead drive about 11 miles up the West Fork road south of Darby to the Lavene Creek Road and follow the signs for about 5 miles to where the trail takes off. The final 2 miles to the summit are above timberline and especially scenic.

How to get there: *North End:* From Lolo, 10 miles south of Missoula on US 93, drive about 9 miles west on US 12. Turn left (south) on FR 451 and drive about 4 miles to the South Fork Lolo Creek trailhead for Trail 311.

South End: During winter drive 4 miles south from Darby on US 93 and head up the West Fork Road (FR 91). Go about 13 miles and turn right on FR 373 before the West Fork Ranger Station. If the road is impassable park at the bottom and begin climbing the northwest-trending ridge to 7,753-foot Boulder Point.

During summer drive 4 miles south from Darby on US 93 and go about 6 miles up the West Fork Road. Just past the Trapper Creek CCC Center, turn right on FR 5634 and drive 9 to 10 miles to the Baker Lake trailhead for Trail 234.

24B SELWAY-BITTERROOT WILDERNESS COMPLEX

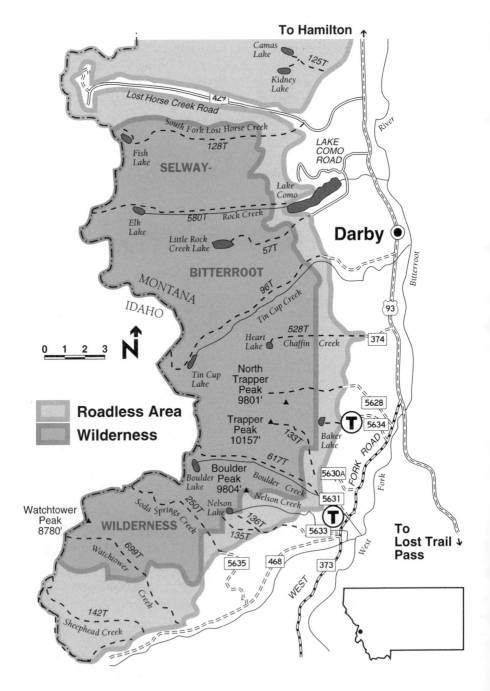

DAY HIKE, OVERNIGHTER, OR EXTENDED BACKPACK - NORTH END

Northern Bitterroot Traverse

Distance: 10 to 16 miles out-and-back; 30 to 40 miles point-to-point.
Difficulty: Moderate day hike/moderately strenuous point-to-point traverse.
Topo maps: Dick Creek-MT/ID; St. Joseph Peak-MT/ID; and Saint Mary Peak-MT.

The first part of the South Fork of Lolo Creek trail passes through 1 mile of cutover Plum Creek land, but soon the trail begins winding through heavy forest and climbing rocky ridges overlooking the South Fork. Broad, wet meadows are reached just inside the Wilderness boundary and continue off and on for miles with abundant camping spots and chances to see moose, elk, black bear, and other wildlife.

For an extended point-to-point trip cross over the Bitterroot Divide to Bass Lake and continue 8 miles down Bass Creek Trail 4 to the campground. For an even longer trip, go south over the ridge on Trail 301 to Kootenai Creek, take a short side trip to the lakes, then drop 12 miles down Kootenai Creek on Trail 53 to the trailhead. Allow 3 to 4 days and set up a car shuttle for this excursion.

WINTER SKI/MOUNTAINEERING DAY TRIP - SOUTH END

Boulder Peak

Distance: 10 miles.
Difficulty: Strenuous.
Topo map: Boulder Peak-MT.

The ridge leading directly to Boulder Point is moderate and not normally prone to avalanche hazard. If access permits, a better route is up the ridge just west of Ward Creek, which levels out toward the top and ties into the main Boulder Peak summit ridge about 1 mile west of Boulder Point. Upon reaching the main ridge the going is fairly easy for 1.5 to 2 miles west to the 9,804-foot summit, which provides a stunning view of the main Bitterroot Divide and several frozen lake basins to the west. The nearly 4,000-foot descent offers moderate telemarking slopes through open subalpine forests.

THE BASS CREEK DRAINAGE IN THE SELWAY-BITTERROOT WILDERNESS.

SUMMER DAY HIKE - SOUTH END

Baker Lake
Distance: 2 miles out-and-back.
Difficulty: Easy.
Topo maps: Trapper Peak-MT and Burnt Ridge-MT.

Baker Lake, on the edge of the wilderness boundary below Trapper Peak, is an ideal destination for kids, older folks, or anyone wanting a short, easy, 1-mile hike into beautiful country. Unfortunately, the shoreline has been marred in the past by fire rings, so bring your portable stove for cooking if you plan to spend the night.

Blue Joint

25

Location: 25 miles southwest of Darby.
Size: 65,370 acres in Montana; Blue Joint is a contiguous part of the 2.4 million-acre Frank Church/River of No Return Wilderness in central Idaho.
Administration: USDAFS—Bitterroot National Forest.
Management status: Congressional Wilderness Study Area plus contiguous national forest roadless land.
Ecosystems: Middle Rocky Mountain coniferous forest-alpine meadow province, Idaho Batholith section, characterized by glaciated mountains with partially developed cirques and large U-shaped valleys; Lower Tertiary and mesozoic granite; Douglas-fir and western ponderosa forest types; and many perennial streams and wet meadows.
Elevation range: 4,900 to 8,637 feet.
System trails: 70 miles.
Maximum core to perimeter distance: 5 miles.
Activities: Hiking, backpacking, cross-country skiing, horseback riding, fishing.
Modes of travel: Foot, skis, and horse.
Maps: 1989 Bitterroot National Forest Visitor Map; 1984 Frank Church-River of No Return Wilderness-North contour map; Nez Perce Peak-ID/MT; Bare Cone-MT; Painted Rocks Lake-MT; Blue Joint-ID/MT; Horse Creek Pass-MT/ID; and Alta-MT /ID.

OVERVIEW: The Nez Perce Road is all that separates Blue Joint from the Selway-Bitterroot Wilderness. Plus, Blue Joint is part of another vast wildland—the 2.4 million-acre Frank Church-River of No Return Wilderness that extends deep into central Idaho with 17 miles of common boundary along the Bitterroot Divide. History comes alive with a segment of the Southern Nez Perce Indian Trail traversing this stretch of the divide, which is also next to the historic Magruder Corridor.

With elevations ranging from 4,900 to over 8,600 feet, half of the Blue Joint exceeds 7,000 feet. The rocky, grassy spine of Razorback Ridge splits the country between the northwest and southwest. Douglas-fir and ponderosa pine grow on the warmer, lower slopes with lodgepole pine on cooler midslopes on up to whitebark pine holding onto high, narrow ridges. Forest fires a century ago burned most of the Blue Joint drainage, producing a vast even-aged forest of spindly lodgepole pine—in contrast with the surrounding forest. Spacious, open meadows, a rarity in the Bitterroot Range, spread across the headwaters of Deer and Blue Joint creeks. Major features include 7,922-foot Castle

25 BLUE JOINT

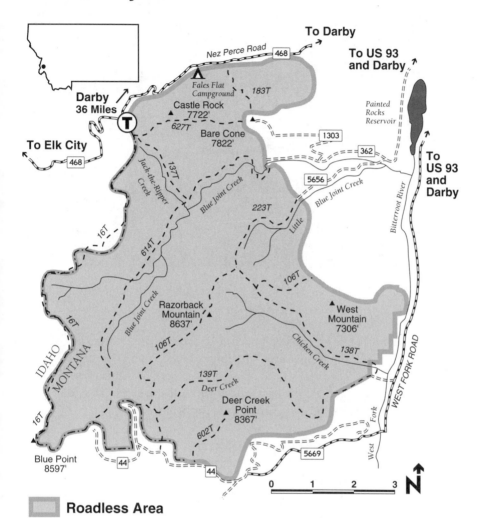

Roadless Area

BLUE JOINT MEADOWS.

Rock, remnant of a volcanic plug, and a natural rock arch east of the confluence of Jack the Ripper and Blue Joint creeks.

The indigenous, genetically pure bighorn sheep herd in the southern breaks of the Selway-Bitterroot Wilderness also uses the northern edge of Blue Joint near Castle Rock, where the rocky terrain is used for lambing.

RECREATIONAL USES: In general, a lack of high lakes and jagged peaks accounts for light recreational use, most of which is for big-game hunting. Day hiking, horseback riding, backpacking, camping, fishing, and some cross-country skiing are rising in popularity. The major attractions are the larger streams and meadows, and the high alpine/subalpine ridges, notably the State Line-Bitterroot Divide and Razorback. Most of the creek bottoms are tightly enclosed by steep sideslopes climbing to narrow ridges, with most of the slopes exceeding 60 percent. As a result, most recreational use is confined to stream bottoms and ridgetops. Nearly 4,000 vertical feet separate where Blue Joint Creek leaves the roadless area from the top of its highest point—centrally located 8,637-foot Razorback Mountain. Two outfitters provide fall hunting camps and three other outfitters offer day trips. Variations of day, overnight, and extended trips abound with ten well-distributed trails totaling 70 miles. In addition, State Line Trail 16 connects with several other trails leading west into the adjacent Frank Church-River of No Return Wilderness.

Blue Joint is part of the largest expanse of undeveloped wildland in the Lower Forty-eight—more than 2.5 million acres, which includes the 2.23 million acre FCRNR Wilderness reaching deep into central Idaho. And just across the Darby-Elk City Magruder Corridor road to the immediate north is the 1.3 million-acre Selway-Bitterroot Wilderness. Part of Blue Joint's attraction is that it is strategically located at the east-central edge of the largest wildland complex in the continental United States (the Greater Salmon-Selway).

How to get there: From US 93, 4 miles south of Darby, drive about 16 miles up the West Fork of the Bitterroot River on West Fork Road (FR 91). Keep to the right on FR 468 for another 16 miles to Nez Perce Pass, which is where the trailhead is located for Trail 16, winding south from the pass along the Bitterroot-State Line divide.

BACKPACKING OR HORSE-PACKING LOOP

Blue Joint Meadows
Distance: 20- to 22-mile loop (3 days).
Difficulty: Moderate.
Topo maps: Nez Perce Peak-ID/MT; Bare Cone-MT; and Blue Joint-ID/MT.

From Nez Perce Pass head south on State Line Trail 16, climbing steeply for the first mile to where the trail intersects with the Jack the Ripper Creek Trail, which will be used on the return leg. Continue south with expansive views west to the dense forests of the FCRNR Wilderness in Idaho and back north to the craggy peaks of the Selway-Bitterroot. The trail winds on an easy contour through a lodgepole pine forest with beargrass and grouse whortleberry ground cover. After about 8 miles the trail reaches Two Buck Spring at an elevation of 7,400 feet. The spring is a good—and sole—source of water along the divide. It is also a fine camping spot, and with room enough for three or four tents it has been used in the past for hunting camps.

The next day drop down to Blue Joint Meadows by traversing cross country across open hillsides to the forks of a side tributary, then down a gorgeous stream bottom with a well-defined game trail weaving through an open, scattered forest. By the time you reach the lush, grassy meadows along Blue Joint Creek you will have dropped 1,200 feet and covered about 2.5 miles from Two Buck Spring. The 6,200-foot high meadows are a wonderful place in which to camp, fish, and listen to coyote music, with a good chance of seeing elk grazing in grassy parks along the divide to the north.

On the third day head down Blue Joint Creek Trail 416 for 4 miles of what seems like more climbing than dropping. Take a left up Jack the Ripper Creek on Trail 137 and continue through a lovely mile-long meadow and open lodgepole forest for another 4 miles to the State Line Divide. At this point a steep, 1-mile descent will have you back at the Nez Perce Pass trailhead, thereby completing the loop.

Allan Mountain

26

Location: 12 miles south of Darby.
Size: 153,367 acres, 102,386 acres of which are in Montana.
Administration: USFS—Bitterroot and Salmon national forests.
Management status: Roadless non-wilderness with a small amount of peripheral land allocated to future development in the forest plan.
Ecosystem: Middle Rocky Mountain coniferous forest-alpine meadow province, Idaho Batholith section, characterized by moderately glaciated mountains and large U-shaped valleys; Lower Tertiary and Mesozoic granite; Douglas-fir and western ponderosa forest types; and with many perennial streams. The roadless area contains the southernmost range of subalpine larch.
Elevation range: 4,600 to 8,909 feet.
System trails: 75 miles (includes a segment of the State Line Trail).
Maximum core to perimeter distance: 3.5 miles.
Activities: Hiking, backpacking, horseback riding, cross-country skiing, fishing.
Modes of travel: Foot, horse, and skis.
Maps: 1989 Bitterroot National Forest Visitor Map; Piquett Creek-MT; Medicine Hot Springs-MT; Sula-MT; Piquett Mountain-MT; Overwhich Falls-MT/ID; Lost Trail Pass-MT/ID; Henderson Ridge-MT/ID; Allan Mountain-ID/MT; and Shoup-ID/MT (1:24,000 topo maps).

OVERVIEW: The large, interstate Allan Mountain roadless area is a crucial biological link for wildlife migrating between the vast central Idaho wilderness and the Continental Divide ecosystems that extend from Yellowstone, through Montana, and northward into Canada. The Montana side of Allan Mountain drains into the upper West Fork of the Bitterroot River. The centerpiece of this Bitterroot Divide wildland corridor is the spectacular 200-foot Overwhich Falls, which is close to where the stream cuts back to the south through erosive soils and bedrock just below the headwaters of Fault Creek.

About 60 percent of Allan Mountain lies above 7,000 feet, where the forest is mostly lodgepole pine, subalpine fir, and whitebark pine. Hearty subalpine larch reaches the southern limits of its range, grasping steep, narrow ridges. Large grassy parks favored by deer and elk were established by fires in 1917 and again in 1919. Other wildlife includes mountain goat, moose, black bear, wolverine, and old growth-dependent pine marten. Native cutthroat trout thrive in the cold, clear waters of fast streams. A branch of the southern Nez Perce Indian Trail traversed this portion of the Bitterroot Divide.

26 ALLAN MOUNTAIN

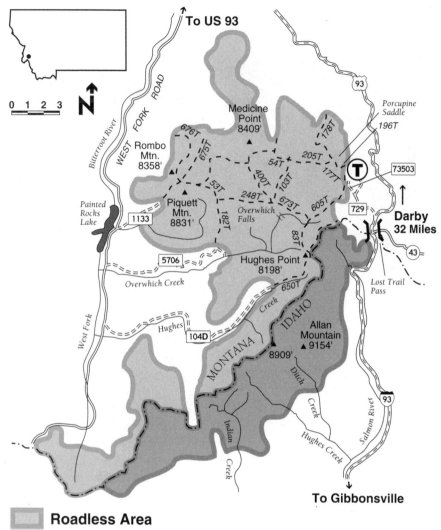

To US 93

West Fork Road

Bitterroot River

93

Porcupine
Saddle
196T

Medicine
Point
8409'

676T

178T

205T

177T

73503

T

54T

400T

1037T

Rombo
Mtn.
8358'

675T

53T

Painted
Rocks
Lake

1133

Piquett
Mtn.
8831'

182T

248T

673T

605T

*Overwhich
Falls*

729

**Darby
32 Miles**

83T

5706

Hughes Point
8198'

Overwhich Creek

650T

43

*Lost Trail
Pass*

Creek

MONTANA

IDAHO

West Fork

Hughes

104D

Allan
Mountain
▲ 9154'

8909'

Ditch

Creek

93

Indian

Creek

Hughes Creek

Salmon River

To Gibbonsville

Roadless Area
Roadless Area (Idaho)

ABOVE SHIELDS CREEK IN THE ALLAN MOUNTAIN ROADLESS AREA.

RECREATIONAL USES: Recreational use is lighter here than in any of the nearby Wilderness and roadless areas. Activities include hunting, hiking, backpacking, horseback riding, fishing, camping, and ski touring. The major attractions are Overwhich Falls, trails and campsites along major streams, a handful of isolated mountain lakes, and several ridgeline trails that lead into varied subalpine country. The more scenic high trails include the State Line and the Saddle to Piquett Mountain route. There are five outfitter hunting camps on the Montana side of the roadless area. In the northwest corner Piquett Mountain is especially striking, with two glaciated lake basins holding four small tarns on its northeast side. The trails are well maintained and are concentrated more in the north end. They are suitable for both foot and horse travel. There is some opportunity for cross-country travel, such as bushwhacking to 8,003-foot Falls Point overlooking Overwhich Falls to the south. Cross-country skiers will find easy access from Lost Trail Pass on US 93. Take the ski lift to the top of Lost Trail Ski Area and head north on the unplowed road toward Saddle Mountain. Experienced backcountry skiers can work the State Line Divide south of the Saddle Mountain road into the roadless area for several miles. Steep terrain and dense forest confine the route to an out-and-back trip.

HOW TO GET THERE: From Darby drive 24 miles south on US 93. Turn right (west) toward the Indian Trees campground and make an immediate left onto FR 729. Continue about 0.75 mile to West Camp Creek Road. Turn left and drive another 0.75 mile to FR 8112. Stay to the right on FR 8112, climbing up through the Saddle Mountain burn and clearcuts for about 6 miles to the Porcupine Saddle spur road (FR 73503). Follow it 1 mile to the trailhead for Porcupine Saddle Trail 196.

BACKPACK OR HORSE-PACKING TRIP

Porcupine Saddle to Overwhich Falls

Distance: 20-mile loop (2 to 3 days).
Difficulty: Moderately strenuous.
Topo maps: Medicine Hot Springs-MT; Sula-MT; Overwhich Falls-MT/ID; and Lost Trail Pass-MT/ID.

This trip provides an enjoyable introduction to the heart of the Allan Mountain country—a little known stretch of the Bitterroot Divide.

Begin the loop to Overwhich Falls by starting out on the Porcupine Saddle Trail 196 (elevation 7,000 feet). The trail winds through a lodgepole pine forest for 0.75 mile to Porcupine Saddle. Turn left on Warm Springs Ridge Trail 177, and go south to where it merges first with Trail 673 and then with Trail 605 along the ridge above Shields Creek.

The trail climbs to 8,040 feet in a heavily forested north aspect that often retains deep snowpack into late June. There are two refreshing springs about a mile apart along the otherwise dry ridge north of Shields Creek. When Trail 605 reaches the confluence of Shields and Overwhich creeks the trail designation changes to 673 for the remaining 2.5 miles down to Overwhich Falls. This stretch of Overwhich Creek above the falls is lined with more than a mile of lush meadows ideal for camping, as evidenced by several hunting camps scattered along the bottom.

For a great photo-op of the falls, scramble down to the creek below the waterfall. Exercise caution—the slope is extremely steep with loose rock. An easier but more distant photo point of the entire falls, with its narrow top and fanned-out bottom, is found by walking above Overwhich Creek on an unmarked side trail about 100 yards below the three-way trail junction.

Continuing the loop, there are a couple of good campsites at Pass and Capri lakes on Trail 400 about 1.5 miles northwest of the falls.

The next day return to the three-way trail junction of Trails 400, 673, and 103 and take Trail 103 north for the 300-foot climb to the head of Warm Springs Creek. Drop down this woodsy path for another 2.5 miles to the mouth of Porcupine Creek. After crossing the stream, take a right on Porcupine Creek Trail 205 on the edge of a meadow. About 0.5 mile up Porcupine Creek the trail arrives at a recently renovated Forest Service cabin, complete with a new fire pit, bridge, and outhouse. Contact the Sula Ranger District if

OVERWHICH FALLS.

you're interested in possible cabin rental. In another mile the trail crosses Lightning Creek and then begins a series of steep switchbacks through open parks, ridges, and forest to the head of Porcupine Creek. Here it joins the main ridge trail (177) leading southeast back to Porcupine Saddle and the trailhead. The 3.5 miles from the mouth of Porcupine to its head is the hardest part of the circuit with an elevation gain of 2,100 feet. Much of the loop is high and dry so carry plenty of drinking water. There have been sporadic reports of giardia so be sure to boil or filter any water obtained from main streams. Ample pure water from springs can be relied on at least into early summer.

Anaconda-Pintler/ Sapphires Wilderness Complex

27

Location: 20 miles southeast of Hamilton; 25 miles southwest of Philipsburg; 13 miles north of Wisdom.

Size: 363,954 acres.

Administration: USDAFS—Beaverhead, Deerlodge, and Bitterroot national forests.

Management status: Wilderness (157,874 acres); Sapphires Congressional Wilderness Study Area (107,000 acres); and the remainder roadless non-wilderness, some peripheral lands of which are allocated to future development in the forest plans.

Ecosystems: Middle Rocky Mountain coniferous forest-alpine meadow province, Bitterroot Valley section (north) and Beaverhead Mountain section (south), characterized by complex, high, and strongly glaciated mountains with sharp alpine ridges and cirques; Precambrian granite with sedimentary and volcanic rocks; Douglas-fir forest type along with smaller areas of sagebrush steppe and alpine vegetation; numerous perennial streams, wet meadows, and moderate- to high-elevation lakes.

Elevation range: 5,300 to 10,793 feet.

System trails: 390 miles.

Maximum core to perimeter distance: 5.5 miles.

Activities: Hiking, backpacking, horseback riding, cross-country skiing, fishing.

Modes of travel: Foot, horse, and skis.

Maps: 1993 Beaverhead/Interagency Travel Plan Map; 1989 Bitterroot National Forest Visitor Map; 1990 Deerlodge National Forest Visitor Map; and 1983 Anaconda-Pintler Wilderness contour map (see appendix for a listing of the 16 1:24,000 topographic maps covering the complex).

OVERVIEW: The Anaconda-Pintler Wilderness is the central jewel in this wild crown, surrounded by contiguous roadless lands that include the Sapphire Range—the crest of which is a northern spur off the Continental Divide. The wilderness core is bisected by 50 miles of the Great Divide where it makes an east-west deviation from its mostly north-south orientation. A vertical mile separates remnant old-growth forests from the loftiest summit in the Anaconda Range—10,793-foot West Goat Peak—where the effects of past glaciation dominate the land.

27 ANACONDA-PINTLER/SAPPHIRES WILDERNESS COMPLEX

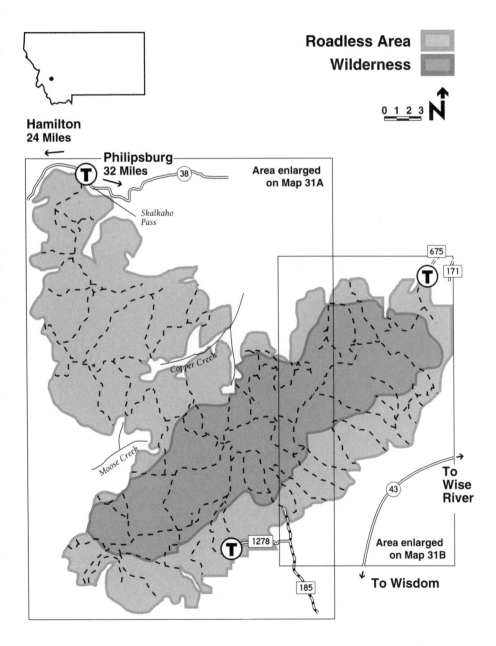

27A ANACONDA-PINTLER/SAPPHIRES WILDERNESS COMPLEX

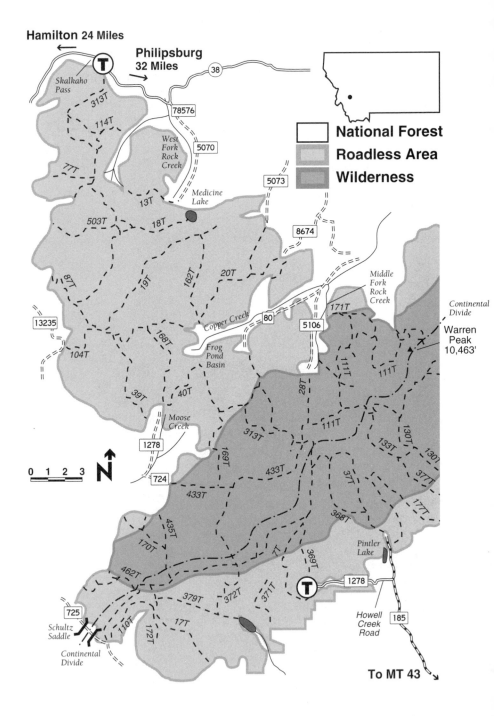

27B ANACONDA-PINTLER/SAPPHIRES WILDERNESS COMPLEX

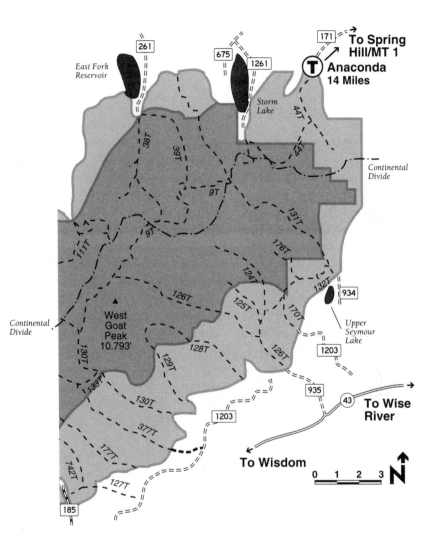

This secluded stretch of the Great Divide gives rise to some of the world's finest trout streams, including Rock Creek and the Big Hole River. Cirques and hanging valleys with dozens of alpine lakes, long U-shaped forested valleys, and glacial moraines form a wilderness wonderland. Year-round snowbanks feed tumbling streams that rest only briefly in deep, canyon-lined pools. Inhabitants of this high country include mountain goats, flying squirrels, and thirteen varieties of raptors.

The precious gem of the Sapphire Range extends northward from the Continental Divide. These more gentle mountains contain exposed bedrock and granite spires laced with open whitebark pine and subalpine larch, lending an alpine flavor to 40 miles of high crest. Glacial scouring has carved steep, rocky basins that nestle fifteen small lakes and countless potholes in the headwaters of the west-side Bitterroot River and east-side Rock Creek. The roadlessness of this linear wildland harbors spacious streamside meadows and old-growth forests uncommon elsewhere in the range. The undeveloped area is wild, big, and diverse enough to support at least 1,000 elk, along with moose, bighorn sheep, wolverine, and pileated woodpecker.

An entry from the journal of noted Montana conservationist Bud Moore during an extended backpack along the crest lends insight into the real treasure of the Sapphires: " . . . the forest is primeval and intimate yet a vista here and there lets the traveler orient to the great space around him. Glimpses of the high country far to the north spur him on and lend bigness to the country."

Majestic 10,641-foot Mount Evans on the Continental Divide towers over the roadless Storm Lake country on the northeast corner of the Wilderness. Dozens of glistening blue-black tarns are hidden in dished-out cirques below which U-shaped valleys end in undulating moraines. Black and gray crags fall sharply off horn peaks along the divide, where both mountain goats and snowfields remain most of the year.

The north end of the Big Hole Valley meets rolling, forested foothills with gently rounded ridges and open parks cut by streams born in the Anaconda-Pintler Wilderness. An uneven-aged lodgepole pine forest is broken by tiny, secret openings perfect for elk spring calving and summer range. The land is high, so usually by mid-November most of the elk have crossed the Continental Divide to their winter range in the Bitterroot. A key feature in the North Big Hole region of the complex is a large, subalpine meadow known as Clam Valley. Meandering Clam Creek cuts deeply through the center of the open park, providing the only habitat for a rare species of freshwater clam that may have been isolated by the most recent retreat of glaciers.

This then is the Anaconda-Pintler Wilderness Complex—a vast unbroken wildland that remains free and wild from the Skalkaho south to the Big Hole.

RECREATIONAL USES: The Anaconda-Pintler Wilderness forms the wild heart of the seventh largest contiguous wildland in Montana, with the spur of the Sapphire Range thrusting northward. Compared to most wildernesses much of the "A-P" is lightly used. Except for hunting season, the Sapphires and North Big Hole components receive even less use. Elk are the most sought-after game, from the early September archery season when the bulls are in rut until around mid-November when the first serious taste of winter drives most of the elk to lower country. The diversity within the complex is astounding, with a corresponding mix of cross-country skiing, backpacking, hiking, fishing, and horsepacking.

Although there are some superb ski tours into such places as Upper Seymour Lake, most of the visitation occurs from midsummer to fall. The dozens of alpine lakes often remain frozen into early July. The Sula Ranger District rents out the eight-person capacity East Fork Guard Station year-round. This cabin is only 1.5 miles from the wilderness boundary on the East Fork of the Bitterroot. Expect to ski in about 0.75 mile during winter. The Philipsburg Ranger District rents the four-person capacity Moose Lake Guard Station throughout the year as well. Depending on snow conditions, visitors may need to hike or ski about 0.25 mile to this cabin, which is located on the southeast edge of the Sapphires Wilderness Study Area.

Johnson Lake is the most heavily used destination in the wilderness. Rainbow Lake receives some of the overflow use from Johnson Lake despite a steep 1,500-foot climb between the two. Heavy fishing pressure is most evident at Edith, Johnson, Phyllis, and Carpp lakes. There is a Forest Service cabin at Mystic Lake which, for whatever reason, seems to attract even more use to this popular spot. The Deerlodge National Forest portion of the wilderness in the northeast corner receives the most use due to ease of access. The northside road parallels the forest boundary and accesses all the trails between the East Fork of Fishtrap Creek west to the Mudd Creek Ridge trail.

The most heavily used trailheads on the south side of the wilderness are West Fork LaMarche Creek by way of the Sundance Lodge private inholding; West Fork Fishtrap Creek; East Fork Thompson Creek; and, to a lesser extent, Mussigbrod Lake. From the north the most heavily used trailheads are the Middle Fork of Rock Creek; Falls Fork of Rock Creek leading up to Johnson and Edith Lakes; and the Carpp Lakes Trails 110 and 111. To protect wilderness values party size is limited to no more than fifteen people and twenty head of stock.

For an exceptional high-country adventure, take the "Hi-Line" trail along and near the Continental Divide across the entire east-west length of the wilderness. Be prepared for some very steep pitches on the western end of this trail between Surprise and Hope lakes. Several stretches can be hazardous for pack stock when wet. Forage is scarce throughout most of this lofty wilderness so it's a good idea to pack in feed when traveling with stock.

SNOW COMES EARLY AT WARREN LAKE IN THE ANACONDA-PINTLER WILDERNESS COMPLEX.

Those looking for solitude and challenge will find ample opportunities for cross-country travel in the higher country. Almost all of the 10,000-foot-plus peaks offer invigorating scrambling along with miles of interconnected ridges with unlimited vistas of a sea of surrounding mountain ranges.

HOW TO GET THERE: *Northern access:* From Hamilton drive 3 miles south on US Highway 93. Turn east on MT 38 (Skalkaho Road) and drive 20 miles to Skalkaho Pass. Continue east over the pass for 0.5 mile and take the first right turn. Go less than 0.25 mile to the trailhead for the Sapphire Crest Trail 313 heading south.

From Philipsburg drive 6 miles south on MT 1 and turn right onto MT 38. Drive west about 25 miles toward Skalkaho Pass. Turn left about 0.5 mile before reaching the pass and drive the remaining 0.25 mile to the trailhead.

Eastern Access: From Anaconda drive 10 miles west on MT 1 to Spring Hill. Turn south on Twin Lakes Creek Road (FR 5131) and go about 3 miles. Turn left on FR 171 and continue about 0.5 mile to the national forest boundary. From here Trail 44 heads up the Twin Lakes Creek drainage.

NORTH SIDE DAY HIKE OR SKALKAHO TO BIG HOLE BACKPACK

Sapphire Crest

Distance: 60 miles point-to-point, or any length out-and-back day hike for as long as time and energy permits.

Difficulty: Moderately strenuous.

Topo maps: Skalkaho Pass-MT; Kent Peak-MT; Whetstone Ridge-MT; Gibbons Pass-MT; Kelly Lake-MT; and Mussigbrod Lake-MT.

Trail 313 makes for a good day hike or a six- to eight-day ramble along the top of the Sapphires. From the trailhead climb 200 feet to the Sapphire Crest and continue south 2 miles on Trail 313 to the open ridge of an unnamed point at 8,168 feet. This ridge offers the first unobstructed views of the vast, densely forested Bowles Creek drainage and points beyond. Farther along the up-and-down divide, campsites close to tiny springs can be found in the head of Bowles Creek, in the very upper reaches of Railroad Creek, and in a delightful meadow at the head of the West Fork of Rock Creek about 9 miles south of Skalkaho Pass. The undulating crest winds through gnarled whitebark pine clinging to granitic soils. After another 3 miles the bouldery apex of 7,650-foot Signal Rock offers the first clear view of the jagged Continental Divide far to the south. The trail holds its grade for another 3 miles to the 3-way junction with trails 18 (east) and 503 (west), at which point Trail 313 drops 300 feet into the Jerry Lake basin before gaining another 700 feet just south of 8,884-foot Congdon Peak. A quick scramble to the rock rubble summit produces a strong sense of being at the parting of the waters between the Bitterroot River and Rock Creek. Continuing south the trail plummets west more than 1,400 feet to avoid the talus and scree of 8,998-foot Kent Peak. This highest point on the Sapphire divide can be climbed easily from Kent Lake. Nearby Trout Lake is actually a fishless frog pond surrounded by a soft, grassy meadow ideal for camping. Southward, the trail regains 800 feet to reach 8,400-foot Rooster Comb. The trail is hard to find just south of Rooster Comb; simply climb to the obvious point at 8,633 feet where the path becomes more evident. En route, Mosquito Meadows is a lovely alpine campsite. Trail 313 circles around the south edge of Shadow Lake, a deep tarn guarded by sheer rock cliffs to the west. Soon you'll come to Frogpond Basin, with its interesting assemblage of mining artifacts, lore, and history. After entering the wilderness boundary at a nameless point at 8,170 feet on a high divide, Trail 313 skirts a long ridgeline before dropping to meadow-lined Kelly Lake. Continue around the head of the drainage below Hidden Lake and then climb nearly 1,000 feet in 1 mile to the junction with Trail 9 on the Continental Divide at an elevation of 8,750 feet. Take Trail 9 to the turn off for Mystic Lake, where you'll pick up Trail 369 for the final 5- to 6-mile descent to the trailhead on the East Fork of Thompson Creek located at the gated closure on the Howell Creek Road. And there

SIGNAL ROCK ALONG THE CREST OF THE SAPPHIRE MOUNTAINS.

you have it. By hiking the high Sapphire crest, crossing the Great Divide into the more rugged Anaconda-Pintler Wilderness, and then dropping to the rolling lodgepole pine-covered foothills along the north edge of the Big Hole Valley, you will experience 60 miles of unbroken wildness from the Skalkaho to the Big Hole.

East Side Day Hike or Overnighter

Lake of the Isle and Mount Evans
Distance: 9 miles (Lake of the Isle) or 13 miles (Mount Evans) round-trip.
Difficulty: Moderate.
Topo map: Mount Evans-MT.

For this out-and-back trip, head up Trail 44, which begins as a jeep trail. The trail climbs moderately up a forested valley. After about 3 miles take the left-hand trail just below Lower Twin Lake and continue on for an 850-foot climb over the next 1.5 miles to aptly named Lake of the Isle. This alpine jewel sits at the base of a rocky spur ridge that juts north from the Continental Divide. The imposing north face of 10,641-foot Mount Evans towers 1.5 miles to the south. If you don't mind getting your feet wet look for an old log raft along the shore and pole yourself out into the lake for as far as you dare. The more ambitious can hike another mile up to the unnamed upper lake at 8,750 feet. This is also the best route to the commanding summit of Mount Evans by way of a saddle 1 mile northeast of the peak.

Humbug Spires

Location: 26 miles south of Butte.
Size: 11,335 acres.
Administration: Bureau of Land Management—Headwaters Resource Area.
Management status: Wilderness Study Area/roadless recreation.
Ecosystems: Middle Rocky Mountain steppe-coniferous forest province, characterized by steep mountains with alluvial terraces and floodplains; Precambrian granite spires and outcroppings; sagebrush steppe and Douglas-fir forest type; complex drainages and often intermittent or seasonal streams.
Elevation range: 5,800 to 8,069 feet.
Miles of system trails: 3 miles.
Maximum core to perimeter distance: 2 miles.
Activities: Hiking, backpacking, horseback riding, fishing, rock climbing, cross-country skiing.
Modes of travel: Foot, skis, horse.
Maps: 1993 BLM Humbug Spires 1:24,000 black & white contour map; Tucker Creek-MT; Mount Humbug-MT; Melrose-MT, and Wickiup Creek-MT (1:24,000 topo maps).

OVERVIEW: Humbug Spires is a land of dense forests, meadows, and canyons surrounded by bunchgrass and sagebrush foothills on the edge of the Big Hole River Valley between the Highland and East Pioneer mountains. The main artery—Moose Creek—flows through a narrow boulder-strewn canyon, changing to a series of pools, beaver ponds, and cascades. This wild enclave harbors several rare plants on the brink of extinction, including Idaho sedge, Kelsey's milk-vetch, and Rocky Mountain Douglasia.

Weathering and erosion of the central granitic core have produced the unique spires for which Humbug is named. The size and distribution of these granite spires is without parallel in the Northwest, providing what is likely the highest quality hard-rock climbing in Montana. No fewer than nine spires rise between 300 and 600 feet, with at least another fifty less than 300 feet high. The largest individual spire is called The Wedge. Another spire, The Crown, is overhung on all sides and has never been climbed, making its top among the last of Montana's truly untracked wildernesses.

RECREATIONAL USES: Readily accessible from I-15 south of Butte, the primary recreational activities here are hiking, stream fishing, rock climbing, backpacking, horseback riding, hunting, and cross-country skiing or snowshoeing.

28 HUMBUG SPIRES

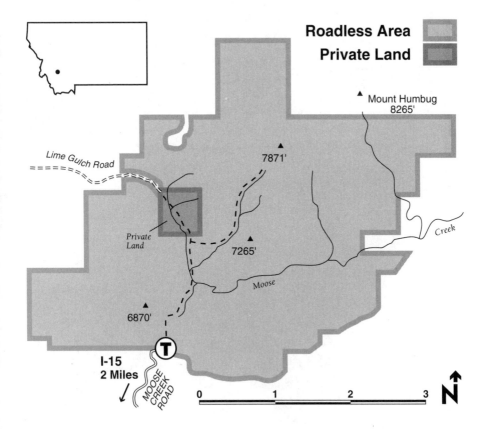

Humbug Spires is the most impressive outcropping of quartz monzonite within the Boulder Batholith, a huge, late-Cretaceous granitic intrusion. Rock climbing on the spires may be the most popular activity. Because of weathering, many of the spire walls have smooth, almost featureless surfaces which are hard to climb. Most routes are limited to vertical cracks, the majority of which vary from 5.5 to 5.7 in difficulty, with some of the more challenging routes reaching 5.12. Routes can be found for all climbing levels, from beginner to expert.

HUMBUG SPIRES NORTH OF MOOSE CREEK.

Most travel is along stream bottoms or ridges, either on horse or foot for either day or overnight trips. Although an established trail heads up Moose Creek, most of Humbug Spires is trailless and undeveloped. A maze of game trails and cross-country openings beckon to the more adventurous. Water runs year-round in most of the Moose Creek tributaries, but it should be treated by filtration or boiling as a precaution.

Moose Creek is populated with brook and rainbow trout in the lower reaches, and cutthroat only in the upper portions where they are protected by the barrier of waterfalls.

HOW TO GET THERE: Take the Moose Creek exit off Interstate 15, about 27 miles south of Butte. Drive northeast up Moose Creek Road to the Moose Creek trailhead at road's end. The low-standard MacLean Creek Road to the right is closed from December 2 to May 15 to protect soils, water quality, and wildlife.

HUMBUG SPIRES, A ROCK CLIMBER'S PARADISE.

DAY HIKE

Moose Creek Ramble

Distance: 8 to 10 miles out-and-back with an optional 10- to 12-mile loop.
Difficulty: Moderate.
Topo maps: Tucker Creek-MT; Mount Humbug-MT; and Melrose-MT.

To find the hiking trail, cross the footbridge just downhill from the restroom at the trailhead. The main trail heads northeast along Moose Creek, passing through groves of Douglas-fir more than 250 years old. After about 1.5 miles the trail forks. To avoid a 160-acre private inholding, which is posted against trespassing, take the right fork marked by white arrows. The trail goes up a small side drainage and over a ridge, quickly joining the northeast fork of Moose Creek. From here many game trails lead in all directions to the rock spires dotted throughout the northern portion of the roadless area. To access The Wedge, one of the more striking spires, continue 1.3 miles up the main trail along the intermittent stream. The Wedge is about 100 yards uphill from an abandoned miner's cabin at the head of the drainage. Up to this point the climbing is moderate—about 1,500 feet over 4 miles. To add a bit of adventure as well as a loop route, follow openings and game paths to the east and southeast, winding around and perhaps scrambling on some of the granite spires en route. A ridge between two south-flowing tributaries to the main southeast branch of Moose Creek provides an enjoyable and scenic loop back down to Moose Creek. Upon reaching the bottom it is another 2 miles down to the main trail. In places the narrow, steep canyon requires climbing above the rock walls, but most of this cross-country portion of the loop can be negotiated without difficulty.

Tobacco Roots

Location: 9 miles south of Whitehall and 11 miles east of Twin Bridges.
Size: 96,562 acres.
Administration: USDAFS—Beaverhead and Deerlodge national forests.
Management status: Roadless non-wilderness with potential mining and some lands allocated to future development in the forest plans.
Ecosystems: Middle Rocky Mountain coniferous forest-alpine meadow province, characterized by complex and high, steep, glaciated mountains with sharp ridges and cirques; Precambrian granite; Douglas-fir forest type with sagebrush steppe and smaller areas of alpine vegetation; and complex drainage pattern with numerous high lakes.
Elevation range: 5,140 to 10,604 feet.
System trails: 46 miles.
Maximum core to perimeter distance: 2 miles.
Activities: Hiking, backpacking, horseback riding, cross-country skiing, fishing.
Modes of travel: Foot, ski, and horse.
Maps: 1993 Beaverhead Interagency Travel Plan Map; 1990 Deerlodge National Forest Visitor Map; Waterloo-MT; Manhead Mountain-MT; Old Baldy Mountain-MT; Noble Peak-MT; Potosi Peak-MT, Copper Mountain-MT; and Ramshorn Mountain-MT (1:24,000 topo maps).

OVERVIEW: The higher reaches of the isolated Tobacco Root Mountains are somewhat fragmented by old mines and mining roads. Still, wildness prevails in what is likely the densest concentration of high peaks in Montana, where twenty-eight rocky pinnacles exceed 10,000 feet—heaven on earth for a stable mountain goat population. Dozens of small alpine tarns are nestled in hanging basins below the high peaks. The most rugged topography in the range lies along the glacial cirque head of Indian Creek, which supplies much of Sheridan's municipal water.

From elk, antelope, and deer winter range of mixed grassland, sagebrush, and juniper the land climbs to lodgepole, Douglas-fir, and spruce on up to whitebark pine and finally to matted alpine trundra. Small wet meadows, usually ringed by granite outcrops, grace every U-shaped valley. In contrast to the sharp peaks of the main Tobacco Roots, the eastern slopes of the range are relatively gentle, with undulating ridges and dissected foothills where raptors and mountain lions hunt their prey.

29 TOBACCO ROOTS

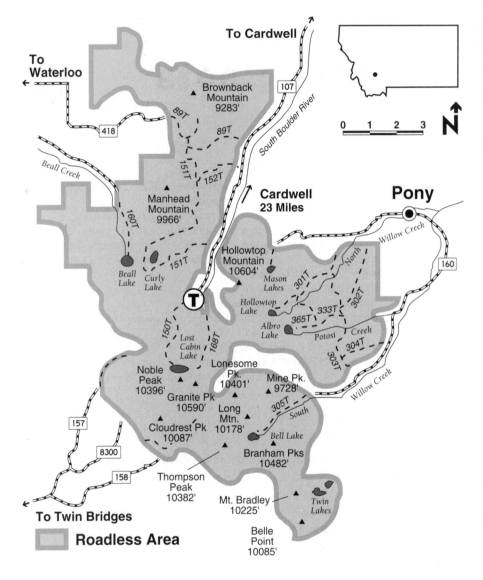

To Cardwell

To Waterloo

Brownback Mountain 9283'

107

89T

418

89T

South Boulder River

Beall Creek

151T

152T

Manhead Mountain 9966'

160T

Cardwell 23 Miles

Pony

Willow Creek

North

160

151T

Hollowtop Mountain 10604'

301T

302T

Mason Lakes

Beall Lake

Curly Lake

T

Hollowtop Lake

333T

365T

Albro Lake

Potosi Creek

304T

303T

150T

Lost Cabin Lake

168T

Noble Peak 10396'

Lonesome Pk. 10401'

Mine Pk. 9728'

Granite Pk 10590'

Long Mtn. 10178'

305T

South

Willow Creek

157

Cloudrest Pk 10087'

Bell Lake

8300

Branham Pks 10482'

158

Thompson Peak 10382'

To Twin Bridges

Mt. Bradley 10225'

Twin Lakes

Roadless Area

Belle Point 10085'

0 1 2 3

N

RECREATIONAL USES: Backpacking, hiking, horseback riding, camping, hunting, and fishing are popular amidst the grandeur of the classic alpine setting of the high Tobacco Roots. Clear streams and sparkling mountain lakes surrounded by scoured peaks, ridges, and cliffs entice the backcountry traveler. The main dividing ridge has several semi-technical peaks that challenge all but the most seasoned climbers. Lack of plowed road access and high avalanche danger in some of the steeper canyons discourage backcountry winter travel. However, it is possible to drive to the small community of Pony on the northeast edge of the range and ski southwest up Willow Creek Road 191 to the glacial lake basins of Hollowtop and Skytop lakes. In stable snow conditions ski mountaineers can climb west up to the high saddle between Mount Jefferson and the apex of the Tobacco Roots, 10,604-foot Hollowtop Mountain. From the saddle it's a moderately steep but steady walk up along the main divide to either or both summits.

HOW TO GET THERE: From I-90 about 31 miles east of Butte take the Cardwell exit and drive 4 miles south on MT 359 to the South Boulder River Road 107. Continue south up the South Boulder River Road about 20 miles to Bismark Reservoir and the trailhead for Lost Cabin Lake Trail 150 on the left (south) side of the road. The road worsens as you head south, but careful driving with a two-wheel-drive vehicle will get you there if the road is reasonably dry.

DAY HIKE OR OVERNIGHTER

Lost Cabin Lake and the Tobacco Root Divide
Distance: 8 miles out-and-back.
Difficulty: Moderate trail hike with strenuous but non-technical side climbs.
Topo map: Noble Peak-MT.

Begin hiking south at the Lost Cabin Lake trailhead on Trail 150. This beautiful alpine gem sits in a cirque 4 miles up with a modest elevation gain of 1,200 feet. Numerous split log bridges mark each stream crossing. A lush subalpine meadow defines the halfway point. The meadow is cut by a deep, meandering stream full of small cutthroat. Keep an eye out for elk around the edges. With a north exposure the upper basin often contains snow into mid-July. The nearly 9,000-foot high lake is surrounded by scattered subalpine fir and spruce, overlooked by 10,396-foot Noble Peak and the imposing crest of the range. The view to the west is overpowering, with the massive rock cliffs of Spuhler Peak's northeast ridge. There are several good tent sites near the outlet, but with no fish Lost Cabin receives comparatively few visitors. The open, rocky slope east of the lake provides a good route to the main divide which rises about 1,000 feet above the lake basin. Corniced snowbanks and steep rocks guard Noble

LOST CABIN LAKE, HIGH IN THE TOBACCO ROOTS.

Peak to the west. After a bit of hand-over-hand rock climbing you'll be on the summit looking 1,500 feet straight down to the narrow upper cirque of Lost Cabin Lake. To the west, the 1,300-foot drop to Noble Lake is made easily down a series of small hanging ledges and valleys. The lake itself has an old cabin and low-standard road to it. It abounds with small cutthroat. Back on the divide and to the east the second highest summit in the range—10,590-foot Granite Peak—is a steep but easy walk up. If you've come this far by all means hike north on the ridge between Lost Cabin Lake and Louise Lake, climbing the prominent 10,353-foot Middle Mountain on its gentler east side. After soaking up the 360-degree mountainscape, continue northeast about 0.25 mile, dropping down to a saddle, for a grand view of Louise Lake. This is prime mountain goat country and you're standing right where they're most likely to be.

East Pioneers 30

Location: 21 miles northwest of Dillon.
Size: 145,682 acres.
Administration: USDAFS—Beaverhead National Forest; Bureau of Land Management—Dillon Resource Area (1,139 acre Farlin Creek WSA on southwest edge of East Pioneers).
Management status: Roadless non-wilderness with some peripheral lands allocated to future development in the forest plan; small BLM WSA on southwest corner.
Ecosystems: Middle Rocky Mountain coniferous forest-alpine meadow province, characterized by complex and high, steep, strongly glaciated mountains with sharp alpine ridges and cirques; Precambrian granite; Douglas-fir forest type with sagebrush steppe and smaller areas of alpine vegetation; and numerous perennial streams and high mountain lakes.
Elevation range: 6,400 to 11,154 feet.
System trails: 80 miles.
Maximum core to perimeter distance: 3 miles.
Activities: Hiking, backpacking, horseback riding, cross-country skiing, fishing.
Modes of travel: Foot, skis, horse.
Maps: 1993 Beaverhead/Interagency Travel Plan Map; Vipond Park-MT; Cattle Gulch-MT; Maurice Mountain-MT; Mount Tahepia-MT; Elkhorn Hot Springs-MT; Torrey Mountain-MT; Polaris-MT; and Ermont-MT (1:24,000 topo maps).

OVERVIEW: The markedly glaciated East Pioneers are a geological puzzle with sharp peaks and steep rock walls. High cirque basins hold more than thirty sparkling trout-filled lakes surrounded by jagged summits and U-shaped glacial trough valleys. Wet seeps and meadows are the telltale signs of higher water tables in the southern reaches of the range.

The land rises abruptly for a vertical mile from Rock Creek to the imposing main dividing ridge, slicing north-south for 25 serpentine miles. The crest is distinguished by the loftiest peaks on the Beaverhead Forest—11,154-foot Tweedy Mountain and Torrey Mountain at 11,147 feet. The west slope is steep with dissected sidehills breaking rapidly to the Wise River. The east side rolls down gradually along foothills to the Big Hole River.

Large changes in elevation contribute to a wide range of flora and fauna. On a typical ascent to the high country you would probably start out in a grass-and-sagebrush park. Climbing up through a lodgepole/subalpine fir forest, you

30 EAST PIONEERS

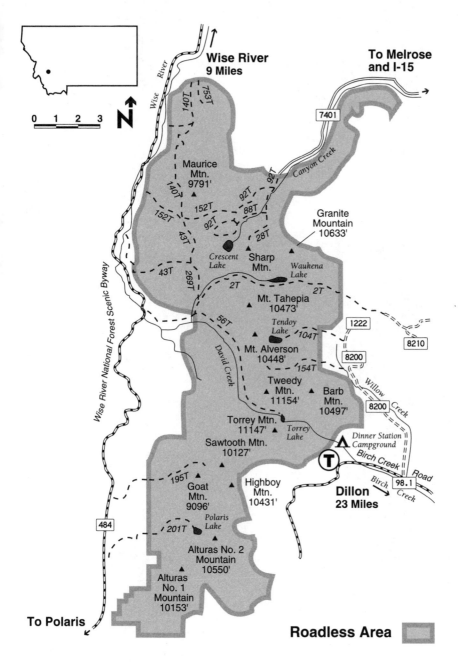

Roadless Area

Backcountry skiing below Barb Mountain in the East Pioneers.

would eventually top a windswept ridge or headwall adorned with whitebark pine. Upper timberline would be around 9,000 feet with hearty shrublike trees and alpine tundra. Mountain music would consist of the wind, a pika's whistle, or the cry of a raptor.

Mountain goats make a good living along cliff faces from Torrey Mountain northeast to a linear plateau north of Canyon Creek, known as the "Elephant's Trunk" because of its shape as seen on a map. Sawtooth and Hidden lakes harbor colorful golden trout, and rare arctic grayling fin the frigid waters of Grayling Lake.

RECREATIONAL USES: With the exceptions of Canyon Creek and David Creek, the East Pioneers receive fairly light recreational use, most of which is seasonal. Fall hunting is popular at nearby guest ranches that outfit hunters for deer, elk, and other species by special permit. Summer backpacking and horse trips into the many high lake basins have gained in popularity. Cross-country skiing is a distant third, in part because of the steep, rugged terrain and the high avalanche hazard throughout much of the higher country. The Wise River Ranger District rents out the Canyon Creek cabin, which is on FR 187 about 13 miles west of Melrose. Winter access varies with snow conditions but it is normally possible to reach this four-person cabin with a four-wheel-drive vehicle. Otherwise, the road may be blocked 6 miles below the cabin. The cabin itself is about 4 miles from the campground at the end of the road. To the south, the Dillon Ranger District rents the three-person capacity Birch Creek cabin, 20 miles northwest of Dillon just off the Birch Creek Road before the Aspen picnic ground (see the ski tour outlined below).

Climbers are lured to the fractured rock faces of David Creek and Barb Mountain for the challenge of technical rock climbing. Barb Mountain (10,497 feet), especially impressive with its north face adorned by hoodoos and rock spires, is named for the fishhook-like barb at its pinnacle.

Besides the golden trout at Sawtooth and Hidden lakes and arctic grayling at Grayling Lake, more than thirty high lakes also support trout.

Established trails tend to go east-west up and down rock-strewn drainages, typically starting out as a closed jeep track and gradually changing to a foot and horse path. Drainages are not interconnected with north-south trails, which makes cross-country travel difficult. A number of lake basins are trailless, such as Barb, which increases the odds of finding solitude and unexpected discoveries.

For a transmountain point-to-point trip, here are the major east-side trailheads that serve as jumping off places for trails crossing the crest of the range to the Wise River:

1) Canyon Creek—a privately owned guest ranch is located here along with a Forest Service campground farther up at the end of FR 7401. Several trails

lead to the southwest, including Trail 92 to the Canyon Lake complex, Trail 28 to popular Lion Lake, and Trail 152 up to and down Gold Creek to the Wise River.

2) Rock Creek—FR 8210 goes to a Forest Service campground at Brownes Lake. A lower standard road continues another 2 miles to the start of Trail 2 to Waukena Lake. Trail 2 crosses the crest to Tahepia Lake and Mono Creek campground on the Wise River. The heavily used David Creek Trail 56 climbs southeast from the campground for about 10 miles to Torrey Lake.

Other popular destinations are:

1) Willow Creek Trail 154 to Gorge Lakes; and
2) the cluster of high lakes at the head of Birch Creek reached from Trail 72.

HOW TO GET THERE: From Dillon drive 11 miles north on I-15 and take the Apex exit. Drive about 10 miles west on the Birch Creek Road (FR 98.1). After passing the Aspen picnic ground stay to the left on FR 98 another 2 miles to the Dinner Station campground on Birch Creek.

ONE-DAY SKI MOUNTAINEERING TOUR

Torrey Mountain
Distance: 12 miles round-trip.
Difficulty: Strenuous.
Topo map: Torrey Mountain-MT.

This ski ascent is nontechnical but should be attempted only in stable snow by experienced, well-conditioned backcountry skiers. At 11,147 feet, Torrey Mountain in the south end of the East Pioneers is only 7 feet lower than the highest point just to the north—Tweedy Mountain. Torrey offers an exhilarating late winter/early spring ski climb.

In most years it is possible to drive all the way up the Birch Creek Road to the Dinner Station campground. From there, head up one of the obvious main east ridges of Torrey Mountain. The climb will begin by hiking on alternating patches of bare ground and postholing through mounds of snow. The snow becomes consistent starting at about 8,000 feet elevation in a dense lodgepole pine forest for the next 3 miles. Suddenly, the gentle ridge climbs abruptly through scattered whitebark pine leading to an open, avalanche-prone slope. There is no way to avoid crossing this slope so turn around here if conditions appear unsafe. If the snow is stable cautiously traverse the slope one at a time. The next 2,400 feet up the main east ridge provides good going with spectacular views of the upper Birch Creek lake basin encircled by jagged peaks—Sawtooth, Highboy, and Tent—all over 10,000 feet. Soon you will be on the rock-strewn summit. Two miles northeast rises Tweedy—separated by a knife

EL CAPITAN, IN SOUTHWEST MONTANA'S BITTERROOT RANGE.
MICHAEL S. SAMPLE

GLACIAL PONDS NEAR THE
CONTINENTAL DIVIDE IN THE
CENTENNIAL MOUNTAINS.
MICHAEL S. SAMPLE

NEWBORN MULE DEER FAWN,
NATIVE TO THE SELWAY-
BITTERROOT WILDERNESS.
BILL CUNNINGHAM

THE ABSAROKA RANGE IN SOUTH-
CENTRAL MONTANA.
MICHAEL S. SAMPLE

.

COYOTES LIVE AND HUNT
THROUGHOUT ALL OF MONTANA'S
WILD COUNTRY.
MICHAEL S. SAMPLE

THE PRYOR MOUNTAINS IN SOUTH-CENTRAL MONTANA.

MICHAEL S. SAMPLE

A WINTER ASCENT OF
11,141" EIGHTEENMILE
PEAK–HIGHEST POINT ON
MONTANA'S SHARE OF THE
CONTINENTAL DIVIDE.
BILL CUNNINGHAM

ROCKY MOUNTAIN BIGHORN
SHEEP ARE FOUND IN THE
MORE RUGGED REACHES OF
MONTANA'S WILD COUNTRY.
MICHAEL S. SAMPLE

A MAZE OF PLATEAUS, COULEES AND DEEP CANYONS MAKE UP WILD BADLANDS IN SOUTHEASTERN MONTANA.

NEGOTIATING A MOUNTAIN GOAT TRAIL IN THE UPPER GREEN FORK, IN THE SCAPEGOAT WILDERNESS.

THE LEE METCALF WILDERNESS, WITH A VIEW OF THE HILGARD RANGE IN THE DISTANCE.
BILL CUNNINGHAM

THE SECURITY PROVIDED
BY MONTANA'S WILD
COUNTRY FOR ELK
CALVING IS CRUCIAL TO
THE FUTURE OF OUR
LARGE HERDS OF ELK.
MICHAEL. S. SAMPLE

Echo Peak in the Hilgard Range of the Lee Metcalf Wilderness.

BILL CUNNINGHAM

ridge of technical rock. Straight below and to the north sits sizable Torrey Lake in a cirque at the head of David Creek. Grand vistas of mountain ranges spread out in every direction—the more gentle adjacent West Pioneers, the Great Divide ranges of the Beaverheads, Anaconda-Pintlers, Italian Peaks, Lima Peaks, and Centennials, along with the Highland, Ruby, Snowcrest, Tobacco Root, Madison, and Gravelly ranges.

West Pioneers

Location: 4 miles east of Wisdom, 2 miles northeast of Jackson, and 4 miles west of Wise River.
Size: 239,572 acres (includes a 148,000-acre Wilderness Study Area).
Administration: USDAFS—Beaverhead National Forest; Bureau of Land Management—Butte District.
Management status: 148,000-acre Congressional Wilderness Study Area core surrounded by an additional 90,352 acres of roadless non-wilderness lands, some of which is allocated to future development in the forest plan.
Ecosystems: Middle Rocky Mountain coniferous forest-alpine meadow province, characterized by complex and high, gentle to moderately steep mountains with sharp ridges and partially-developed cirques along the main divide; Precambrian granite; Douglas-fir forest type with sagebrush steppe and small, isolated areas of alpine vegetation; numerous perennial streams with a complex drainage pattern, abundant parks and wet meadows.
Elevation range: 5,850 to 9,497 feet.
System trails: 245 miles.
Maximum core to perimeter distance: 5 miles.
Activities: Hiking, backpacking, horseback riding, mountain biking, cross-country skiing, fishing.
Modes of travel: Foot, horse, mountain bike, and skis.
Maps: 1993 Beaverhead/Interagency Travel Plan Map; Pine Hill-MT; Foolhen Mountain-MT; Dickey Hills-MT;; Proposal Rock-MT; Shaw Mountain-MT; Stine Mountain-MT; Stewart Mountain-MT; Odell Lake-MT; Maurice Mountain-MT; Jackson Hill-MT; Maverick Mountain-MT; and Elkhorn Hot Springs-MT (1:24,000 topo maps).

OVERVIEW: The rounded West Pioneers, on the sunrise side of the Big Hole Valley, are so different from the ruggedly alpine East Pioneers that it's hard to believe the same major mountain mass encompasses both ranges. The Pioneers are divided by the Wise River, a major north-flowing tributary of the Big Hole. The West Pioneers is one of Montana's largest unprotected roadless areas.

With steep mountain goat rocks in the north and gentler terrain to the south, the land ascends to 9,497-foot Stine Mountain. Seventy percent of the high-quality water produced comes from snow melting into sparkling, fish-filled lakes along the crest, draining to wet meadows and parks and, finally, flowing to the Big Hole River. Sagebrush and grassland complement dense lodgepole pine forests, with big old spruce in the bottoms. Giant whitebark pines

31 WEST PIONEERS

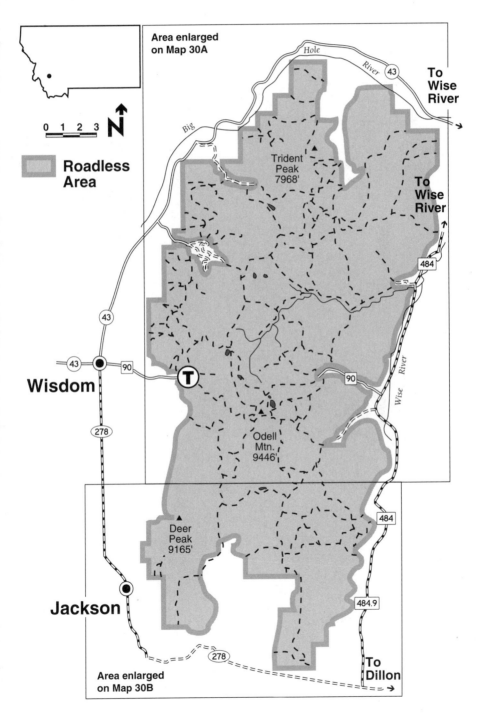

Area enlarged
on Map 30A

To
Wise
River

To
Wise
River

Roadless
Area

Trident
Peak
7968'

43

484

Big

Hole

River

43

43   90

90

Wisdom

278

Wise River

Odell
Mtn.
9446'

T

Deer
Peak
9165'

484

484.9

Jackson

278

To
Dillon

Area enlarged
on Map 30B

31A WEST PIONEERS

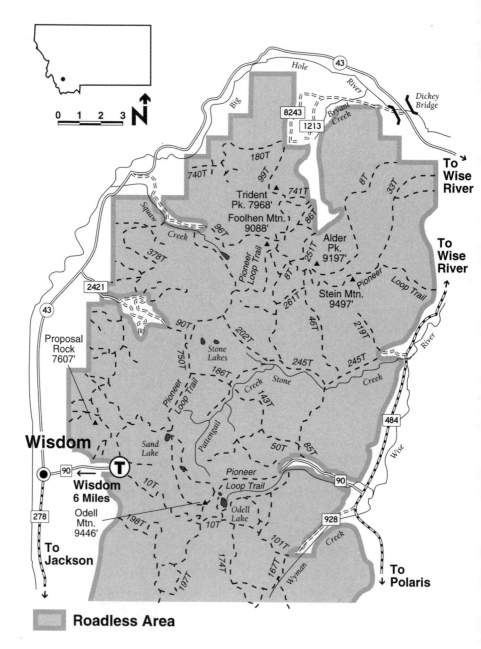

Roadless Area

along windswept ridges are some of the oldest in Montana. Western larch grow near the head of Osborne Creek—the easternmost extension of the species. The longest-living stand of lodgepole pine known—500 years old—survives in the undisturbed Effie Creek drainage. Adding to this ecological significance is a pure-strain lake population of arctic grayling, likely the last outside Alaska. They reproduce in Odell Lake, Schwinegar Lake, and in one of the Bobcat Lakes. Old Tim Creek, lined by meadows for much of its course, contains remnant pure-strain native cutthroat trout.

Elk make a year-round living in this large, diverse land, from foothill winter foraging to calving grounds, and from summer grazing to fall security in lodgepole/spruce thickets. Overall, these gentle mountains have a comfortable, sublime feel—as inviting to the human visitor as it is for the newborn elk calf.

RECREATIONAL USES: A moderate amount of dispersed recreation occurs here. Hunting is the dominant activity, with some peripheral areas on the north and west sides receiving heavy elk hunting pressure. An increasing number of backpackers are drawn to the lakes for fishing and camping, most of which are in the central high-ridge country. The roadless area is big enough to absorb a week-long backpacking or horse trip, yet gentle enough for weekend family outings close to roadheads along the Wise River and from the Big Hole Valley. Unlike its more rugged neighbors to the immediate west, north and east the West Pioneers are distinguished by moderately rolling forest-covered hills and ridges interspersed with huge parks and meadows—ideal for easy hiking and backpacking. This landscape is also well suited for extended or day-trip cross-country skiing, although distances from the ends of plowed roads to the interior are substantial in most cases. One exception is the road to Elkhorn Hot Springs, which is close to trails leading into the southeast corner near Maverick Mountain and Crystal Park.

From December 1 to August 31 the Wise River Ranger District rents out the four-person capacity Foolhen Cabin which is within the northern boundary of the study area. At the end of 12 miles of unplowed road, the cabin is used mostly by snowmobilers. During summer the trail distance from the end of the Bryant Creek road is 2.5 miles.

HOW TO GET THERE: From MT 43 on the north end of Wisdom head east on Steel Creek road about 6 miles to the Steel Creek campground, which is the trailhead for Trail 10.

31B WEST PIONEERS

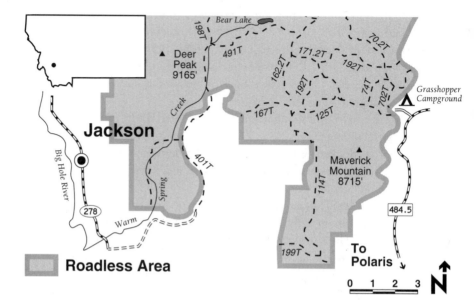

Bear Lake
198T
▲ Deer Peak 9165'
491T
171.2T
70.2T
162.2T
192T
192T
74T
702T
Grasshopper Campground
167T
125T

Jackson

Creek

Big Hole River

401T

Spring

Maverick Mountain 8715' ▲

114T

278

Warm

484.5

199T

To Polaris

Roadless Area

0 1 2 3 **N**

BACKPACK OR HORSE-PACKING TRIP

Steel Creek Loop
Distance: 20 miles (3 days).
Difficulty: Moderate.
Topo maps: Proposal Rock-MT; Stewart Mountain-MT; and Odell Lake-MT.

From Steel Creek campground go past the drift fence and on up the Steel Creek jeep track a short distance to the beginning of the Odell Lookout Trail 10, which switchbacks up the slope to the right. After a 1-mile climb through open forest the trail skirts southeast above large and lush Moose Meadows where moose, deer, and elk are sometimes seen during very early or late daylight hours. The trail then climbs steeply up one of the upper tributaries of Steel Creek through wet spruce glades and scattered giant Douglas-fir—survivors of the last major fire. Continue on to about mile 8 with a short side trip to the crown of the West Pioneers—9,446-foot Odell Mountain. The view from this large, rounded summit provides an excellent perspective on the heart of these meadow-lined mountains.

ANGLING FOR BROOKIES IN **WARM SPRINGS CREEK**—SOUTH END OF THE **WEST PIONEERS**

With about 3,000 vertical feet under your belt take the mellow descent to one of the forest lakes immediately east of the peak and make camp for the night. Continuing north on Trail 245, Baldy Lake is well worth a stop. Baldy is one of several lakes nestled in the talus rock at the base of the long ridge that culminates at the top of Odell Mountain. Sand Lake, a couple of miles north, is the site of an outfitter hunting camp and a nice spot to spend another night. Fishing can be good at times in both Baldy and Sand lakes, but the greatest attraction is simply relaxing in the sublime beauty of the West Pioneers. On the third day take the Sand Lake trail west and then south about 6 miles, ending up at the Steel Creek guard station just below the campground.

West Big Hole

Location: 14 miles southwest of Wisdom and 12 miles west of Jackson.
Size: 214,000 acres; 130,782 acres of which are in Montana.
Administration: USDAFS—Beaverhead and Salmon national forests.
Management status: Roadless non-wilderness, with some peripheral lands allocated to future development in the forest plan.
Ecosystems: Middle Rocky Mountain coniferous forest-alpine meadow province, characterized by complex and high, steep, strongly glaciated mountains with sharp alpine ridges and cirques; Precambrian granite; Douglas-fir forest type with sagebrush steppe and smaller areas of alpine vegetation; and a complex drainage pattern with numerous perennial streams and high lakes.
Elevation range: 6,500 to 10,621 feet.
System trails: 65 miles.
Maximum core to perimeter distance: 5 miles.
Activities: Hiking, backpacking, horseback riding, cross-country skiing, mountain biking, fishing.
Modes of travel: Foot, horse, skis, and mountain bike.
Maps: 1993 Beaverhead/Interagency Travel Plan Map; Big Hole Pass-ID/MT; Isaac Meadows-MT; Jumbo Mountain-MT/ID; Homer Youngs Peak-MT/ID; Miner Lake-MT; Bohannon Spring-ID/MT; and Goldstone Pass-MT/ID (1:24,000 topo maps).

OVERVIEW: Local ranchers and outdoor enthusiasts have been working together for more than a decade to protect the West Big Hole from roads and logging in the middle and lower slopes of this Continental Divide wild country. Rising from the sunset side of the broad Big Hole, these snowy southern Bitterroot Mountains reach over 10,000 feet along the divide before dropping sharply into Idaho. From high sagebrush plains the lodgepole pine-covered foothills on the Montana side of the West Big Hole ascend gradually, merging into glaciated U-shaped canyons and finally thrusting steeply to the Great Divide. The centerpiece is the apex of the range—the rock-strewn mass of 10,621-foot Homer Youngs Peak, which actually rises just east of the Continental Divide. Nearly thirty dark blue alpine lakes are cupped in lush hanging valleys where a myriad of wildflowers explode in color by mid-July along the edges of lingering snowfields. In the lower country visitors can savor the quiet joy of a subalpine meadow and the peace of a meandering stream and deep pools teaming with brookies. Wildlife match the landscape, with black bear,

32 WEST BIG HOLE

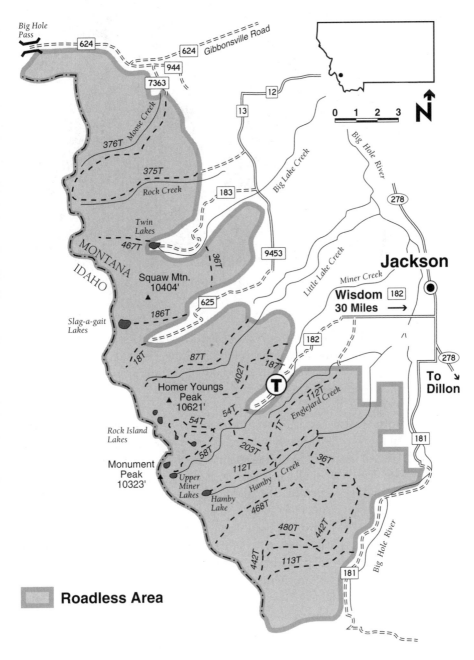

Roadless Area

ALONG THE CONTINENTAL DIVIDE ABOVE GENEVA LAKE, IN THE SOUTH END OF THE WEST BIG HOLE.

mountain lion, elk, deer, moose, goat, and wolverine relying on a diverse mix of forest, meadow, park, and alpine tundra habitats. This exhilarating 40-mile stretch of high snow country is an especially important producer of pure water for fish and downstream users.

RECREATIONAL USES: There are four Forest Service campgrounds along the eastern edge of the West Big Hole: South and North Van Houten, Miner Lake, and Twin Lakes. All are filled up during summer holidays; Twin Lakes is the most heavily used. The Wisdom Ranger District rents the four-person capacity Twin Lakes cabin during winter, but demand has been low for this remote, hard-to-get-to outpost.

Overall, recreational use has been rising, with archery hunting showing the most increase. A typical use pattern is for groups to camp in campgrounds or along the roads, traveling the trails and fishing the lakes on weekends. The heaviest use drainages are Miner Creek and Slag-a-Melt. Winter cross-country skier use is light because of a lack of plowed roads near the national forest boundary. However, a chained-up 4-wheel-drive vehicle can usually reach West Big Hole trailheads along the Foothills Road (FR 945) in December before the snow gets too deep. Most of the valley floors provide great backcountry ski touring and are wide enough to avoid avalanche hazards.

Outfitted use is low, consisting of a small amount of guided backpacking along with a few day horseback rides into Lower Hamby and Rock Island lakes. A key feature of the West Big Hole is its remote accessibility. Only a few hours travel time separates most of the trailheads from the heads of basins below the Continental Divide. The stream bottoms are fairly level well up to their headwaters, before meeting the sharp incline of the Great Divide. Most of the access to the West Big Hole is provided by the Foothills Road (FR 945) going south from MT 43, or via the Twin Lakes, Miner Lake, Van Houten Lake, and Bloody Dick roads. Despite long shuttles, point-to-point treks are best done with two vehicles because the chances of hitching a ride on these lightly traveled roads are slim.

About 40 miles of the Continental Divide National Scenic Trail wind along the rugged alpine crest of the West Big Hole. The CDNST can be reached at Big Hole Pass from the Gibbonsville road on the north end, or from trails that lead out from Twin Lakes, Lena Lake, Darkhorse, Jahnke, Little Lake, Rock Creek, and Van Houten.

HOW TO GET THERE: From Wisdom drive 18 miles south on MT 278 to Jackson. Continue about 0.5 mile south of Jackson, turn right (west) on FR 182, and drive about 12 miles to Miner Lake Campground. Begin your exploration of the West Big Hole from the campground or, with a high-clearance vehicle, drive an additional 3 miles of very rough, rocky road to the gate closure, which is the trailhead for Trail 54.

LOOKING EASTWARD DOWN THE GENEVA-HAMBY LAKE DRAINAGE, FROM THE GREAT DIVIDE.

Day Hike or Overnighter

Homer Youngs Peak
Distance: 10 miles out-and-back.
Difficulty: Strenuous.
Topo maps: Homer Youngs Peak-MT/ID and Miner Lake-MT.

The highest point in the West Big Hole—10,621-foot Homer Youngs Peak—towers above the 10,000-foot crest of the Continental Divide to the immediate west. The most direct approach to the summit is to take the overland Trail 187 north from the Miner Lake Road about 0.5 mile below the closure. As soon as you reach the main ridge above Miner Creek, head west on the main east ridge of the peak with first Kelly Creek and then Heart Lake on your right to the north. This is a vigorous 8- to 10-mile roundtrip with a vertical climb of 3,500 feet.

To combine climbing with backpacking leave from the gated road closure on the Miner Lake road and head up the old jeep tracks, which soon turn into Trail 54. Climb steeply for 1,300 feet over a distance of 3 miles to lower Rock Island Lake, which has several choice but heavily used campsites. From there, hike to the upper lake and then onto the 9,055-foot saddle on the prominent southwest ridge of Homer Youngs Peak. The saddle can be reached by picking your way up the slope cross country or by finding a faint trail toward the head of the upper lake. This is an excellent place to see mountain goats. From the saddle you'll have a 1,600-foot hand-over-hand rock scramble to the summit. With care a safe route without exposure can be found without difficulty. From the top you'll be treated to a panorama of the entire Big Hole watershed along with the Bitterroots, Pintlers, Sapphires, and range after range fading into Idaho. You'll actually be looking west over the top of the Divide to the Salmon River valley in Idaho.

Italian Peaks

33

Location: 50 miles southwest of Dillon and 16 miles southwest of Lima.
Size: About 250,000 acres; 91,277 acres of which are in Montana.
Administration: USDAFS—Beaverhead and Targhee national forests.
Management status: Roadless non-wilderness
Ecosystems: Middle Rocky Mountain steppe-coniferous forest-alpine meadow province, characterized by complex and high, steep mountains with sharp ridges and cirques; Precambrian granite, sedimentary and volcanic rocks; Douglas-fir forest type, sagebrush steppe with small areas of alpine vegetation; complex drainage pattern with many intermittent streams.
Elevation range: 7,480 to 11,141 feet.
System trails: 55 miles.
Maximum core to perimeter distance: 3 miles.
Activities: Hiking, backpacking, horseback riding, fishing, cross-country skiing.
Modes of travel: Foot, skis, and horse.
Maps: 1993 Beaverhead/Interagency Travel Plan Map; Morrison Lake-ID/MT; Island Butte-MT; Caboose Can-MT; Cottonwood Creek-ID/MT; Eighteenmile Peak-MT/ID; Deadman Lake-MT/ID; and Scott Peak-ID/MT (1:24,000 topo maps).

OVERVIEW: The high, wide, and dry Italian Peaks wildland is truly Montana's "hidden corner" at the state's most southern extremity. The centerpiece is Italian Peak itself, a 10,998-foot massif of the Continental Divide with a sheer, overpowering 2,000-foot precipice of shattered limestone. Distinctive ridges define the upper Nicholia Basin where scattered pockets of whitebark pine and spruce surround wet meadows with an undulating landscape of dips and mounds. Most of these remote southern Bitterroots are either above timberline or interspersed with patches of lodgepole pine and Douglas-fir on cooler north-facing slopes.

Here the Great Divide is a narrow, gently sloping grassy ridgetop in the northern reaches, becoming sharper with steep, rocky cirque headwalls south of Morrison Lake. From 11,141-foot Eighteenmile Peak—the highest point on Montana's share of the Continental Divide—one gets the sense of unlimited, uncluttered space. This feeling is especially powerful during winter, when the blurred whiteness of vast valleys and mountain ranges in every direction masks the meager lines of human development.

33 ITALIAN PEAKS

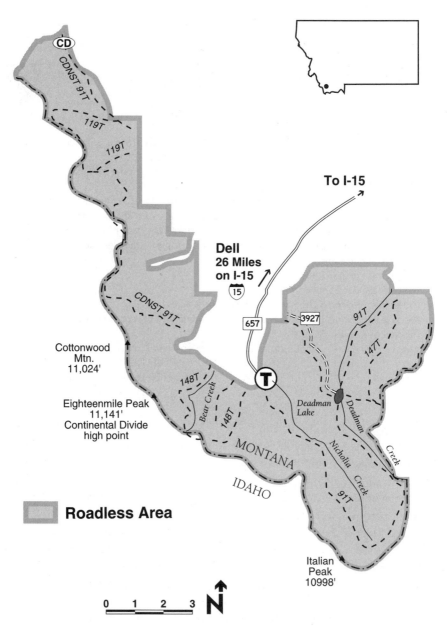

To I-15

Dell
26 Miles
on I-15

CDNST 91T

119T

119T

CD

Cottonwood
Mtn.
11,024'

Eighteenmile Peak
11,141'
Continental Divide
high point

CDNST 91T

657

3927

91T

147T

148T

148T

Bear Creek

Deadman
Lake

Deadman Creek

Nicholia Creek

MONTANA

IDAHO

91T

Italian
Peak
10998'

▭ **Roadless Area**

0   1   2   3   **N**

This austere, mostly treeless land is well suited for mountain goats and sum-mering elk, as a sanctuary for many smaller mammals, and as home for the transitory, endangered gray wolf.

RECREATIONAL USES: Recreational use is light in the Italian Peaks because this lofty Great Divide country is a long ways from anywhere with few people living anywhere near it. Hunting is the most popular activity, with some fishing in Deadman Lake and Nicholia Creek. There are ample opportunities for solitude while hiking, back-packing, and mountain climbing in the more rugged higher country near the divide. About 50 miles of the Continental Divide National Scenic Trail wind through the roadless area. The trail drops off the divide for about 20 miles for a lower and more direct route between the heads of Meadow and Little Deadman creeks.

Although distant from paved roads, it is often possible to drive within 2 or 3 miles of the north boundary during the winter due to little snow on the windswept sage-brush plains. This allows for ski mountaineering trips into the high country during the dead of winter. For example, with a four-wheel-drive vehicle it is possible to get as far as Cottonwood Creek on Nicholia Creek Road (FR 657.1), and from there hike and ski the 15-mile loop to the top of 11,141-foot Eighteenmile Peak, climb-ing about 3,700 feet. This is not a technical route and avalanche danger is low on the main northeast ridge to the summit, but it is a long strenuous ascent for seasoned, well-conditioned climbers. Expect to travel mostly on foot along bare but icy ridges, with only 2 to 3 miles of actual skiing in Bear Creek on the return loop.

HARKNESS LAKES EN ROUTE TO EIGHTEENMILE PEAK.

HOW TO GET THERE: Take the Dell exit off I-15, 45 miles south of Dillon, and get on Big Sheep Creek Road (FR 257), which parallels the west side of the interstate for 1 mile before turning southwest up Big Sheep Creek. Continue on this road about 19 miles to Nicholia Creek Road (FR 657.1). Turn right and drive about 6.5 miles southwest to the national forest boundary. After another 0.5 mile park where the road crosses Bear Creek. If you have a high-clearance vehicle and road conditions permit, you may be able to drive another 1.5 miles to the year-round vehicle closure, which is near where Tendoy Creek Trail 148 takes off from the main Nicholia Creek jeep road (Trail 91). This is also a good place to park for a journey up Nicholia Creek.

MULTI-DAY BACKPACK

Nicholia - Deadman Creek Loop
Distance: 20-mile loop (3 or 4 days).
Difficulty: Moderately strenuous.
Topo maps: Eighteenmile Peak-MT/ID; Deadman Lake-MT/ID; and Scott Peak-ID/MT.

This is a good hike for midsummer through early fall. Begin by heading south up the broad Nicholia Creek valley on Trail 91. After about 0.5 mile this jeep trail turns into an actual hiking or horse trail. The willow-lined riparian bottom has an almost continuous series of beaver dams for several miles. There is a trail junction about 2 miles up, with the original unmarked trail keeping to the right, and the left-hand trail signed, "Deadman Lake 4 miles." Take the left trail, which continues up the main drainage through open meadows and crosses the stream several times. It eventually intersects a well-blazed trail that goes up to the head of Nicholia Creek, crosses over a 9,400-foot pass, and drops into Deadman Creek. Cattle grazing is extensive in the open pastures of Nicholia Creek so all drinking water in this area must be boiled or filtered. As the trail climbs high, limestone cliffs pocketed with caves tower above. Ancient Douglas-fir at 8,000 feet give way to spruce, lodgepole pine, and finally whitebark pine. At 9,000 feet the country opens up to wet meadows fed by tiny springs, favored by summering elk. The head of the drainage is defined by the Continental Divide—rocky, sheer peaks with spectacular cliffs, scree, and mounds of talus cresting to almost 11,000 feet. At 7 miles from the trailhead the upper reaches of Nicholia Creek offer remote sites for an alpine camp.

Italian Peak (10,998 feet) is a worthy destination for a second layover day. The climb is nontechnical but difficult because of loose, small, irregular rock. A chute with a series of ledges just to the west of the summit allows for tough but manageable scrambling on all fours. This is prime sheep and goat country so keep a lookout for these nimble denizens of the high country. An easier route

ALONG THE CONTINENTAL DIVIDE IN THE SOUTH END OF ITALIAN PEAKS.

to and from the summit is from a saddle on the divide about 0.5 mile northwest of the peak.

On the third day hike the good trail on loose rock to the alpine head of Deadman Creek. A short side trip to Divide Lake, just inside Idaho, is well worthwhile. Climb back 250 feet to the divide and descend the narrow, more densely forested Deadman Creek for 6 to 7 miles to Deadman Lake—a 6-acre pond stocked with cutthroat. From there follow a jeep trail (FR 3927) about 4 miles northwest across sagebrush-grasslands to the lower parking area at the confluence of Bear Creek and Nicholia Creek, thereby completing a 20-mile counter-clockwise loop through the alpine heart of Italian Peaks.

Lima Peaks

34

Location: 7 miles south of Lima and 50 miles south of Dillon.
Size: 90,201 acres; 42,701 acres of which are in Montana.
Administration: USDAFS—Beaverhead and Targhee national forests.
Management status: Roadless non-wilderness.
Ecosystems: Middle Rocky Mountain steppe-coniferous forest-alpine meadow province, characterized by complex and high, steep mountains with rounded-to-sharp alpine ridges and cirques; Precambrian granite, sedimentary and volcanic rocks; sagebrush steppe with small areas of alpine vegetation, Douglas-fir forest type; and complex drainage patterns with many intermittent streams.
Elevation range: 6,720 to 10,961 feet.
System trails: 33 miles.
Maximum core to perimeter distance: 3.5 miles.
Activities: Hiking, backpacking, cross-country skiing, horseback riding.
Modes of travel: Foot, skis, horse.
Maps: Beaverhead interagency Travel Plan Map; Gallagher Gulch-MT; Lima Peaks-MT; Fritz Peak-ID/MT; Edie Ranch-ID/MT; and East of Edie Ranch-ID/MT (1:24,000 topo maps).

OVERVIEW: The sharp, grassy ridge of the Continental Divide runs east-west through the Red Conglomerate Peaks, forming the 10,000-foot southern buttress of the Lima Peaks roadless area. The rounded mounds of the four Lima Peaks rise to the north. Steep, rocky slopes on 10,961-foot Garfield Mountain tower above an austere grassland. Isolated stringers of whitebark pine, subalpine fir, lodgepole, and juniper cling to the lee sides of windswept ridges and sheltered draws. This open country is at least 80 percent treeless with rounded ridges and deeply cut streams that often dry up by summer. The north faces of the Lima Peaks are scoured with cirques descending to narrow V-shaped glacial valleys and moraines amidst wide expanses of rolling foothills. Elk calve near the head of Sawmill Creek and summer along the more remote stretches of the Great Divide. Indian pictographs exist along the Middle Fork of Little Sheep Creek.

The best overall view of the Lima Peaks is from the Forest Service East Creek campground, and the best time is October when the peaks are perfectly framed by the blazing yellow of aspen.

34 LIMA PEAKS

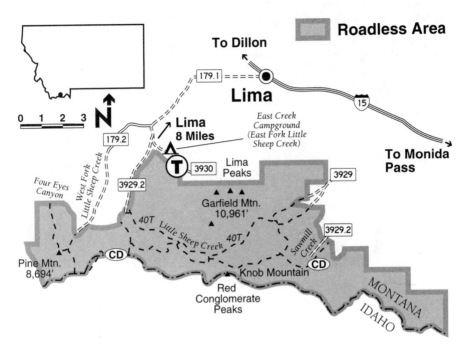

RECREATIONAL USES: Most of the light recreational use occurs during the fall hunting season. There are also opportunities for hiking, backpacking, horseback riding, and cross-country skiing. Because this high and dry country is mostly open sagebrush steppe with scattered forest, these activities can be pursued both on and off trail. Although far from any population center, Lima Peaks are close enough to I-15 to have that curious blend of remoteness and accessibility. This is not deep snow country so the north end can usually be reached by vehicle up Little Sheep Creek. This lofty Great Divide roadless area is well suited for cross-country hiking, peak scrambling, and ski mountaineering in a primitive setting.

HOW TO GET THERE: From the Lima exit on I-15 take the Little Sheep Creek Road (FR 179.1) about 7 miles southwest of Lima to the East Fork Road (FR 3930). Turn left and drive about 1 mile to the East Creek campground.

A WINTER EXCURSION IN THE LIMA PEAKS.

SKI MOUNTAINEERING OR DAY HIKE

Lima Peak
Distance: 7 miles off-trail out-and-back.
Difficulty: Strenuous.
Topo maps: Gallagher Gulch-MT; and Lima Peaks-MT.

Even during winter it is often possible to drive a little way past East Creek campground. Ski about 1 mile up East Creek to a fork in the stream. At this point it will probably be possible to climb without skis up a steep side slope that ties into the main feeder ridge. The ridge leads up to a high, open, broad saddle overlooking the large basin between the high point in the area—10,961-foot Garfield Mountain—and 10,706-foot Lima Peak. Continue hiking across this barren, austere plateau and then climb steeply for another 1,800 vertical feet to the broad top of Lima Peak, encountering a major false summit along the way. A winter ascent is strenuous with snow and ice clinging to broken talus rock all the way to the peak. The windswept snow is usually rock hard, making the descent treacherous. The view from the top provides an excellent perspective on the entire roadless area, including the Red Conglomerate Peaks along the Continental Divide to the south. The isolated, central location of the peak affords 360 degrees of mountain grandeur—from the Grand Tetons, north to the Anaconda-Pintlers, the Madisons, Lionhead, Centennials,

Gravelleys, West Big Hole, East Pioneers, Lemhis, and on to infinity. A summertime traverse from Lima Peak southwest to Garfield Mountain is possible but should not be attempted during winter because of exposed loose rock and ice on the connecting ridge. An average of more than 1,000 vertical feet per mile is gained from the campground to the top of Lima Peak for a total gain of 4,000 feet.

Centennial Mountains/ Red Rock Lakes Wilderness Complex

35

Location: 56 miles southeast of Dillon and 20 miles east of Lima.

Size: About 120,000 acres; including 82,350 acres in Montana.

Administration: U.S. Fish & Wildlife Service—Red Rock Lakes NWR; Bureau of Land Management—Dillon Resource Area; Agricultural Research Service Sheep Experiment Station; and USDAFS—Beaverhead and Targhee national forests.

Management status: Red Rocks Wilderness (32,350 acres); BLM Wilderness Study Area (27,691 acres); Sheep Experiment Station (16,650 acres); and national forest roadless non-wilderness (4,474 acres).

Ecosystems: Middle Rocky Mountain steppe-coniferous forest-alpine meadow province, characterized by complex, high and steep mountains with rounded-to-sharp ridges and cirques; Precambrian granite, sedimentary, and volcanic rocks; extensive lake, marsh, and wetlands system bounded by sagebrush steppe leading up to Douglas-fir forest type and, finally, on up to sizable areas of alpine vegetation; and a complex drainage pattern with numerous perennial and some intermittent streams.

Elevation range: 6,608 to 10,196 feet.

System trails: 30 miles (including about 20 miles of the Continental Divide National Scenic Trail).

Maximum core to perimeter distance: 2.5 miles.

Activities: Hiking, backpacking, horseback riding, cross-country skiing, boating, fishing, wildlife viewing/birding.

Modes of travel: Foot, horse, skis, boat (canoe).

Maps: 1993 Beaverhead/Interagency Travel Plan Map; Lower Red Rock Lake-MT; Elk Springs-MT; Corral Creek-MT/ID; Big Table Mountain-MT/ID; Wilson Creek-MT/ID; Slide Mountain-MT/ID; Upper Red Rock Lake-MT/ID; Mount Jefferson-MT/ID; and Sawtell Peak-ID/MT (1:24,000 topo maps).

OVERVIEW: Red Rock Lakes Wilderness is located in the heart of the wide-open Centennial Valley. This out-of-the-way, virtually undeveloped basin holds an amazing array of interconnecting marshes and waterways. More than 14,000 acres of wetlands provide refuge for some 215 species of birds and other wildlife, including 23 kinds of ducks and geese along with a myriad of shorebirds, sora rails, eagles, and peregrine falcons. The sanctuary was estab-

35 CENTENNIAL MOUNTAINS/ RED ROCK LAKES WILDERNESS COMPLEX

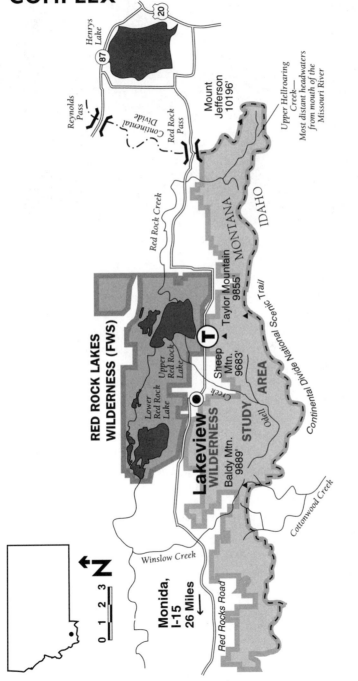

Henrys Lake

Reynolds Pass

Red Rock Pass

Continental Divide

Mount Jefferson 10196'

Upper Hellroaring Creek— Most distant headwaters from mouth of the Missouri River

Red Rock Creek

MONTANA

IDAHO

Taylor Mountain 9855'

RED ROCK LAKES WILDERNESS (FWS)

Upper Red Rock Lake

Lower Red Rock Lake

Sheep Mtn. 9683'

Continental Divide National Scenic Trail

AREA

Lakeview

WILDERNESS

STUDY

Odell Creek

Baldy Mtn. 9889'

Cottonwood Creek

Winslow Creek

N

0 1 2 3 Miles

Monida, I-15 26 Miles

Red Rocks Road

LOWER RED ROCK LAKE WITH CENTENNIAL RANGE TO THE SOUTH.

lished in 1935 to safeguard the rare trumpeter swan, largest of all North American waterfowl.

The huge, shallow Upper and Lower Red Rock lakes are vestiges of an ancient and larger lake. Over the eons the valley has gradually filled with alluvium. This ongoing process will eventually kill the lakes. Red Rock Creek still harbors rare arctic grayling, one of the last native populations outside of Alaska. Moose are hearty year-round residents, but long, snowbound winters force elk, deer, and antelope to lower elevations.

To the immediate south the Centennial Mountains straddle the Continental Divide for 35 miles west of Yellowstone National Park. The more rugged north slopes, which drain into Montana, encompass 50,000 acres of unroaded uplands. The massive upthrust of the range is startling. From an already elevated valley floor of 6,600 feet, this dramatic backdrop to the Red Rock Lakes wetlands shoots upward more than 3,000 feet in less than 1 mile.

This Great Divide range is one of the few in the Northern Rockies that trend east and west, which may partially explain its rich diversity of native flora and fauna. To date, 362 vascular plant species have been found in the Centennials. The land is divided by the northeast-trending Odell Creek fault. The core of the higher and steeper eastern Centennials is Precambrian rock overlain by sedimentary rocks. In contrast, the western Centennials display a variety of earthflows and landslides.

Most wildlife species that were in the range during pristine times are still there, from wintering moose to a large interstate elk herd of 300 to 500 animals. Occasional wolves and grizzlies roam through high, grassy parks, aspen groves, and spruce-fir forests in search of a meal. With its prey base on the adjoining Red Rock Lakes refuge, the endangered peregrine falcon nests on protected cliff faces. The headwaters of secluded Hellroaring Creek, in the southeast corner of this linear east-west wildland, are the most distant source of the Missouri-Mississippi river system, more than 4,000 miles from its mouth downstream.

RECREATIONAL USES: The best time to visit Red Rock Lakes is from about mid-May to October, whereas July to October is prime time for the higher country in the Centennials. Wildflowers are at their colorful peak in both places in July when the meadows explode into pastel seas of shooting stars, buttercup, geranium, lupine, and loco. In the mountains expect to see vibrant displays of columbine, arnica, bluebells, Indian paintbrush, and lupine. About 75 percent of those who visit Red Rocks engage in wildlife viewing. At least 255 bird species have been recorded at the refuge; waterfowl are especially abundant.

Quite properly, travel is restricted in the lakes and marshes when waterfowl nest. However, trumpeter swans can be seen and photographed at close range from mid-July through August at Shambow Pond just north of the Red Rock Pass road. The best way to explore the Wilderness interior of Red Rock Lakes is by canoe. Boats are permitted on Upper Red Rock Lake after July 15 when waterfowl have concluded their nesting. All boating is prohibited on the lower lake during spring and summer to protect nesting swans.

The most popular activity is waterfowl hunting which is limited to Lower Red Rock Lake and surrounding lands. Antelope hunting is permitted in much the same area as well as in other northern portions of the refuge. Trophy-sized rainbow, eastern brook, and Yellowstone cutthroat draw anglers to Red Rock Creek and a few small lakes in the non-wilderness part of the refuge. The lakes and ponds within the Wilderness are inhabited mostly by ling and suckers and are closed to fishing to safeguard wildlife from human disturbance. There are two campgrounds on the refuge.

In the mountains big-game hunting is the most popular activity. Most of the hunting is for elk, deer, and moose and generally requires packing in with horses and mules. Almost all of the more rugged Montana side of the Centennials is closed to off-road vehicles. Hiking, camping, and fishing are growing in popularity, with the favored fishing streams being Hellroaring, Odell, and Tom creeks. The deep snow country of the Centennials is excellent for ski mountaineering and touring but a 25- to 30-mile snowmobile ride is needed just to get to the village of Lakeview during the long winter.

The climate can be extreme, with recorded temperatures varying between 91 degrees Fahrenheit in August and minus 49 degrees F. during January. With fewer than ten frost-free days per year you will need a warm jacket almost every night. The short summers and limited public access inhibit hiking, but there are still good trips to be taken. More than 50 miles of the Continental Divide wind along the crest of the Centennials. Closely following the divide is the Continental Divide National Scenic Trail.

There is legal access from the Price-Peet Road, Jones Creek Road, the Bear Creek Road on the west end, and the Corral Creek Road to the east. In the central portions of the range, BLM and refuge lands provide foot access. Except for the Odell Creek trail, the entire north side of the Centennials is closed to vehicles during winter. There is generally no public access across private lands, particularly in Alaska Basin on the east end.

HOW TO GET THERE: Take the Monida exit off I-15, 14 miles southeast of Lima, and go 26 miles east on the Red Rock Lakes gravel road to the Red Rock Lakes NWR Headquarters at Lakeview (population 8). From the opposite direction Lakeview can be reached from MT 87 by turning at Henry's Lake, Idaho, and traveling 30 miles west on the Red Rock Road.

DAY CANOE TRIP

Upper Red Rock Lake
Distance: 10 miles.
Difficulty: Easy.
Topo map: Upper Red Rock Lake-MT/ID.

On the refuge, for an exploratory trip in the marshes and wetlands of Red Rocks, canoe around the 10-mile shoreline of Upper Red Rock Lake after July 15. Hug the shoreline as best you can; sudden strong winds can make the open water hazardous.

DAY HIKE

Sheep Mountain
Distance: 5 to 6 miles out-and-back.
Difficulty: Strenuous.
Topo map: Upper Red Rock Lake-MT/ID.

This cross-country hike is also part rock scramble and requires good routefinding skills. Begin the hike up Sheep Mountain just west of the Upper Red Rock Lake campground about 5 miles east of Lakeview on the Red Rock road. After crossing the flats climb the first 1,000 feet up through a forest of Douglas-fir. The next 2,000 vertical feet consist of routefinding around, between,

VAST SUBALPINE PARKS AT THE HEAD OF ODELL CREEK IN THE CENTENNIAL
MOUNTAINS.

and on top of a continuous series of rock ledges. Take your time and enjoy the
semi-technical challenge of traveling skillfully and safely through this type of
rugged terrain. After climbing 3,000 vertical feet in only 1 mile the actual summit broadens out into a huge alpine meadow and plateau that is a joy to
wander around in. Sheep Mountain provides one of the best all-around per-
spectives on the complex wetland system of the Centennial Valley and of the
surrounding mountain ranges. Between the summit and the Continental Divide
3 miles to the south are roads and surface disturbance from phosphate mining
some 35 years ago. For a more primitive experience you may wish to return
by way of a different route down the north face.

Snowcrest

Location: 30 miles southeast of Dillon.
Size: 110,000 acres.
Administration: USDAFS-Beaverhead National Forest; Bureau of Land Management-Dillon Resource Area; Montana Department of Fish, Wildlife & Parks; Rocky Mountain Elk Foundation.
Management status: BLM Wilderness Study Area (6,231 acres); roadless non-wilderness; state and private wildlife winter range.
Ecosystems: Middle Rocky Mountain steppe-coniferous forest-alpine meadow province, characterized by complex and high, steep mountains with rounded-to-sharp ridges and partially developed cirques, glacial and fluvial valleys and floodplains; Precambrian granite, sedimentary and volcanic rocks; sagebrush steppe with small areas of alpine vegetation, Douglas-fir forest type; and a complex drainage pattern with some streams being intermittent.
Elevation range: 6,600 to 10,573 feet.
System trails: 66 miles.
Maximum core to perimeter distance 3.5 miles.
Activities: Hiking, backpacking, fishing, cross-country skiing, horseback riding.
Modes of travel: Foot, skis, horse.
Maps: 1993 Beaverhead interagency Travel Plan Map; Home Park Ranch-MT; Swamp Creek-MT; Spur Mountain-MT; Whiskey Spring-MT; Antone Peak-MT; Stonehouse Mountain-MT; and Wolverine Creek-MT (1:24,000 topo maps).

OVERVIEW: From most any high point in the Snowcrest you can see with a single sweeping glance sagebrush foothills, grassy parks, aspen groves, subalpine meadows, barren talus slopes, forests of Douglas-fir and limber pine, twisted whitebark pine clinging to exposed ridges, all the way up to the matted tundra beneath your feet. All this is compacted within an incredibly short distance.

Most impressive is the vast East Fork Blacktail Deer Creek basin—a grand mosaic of heavily forested bottoms, deeply incised streams, rounded grassy knobs, and open parks. Glacial features here are subtle due to the soft sedimentary rocks that make up most of the Snowcrest. Rapid weathering of these rocks causes landslides of hundreds of acres. The east side is the scarp slope of a north-south trending fault with a shorter, steeper, and more dense drainage pattern. The west slope gives rise to fewer, flatter streams.

By late fall up to 2,000 elk are migrating west and north onto 50,000 acres of grassland on the adjacent Blacktail and Robb Creek winter ranges. Here is a place where antelope range to 9,000 feet, where the unearthly calls of summering sandhill cranes pierces the clear mountain air. When traveling this

36 SNOWCREST

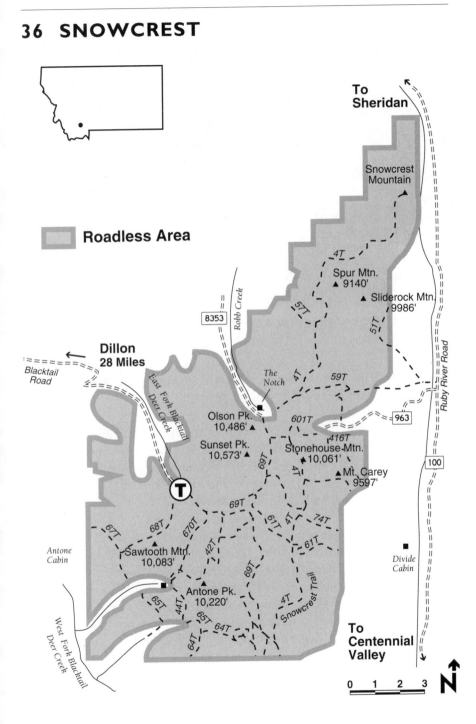

Roadless Area

To
Sheridan

Snowcrest
Mountain

4T

Spur Mtn.
▲ 9140'

▲ Sliderock Mtn.
9986'

8353

Robb Creek

57T

51T

Dillon
28 Miles

Blacktail
Road

The
Notch

4T

59T

East Fork Blacktail Deer Creek

Olson Pk.
10,486' ▲

601T

963

Sunset Pk.
10,573' ▲

416T

Stonehouse Mtn.
▲ 10,061'

100

69T

4T

▲ Mt. Carey
9597'

Ruby River Road

69T

671

68T

670T

42T

61T

4T

74T

61T

Antone
Cabin

Sawtooth Mtn.
10,083'

69T

Divide
Cabin

65T

44T

Antone Pk.
10,220'

65T

64T

4T

Snowcrest Trail

64T

West Fork Blacktail Deer Creek

To
Centennial
Valley

0   1   2   3

N

DIVIDE CABIN, ON THE SOUTHEAST CORNER OF THE SNOWCREST RANGE.

country, you'll have the strange impression of moving in reverse, up out of the mountains onto the plains.

RECREATIONAL USES: At least 70 percent of the annual recreational use centers around hunting in the fall. With one of the largest and most productive elk herds in Montana, the Snowcrest is one of the most heavily hunted areas in the state. There are four licensed hunting outfitters here. Three of them have camps in Devil's Hole, West Fork Ruby, and Lawrence Creek. The fourth is a day-use outfitter who operates during both summer and fall.

As winter snows begin to pile up, cross-country skiers can find tens of thousands of acres of ideal touring terrain in the Snowcrest. The only problem is getting close enough to this remote country by vehicle to make day or overnight ski trips feasible. The Madison District of the Forest Service rents the historic Divide and Antone cabins to the public based on advanced reservations and payment. These picturesque guard stations sit on opposite sides of the Snowcrest Divide along the southern edge; both can sleep four to eight people. Depending on snow conditions, the distance can be 19 miles to Divide and 16 miles to Antone. During the winter of 1987 our party was lucky—we were able to drive almost to the Three Forks Cow Camp on the Ruby—a mere 13 miles from the Divide cabin.

Access to the Snowcrest may be even more limited due to a heavy clay content in the soil that makes roads treacherous when wet. The Forest Service discourages recreational use during the wet spring season to avoid conflicts with elk calving.

During the summer, activities include horseback riding, a rare backpacking party, hiking, and some fishing in the East Fork of Blacktail Deer Creek. The low summer visitation may be partly due to the scarcity of fishable water. The country is high and the mountains impressive, but absent is the traditional magnet—alpine lakes teeming with fish.

Even though the western and southern flanks of the range are bounded by private land, public access routes are available, some of which are passable only by four-wheel-drive vehicle. The major access on the west side is up a primitive road to The Notch—a high saddle in the heart of the Snowcrest with a Forest Service cabin. The East Fork Blacktail Road and a route to Antone Cabin offer access to the southwestern and southern edges. The north-south Ruby River Road provides linear access to the east side. The popular Forest Service Cottonwood campground on the northeastern corner is a good spot to establish a basecamp for day trips into the backcountry.

HOW TO GET THERE: From just south of Dillon drive about 20 miles southeast on the high-standard Blacktail Road to the Blacktail Wildlife Management Area. Then turn left on the East Fork of Blacktail Deer Creek Road and go about 8 miles to a road closure just before the BLM/public lands boundary. This is the trailhead for Trail 69, which heads up the East Fork.

EAST FORK OF BLACKTAIL DEER CREEK—GATEWAY TO THE SNOWCREST.

DAY HIKE OR OVERNIGHTER

East Fork of Blacktail Deer Creek

Distance: 12 to 15 miles out-and-back.
Difficulty: Moderate, with optional strenuous peak climbs.
Topo maps: Antone Peak-MT and Stonehouse Mountain-MT.

The East Fork Blacktail Deer Creek trailhead is the most popular point of entry, offering many day-use and overnight combinations of both the out-and-back and loop variety. Head up East Fork Trail 69, passing several beaver ponds with brook trout. After about 3 miles take the left-hand fork going toward Honeymoon Park. Within 2 more miles you'll cross several springs with level benches on the left ringed by Douglas-fir—ideal campsites. Although the ridgetops are high and dry, much of the Snowcrest is lush with springs. The views up Lawrence Creek and of the expansive East Fork drainage and surrounding Snowcrest peaks are stunning. The 8,000-foot high campsite provides easy access to the highest point in the range—10,573-foot Sunset Peak—as well as 10,486-foot Olson Peak to the immediate north. An open 2-mile, 2,500-foot climb and scramble will get you to the top of Sunset Peak—well named, since it catches the last light of day. The best route is along the dinosaur spine of the south ridge. The mile-long traverse north to Olson Peak provides a grand view of the crest of the Snowcrest Range and a commanding straight-down look at The Notch. Along the way watch for mountain goats in the hanging valley at the head of Robb Creek. Lawrence Creek stretches out across the East Fork to the south.

If time permits make the easy climb up the drainage through a delightful string of forest and meadows to the open summit of 10,241-foot Antone Peak. From the peak it's an easy descent to Antone Pass, and then another mile to the cabin. On the return loop head down Rough Creek on Trail 670 to where it meets the East Fork about 2 miles below your camp. This would be a 14-mile loop from the above described campsite, ideal as a long layover day hike.

Lionhead

37

Location: 10 miles west of West Yellowstone.
Size: 48,180 acres, 32,780 acres of which are in Montana.
Administration: USDAFS—Gallatin and Targhee national forests.
Management status: Roadless non-wilderness, with some peripheral lands allocated to future development in the forest plan.
Ecosystems: Middle Rocky Mountain coniferous forest-alpine meadow province, Yellowstone Highlands section, characterized by high, glaciated mountains with cirques and moraines; Precambrian metamorphic and Tertiary volcanic rocks; Douglas-fir and western spruce-fir forest types; many short, steep streams with lakes at high elevations.
Elevation range: 6,500 to 10,606 feet.
System trails: 28 miles.
Maximum core to perimeter distance: 2.5 miles.
Activities: Hiking, backpacking, rock climbing, cross-country skiing, horseback riding, fishing.
Modes of travel: Foot, skis, and horse.
Maps: 1991 Gallatin National Forest Visitor Map; south end of 1992 Lee Metcalf Wilderness Map-1"/mile contour; Earthquake Lake-MT, Hebgen Dam-MT; Targhee Peak-ID/MT; and Targhee Pass-ID/MT (1:24,000 topo maps).

OVERVIEW: The massive earthquake slide that blocked the Madison River on the northwest corner of the Lionhead country in 1959 tells of the inherent instability of rocks and soils in these Henry's Lake Mountains, which are actually limestone blocks sitting atop layers of shale and Yellowstone volcanics. The Continental Divide winds for 10.5 miles through rolling tundra at the head of four major pristine tributaries to the Madison River within the roadless area. The Lionhead, also dubbed Earthquake, has an unusually large concentration of lofty pinnacles within a small perimeter along the divide, crowned by Lionhead's remote and lofty summit, 10,311-foot Sheep Mountain. Nine subalpine lakes are tucked away in cirque basins, including the largest and most popular, Coffin Lake. Named for Lionhead Mountain on the Continental Divide, this land of dense forests and broad subalpine parks is wild enough for the grizzly and diverse enough for elk and bighorn sheep to spend both summer and winter.

RECREATIONAL USES: The Lionhead is remote yet accessible to within 1 mile of US 191, MT 87, and US 287. Portions of the country are heavily hunted for big game. This lofty Continental Divide country is also explored by hikers,

37 LIONHEAD

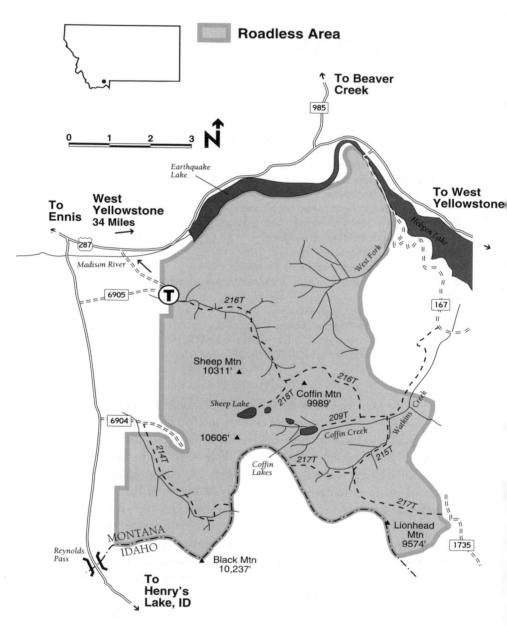

Roadless Area

To Beaver Creek

985

0 1 2 3 N

Earthquake Lake

To West Yellowstone

To Ennis

West Yellowstone 34 Miles

Hebgen Lake

287

Madison River

West Fork

6905 T

216T

167

Sheep Mtn 10311' ▲

Coffin Mtn 9989' ▲

216T

Sheep Lake

218T

209T

6904

10606' ▲

Coffin Creek

Watkins Creek

214T

Coffin Lakes

217T

215T

217T

MONTANA

IDAHO

Lionhead Mtn 9574'

1735

Reynolds Pass

Black Mtn 10,237'

To Henry's Lake, ID

backpackers, and cross-country skiers along with light-to-moderate use by anglers and rock climbers. Rugged topography including steep, forested drainages helps ensure a high degree of solitude. Winter travelers need to be alert to the dangers of avalanches and severe winter storms.

There are several basins with high lakes but all are barren of fish except Upper and Lower Coffin Lakes. Upper Coffin Lake was graveled to provide spawning beds for the introduction of golden trout. Of the 6 miles of fishing streams, Watkins Creek has the most productive stretch. The crest of the Continental Divide and several of the higher ridges to the north provide superb routes for off-trail hiking and moderate rock scrambling.

HOW TO GET THERE: From West Yellowstone drive 8 miles north on US 191/287 and turn left. Continue 22 miles west on US 287 to MT 87. Turn left and go 1.5 miles south, then go left (east) on FR 6905 for 2.5 miles to the trailhead for the Sheep Creek Trail 216.

EARTHQUAKE SLIDE ON THE MADISON RIVER—NORTHWEST EDGE OF THE LIONHEAD ROADLESS AREA.

OVERNIGHTER

Sheep Lake/Sheep Mountain

Distance: 12 to 14 miles out-and-back.
Difficulty: Moderate with optional strenuous climbs.
Topo maps: Earthquake Lake-MT; Hebgen Dam-MT; and Targhee Pass-ID/MT.

Trail 216 on the northwest corner of the roadless area begins at the 6,500-foot mouth of Sheep Creek Canyon. The well-maintained trail crosses three footbridges within the first 2 miles. After 1 mile the canyon narrows and deepens with south-facing rocky slopes and an occasional small meadow in the stream bottom. After switchbacking steeply to the third footbridge the country opens up with more gentle sideslopes. After about 5 miles and at nearly 8,500 feet, the trail angles up through scree and around a small side drainage. Then it rejoins Sheep Creek for the remaining climb to Sheep Lake at 9,071 feet—a 2,600-foot elevation gain over 6 to 7 miles. Except for an old irrigation dam by the lake, the upper basin is wild.

Sheep Lake is barren of fish and, as such, is visited mostly by hunters and a few climbers. In fact, with 10,000-foot peaks on three sides the lake makes an excellent base camp for several days of climbing and rock scrambling. To reach the highest point of 10,606 feet to the immediate southwest, climb the forested ridge on the east side of the lake. This main ridge wraps around to the west for about 1 mile, climbing first to a 10,541-foot bump and then onto to the loftiest summit. The ridge can be traversed without difficulty for another 2 miles north to 10,321-foot Sheep Mountain, where you are likely to see the namesake resident bighorns. There are a couple of rough sections along the ridge that can be bypassed on either side.

To complete a climbing loop double back to the prominent 10,274-foot peak and take its moderate northeast ridge back down to the lake. An easier side trip from the nameless point at 10,606 feet is to hike the broad, open slope to the south for about 1 mile, reaching the Continental Divide at an elevation of 10,250 feet. Walk along the divide 0.5 mile to the southeast for a grand view of the Coffin Lakes basin and all the way down Watkins Creek to Hebgen Lake.

Lee Metcalf
Wilderness
Complex

38

Location: 25 miles southwest of Bozeman and 10 miles north of West Yellowstone.
Size: 352,936 acres (North Madison is 110,240 acres; South Madison is 242,696 acres); 254,944 acres of this total is designated as the four-part Lee Metcalf Wilderness.
Administration: USDAFS—Gallatin and Beaverhead national forests; National Park Service—Yellowstone NP; Bureau of Land Management—Dillon Resource Area.
Management status: 254,944 acres in the Lee Metcalf Wilderness (includes the 6,000-acre Beartrap Canyon unit managed by the Bureau of Land Management); the 36,752 Cabin Creek recreation area; about 20,000 acres in the northwest edge of Yellowstone National Park; and about 41,240 acres of contiguous non-wilderness roadless lands.
Ecosystems: Middle Rocky Mountain steppe-coniferous forest-alpine meadow province, Yellowstone Highlands section, characterized by complex and high, steep mountains with sharp alpine ridges, cirques and moraines along with narrow-to-broad valleys; Precambrian metamorphic granitic rocks along with Tertiary volcanics in the south; Douglas-fir and western spruce-fir forest types along with smaller areas of sagebrush steppe and alpine vegetation; and numerous perennial streams, wet meadows, and high lakes.
Elevation range: 4,400 to 11,316 feet.
System trails: 86 miles in the north unit and 130 miles in the south unit for a total of 216 miles.
Maximum core to perimeter distance: 4.5 miles in the north unit; 5.5 miles in the south unit.
Activities: Hiking, backpacking, mountaineering, cross-country skiing, horseback riding, whitewater rafting and kayaking, fishing.
Modes of travel: Foot, skis, boat, and horse.
Maps: 1993 Lee Metcalf Wilderness Map-1"/mile contour; 1991 Gallatin National Forest Visitor Map; BLM Bear Trap Canyon Wilderness Visitor's Guide-1-1/2"/mile contour; (refer to appendix for a listing of the 26 topographic maps that cover the Lee Metcalf Wilderness complex).

OVERVIEW: In the northwest corner of the Lee Metcalf Wilderness Complex, Bear Trap Canyon—the first BLM Wilderness in the nation—consists of 6,000 acres of wild canyon country along the Madison River. Bear Trap offers 9 miles of possibly the most exciting and challenging whitewater in Montana, and this may be the only wild habitat shared by both rattlesnakes and moose. From the dry canyon, the ecological bridge of Cowboy Heaven sweeps upward for 6,500 feet to the craggy crest of the Spanish Peaks. As one of the greatest elevation gains

38 LEE METCALF WILDERNESS COMPLEX

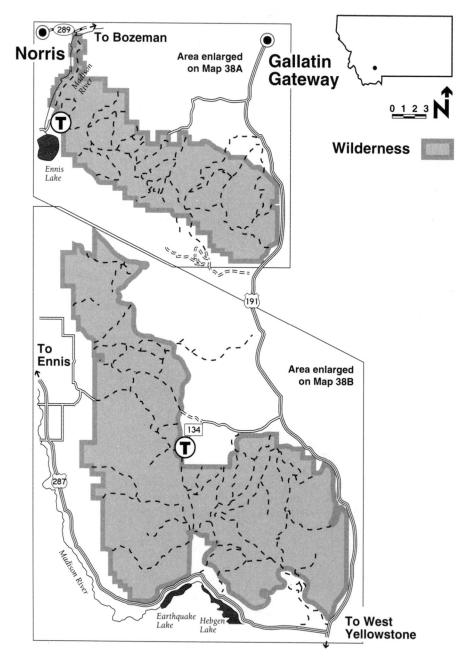

in Montana, this remarkable transition spans the full spectrum of unaltered mountain life zones.

In the Spanish Peaks glaciers carved the valleys into U-shapes, with glacial lakes, knife ridges, near-vertical headwalls, and twenty-five peaks soaring above 10,000 feet. Most of these mountains are made of ancient igneous and sedimentary rocks, converted to gneiss and schist, and they are some of the earth's oldest exposed rocks.

To the south, a vertical mile of glaciated relief imprints the Taylor-Hilgard with jagged pinnacles, U-shaped valleys and alpine cirques. The smooth sedimentary forms of the Taylor Peaks differ dramatically from the rugged igneous Hilgard Peaks farther south. Open foothills on the west face of the Bear Creek Wildlife Management Area are winter range for more than 500 elk. Some of the prominent landmarks along the crest of the Hilgards include the distinctive summits of the Sphinx, the Helmet, Koch Peak, and the chimney spires of 11,316-foot Hilgard Peak—highest point in Montana outside of the Beartooth Range. About 70 gemlike high lakes are pocketed along the divide, most of which are in the more rugged southern reaches near Hilgard Peak.

Vast grassy subalpine basins and lush meadows spread out across a more subdued landscape in the Skyline Ridge country of Cabin Creek and Monument Mountain. As the only portion of the Wilderness adjacent to Yellowstone, the southeast corner of the Madisons is superb living space for elk, moose, sheep, and the threatened, free-roaming grizzly.

RECREATIONAL USES: *Bear Trap Canyon*—As our country's first BLM wilderness, the canyon is noted for its depth and one of the wildest stretches of whitewater in Montana. Access to Bear Trap is limited by steep slopes. The only major trails are one parallel to the river on the east side and one along the canyon rim in the southeast corner. Because recreational use is channeled along the river the narrow corridor is vulnerable to overuse. Solitude may be in short supply with hikers meeting as they go into and out of the canyon. Most of the slopes exceed 60 percent and cross-country travel is difficult. Fishing accounts for about two-thirds of the use during summer and early fall. Bear Trap is more popular for day use due to the lack of level campsites with trees for shade, windbreak, and privacy. However, the canyon is excellent for off-season hiking thanks to low snowpack and easy access.

Spanish Peaks—The most popular activities in this high alpine country are fishing, big game hunting, geological study, rock climbing, hiking, backpacking, horseback riding, cross-country skiing, camping, and uncluttered relaxation. Most of this use occurs between July 1 and October 15, with the heaviest visitation coming on weekends from mid-July through Labor Day and during the fall hunting season. For solitude choose one of the more lightly used trails. Spanish Creek Trail 407 and Cascade Creek Trail 77 receive almost 70 percent

38A LEE METCALF WILDERNESS COMPLEX-NORTH (BEARTRAP CANYON/ SPANISH PEAKS)

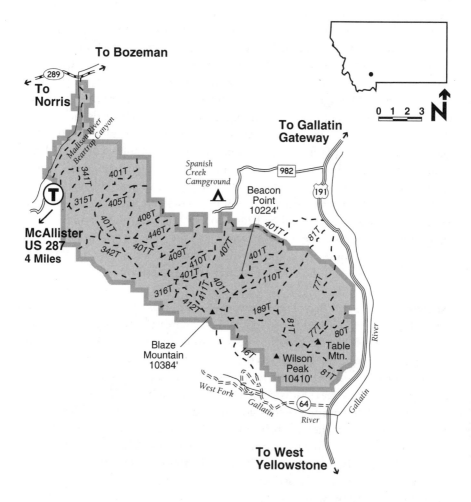

of the use. It is also advisable to avoid the heavily used Spanish Lakes, Mirror Lake, Thompson Lake, Jerome Rock Lakes, Lake Solitude, and Lava Lake. The trails to Lake Solitude and Spanish Lakes are closed to horses. Although improving, these areas show signs of overuse: excess fire rings, tree mutilation, trail erosion, and campsites too close to water bodies. The maximum party size of ten people and fifteen head of stock has helped to maintain wilderness values.

Taylor-Hilgard—major attractions include scenic lakes and peaks, abundant and diverse wildlife, varied geology, and a wide spectrum of recreation, including mountaineering, backpacking, fishing, hunting, and ski touring. The major trailheads on the Gallatin River (east) side include, from north to south, Yellow Mule, Buck Creek, Cache Creek, Taylor Fork, Eldridge Creek, Wapiti Creek, and Potamogeton Park. Solitude is hard to find on the heavily used trails up the West and South forks of Hilgard Creek from the Potamogeton Park trailhead. The Sentinel Creek/Hilgard Basin Trail 202 is a mainline travel corridor during the busy summer season and is overrun during the September bighorn sheep hunt. On the Madison (west) side the only legal trail access is at Bear Creek (Trail 326), about 12 miles south of Ennis, and Papoose Creek (Trail 355), just east of US 287 near the West Fork Rest Area. The Forest Service has an end-of-the-road facility at Indian Creek with informal access across a small strip of private land. In general, the western side of the Madison Range receives comparatively little recreational use because of limited public access.

HILGARD BASIN IN THE SOUTHWESTERN REACHES OF THE LEE METCALF WILDERNESS.

38B LEE METCALF
WILDERNESS COMPLEX-SOUTH

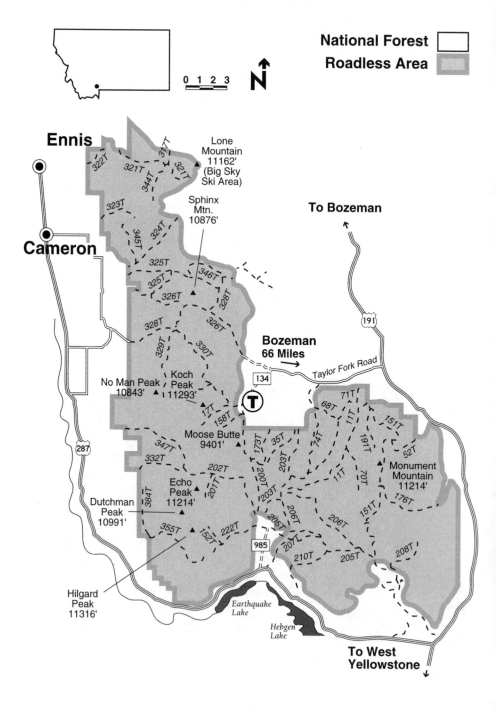

National Forest

Roadless Area

0 1 2 3   N

Ennis

Lone Mountain 11162' (Big Sky Ski Area)

317T
322T
321T
321T
344T

323T

Sphinx Mtn. 10876'

To Bozeman

345T
324T

Cameron

325T

325T
346T
326T
328T

328T
326T

329T
330T

Bozeman
66 Miles

Taylor Fork Road

191

134

No Man Peak 10843'
Koch Peak 11293'

17T
158T

71T
68T
11T
74T
191T
151T

Moose Butte 9401'

347T

332T

202T
201T

35T
203T
200T
203T

52T

Monument Mountain 11214'

287

Echo Peak 11214'

Dutchman Peak 10991'

384T

355T
152T
222T
206T
206T
151T
176T
11T
70T

205T
207T

985

210T
205T
208T

Hilgard Peak 11316'

Earthquake Lake

Hebgen Lake

To West Yellowstone

The Hebgen Lake Ranger District rents the four-person capacity Beaver Creek cabin year-round. During winter Beaver Creek Road 985 is plowed to within 3 miles of the cabin. Located next to West Fork Beaver Creek Trail 222, the cabin is a good base for ski tours into the southern Taylor-Hilgard country when snow conditions are stable.

Monument Mountain—this Skyline Ridge country is more subdued, lacking the jagged peaks and high lakes to the north. Major trailheads include Sage Creek, Monument Creek, Little Spring Creek, Bacon Rind Creek, and Cabin Creek. Cabin Creek Trail 205 leads into the 38,000-acre Cabin Creek Recreation and Wildlife Management Area, which is being managed essentially as wilderness, with the exception of snowmobiling. The four-person capacity Cabin Creek cabin is rented throughout the year by the Hebgen Lake Ranger District. The cabin sits on the edge of a vast subalpine meadow system ideal for ski touring.

HOW TO GET THERE: *North:* From Norris drive about 9 miles south on US 287 to McAllister. Turn left and drive about 4 miles east on the North Ennis Lake Road. Cross the bridge across the Madison River outlet and proceed down the east side of the river about 0.3 mile to a trailhead on the right for the Trail Creek/Barn Creek Trail 341.

Central: From Bozeman drive about 56 miles south on US 191 and turn right (west) on Taylor Fork Road 134. Drive about 8 miles to the first major junction, turn left, and go about 2 miles to the road closure/trailhead for Taylor Creek Trail 17.

DAY HIKE OR OVERNIGHTER

Cowboy Heaven

Distance: 14-mile loop.
Difficulty: Strenuous as a day hike; moderate as an overnighter.
Topo maps: Ennis Lake-MT and Cherry Lake-MT.

Trail 341 begins at an elevation of 4,835 feet and then climbs steeply through grasslands up Trail Creek, opening stunning vistas to the south along the precipitous west slope of the Madison Range. After climbing 1,600 feet over 3 miles the trail splits in a steep park. Stay to the left on Trail 341 and contour another 3 miles through a Douglas-fir forest to an unnumbered trail that quickly gains another 600 feet to Cowboy Heaven—a large top-of-the-ridge aspen parkland which, at 7,600 feet, lies just below the main divide of the Madison Range. This divide is an important wildlife migration link between the prickly pear bottom of Bear Trap Canyon and the alpine tundra of the Spanish Peaks.

SENTINEL CREEK, IN THE HILGARD PEAKS.

If you're going to stay awhile, set up camp near one of several springs on the north side. Continue the loop by going south to the main divide, picking up Trail 315, which angles southwest below 8,042-foot Red Knob. The trail switchbacks down to the Trail Creek Trail 341, leading back to where you began near the Madison River.

DAY HIKE OR OVERNIGHTER

Taylor Creek
Distance: 9 miles out-and-back.
Difficulty: Moderate, with optional strenuous climbs.
Topo map: Koch Peak-MT.

Trail 17 begins at about 7,300 feet, crossing Taylor Creek after about 0.5 mile. For the next mile the trail passes through grassy meadows before climbing above scenic Taylor Falls. Continue past the falls up the main drainage on Trail 17, gaining a moderate 900 feet over the next 3 miles to where the trail ends in a small opening near a spring. Set up camp for as much time as you have to explore the surrounding peaks and lake basins, which avoid overuse by being both fishless and trailless. For a vigorous and rewarding nontechnical rock scramble climb straight up the ridge northwest of camp to 11,293-foot Koch Peak. This is a 2,800-foot ascent of forested ridges, steep scree sideslopes, and talus rock over a distance of about 1.5 miles. The view of the glacier-scoured mountainscape and surrounding ranges is exceptional along this stretch of the main Madison Range divide. Other shorter day trips from the end-of-the-trail include climbing into any one of the three pockets of small alpine tarns to the southwest, west, and northwest. These hanging cirques vary in elevation from 9,400 to 10,000 feet and are excellent choices for solitude, challenging terrain, and scenic grandeur, especially near the precipices of Tunnel Ridge to the west.

Gallatin Range

39

Location: 10 miles south of Bozeman.
Size: 263,440 acres.
Administration: USDAFS—Gallatin National Forest; NPS—Yellowstone National Park.
Management status: Congressional Wilderness Study Area (155,000 acres); Yellowstone National Park; Montana Dept. of Fish, Wildlife & Parks Wildlife Management Area; plus contiguous roadless non-wilderness, some of which is allocated to future development in the forest plan.
Ecosystems: Middle Rocky Mountain coniferous forest-alpine meadow province, Yellowstone Highlands section, characterized by complex and high, steep mountains with rounded-to-sharp alpine ridges and cirques along with narrow-to-broad valleys; Precambrian metamorphic granitic rocks along with Tertiary volcanics in the south; Douglas-fir and western spruce-fir forest types along with smaller areas of alpine vegetation; numerous perennial streams and wet meadows as well as some lakes along the crest.
Elevation range: 5,500 to 10,333 feet.
System trails: 193 miles.
Maximum core to perimeter distance: 5 miles.
Activities: Hiking, backpacking, cross-country skiing, horseback riding, mountain biking, fishing.
Modes of travel: Foot, skis, horse, and mountain bike.
Maps: 1991 Gallatin National Forest Visitor Map; (see Appendix D for a listing of the 16 topographic maps covering the roadless portion of the Gallatin Range).

OVERVIEW: From the Hyalite Peaks just south of Bozeman, the Gallatin Range extends 60 miles into the rugged northwest corner of Yellowstone National Park. The range harbors the largest unprotected wildland in the Greater Yellowstone ecosystem. Squeezed between the narrow Gallatin River canyon on the west and the broad Yellowstone River Valley to the east, the Gallatins rise to more than 10,000 feet along an open, often jagged north-south crest.

Picture a mountainscape first formed by compression and later covered by lava from the Yellowstone volcanic field and you're looking at the Gallatin. Some 6,000 feet of layered andesite, breccia, and conglomerate built the volcanic mound that is today the long, arching ridge of Hyalite Peaks, named for a locally abundant colorless opal.

The extensive Gallatin Petrified Forest near Specimen Ridge along the heads of Tom Miner, Rock, Porcupine, and Buffalo Horn creeks presents an unusual

39 GALLATIN RANGE

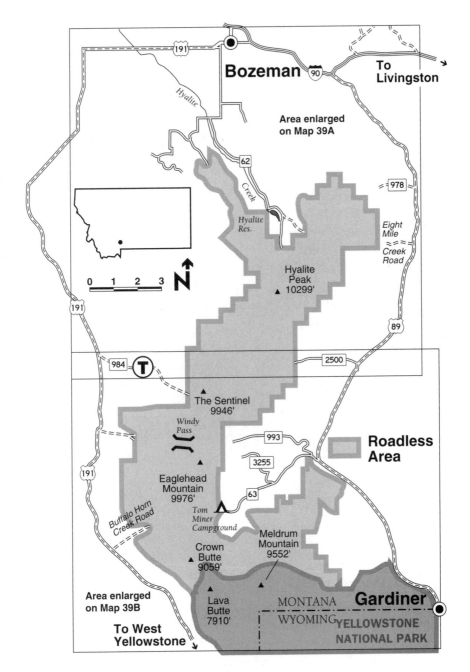

Bozeman

To Livingston

Area enlarged
on Map 39A

Hyalite
Res.

Hyalite
Peak
10299'

Eight
Mile
Creek
Road

0   1   2   3   N

The Sentinel
9946'

Windy
Pass

Roadless
Area

Eaglehead
Mountain
9976'

Tom
Miner
Campground

Meldrum
Mountain
9552'

Buffalo Horn
Creek Road

Crown
Butte
9059'

Area enlarged
on Map 39B

Lava
Butte
7910'

MONTANA   Gardiner

To West
Yellowstone

WYOMING YELLOWSTONE
NATIONAL PARK

39A GALLATIN RANGE-NORTH

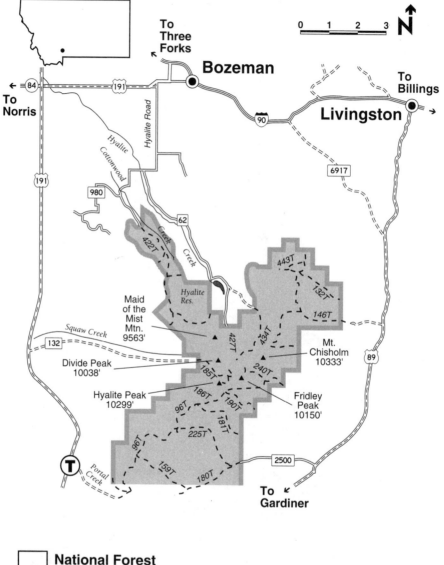

National Forest
Roadless Area

view of trees that were petrified in their original growing positions. Today's living forest is also worthy of note. Broad, open slopes are dominated by big sage, with their northern aspects covered by thick forests of Douglas-fir, aspen, spruce, and lodgepole pine. Tundra, turf, and rock mark the crest where the wind roars like a runaway freight train.

The southern Gallatin is superb grizzly country as well as some of the choicest elk range anywhere, with its blend of grassland forage and dense forest hiding cover. Two bighorn sheep herds of about 150 animals each reside here with another smaller band to the north in the Hyalite Peaks. Along with this stunning array of wild denizens, an almost unnerving volcanic geology lends mystique to this mountain realm.

RECREATIONAL USES: Elk hunting is the number one recreational activity in the Gallatin Range, followed by hiking, backpacking, horseback riding, fishing, and cross-country skiing. Outfitter base camps are in Steele Creek, Porcupine Creek, and Bark Cabin Creek. There is some mountain biking in the Hyalite Peaks, which are also the most heavily used part of the wilderness study area by hikers, backpackers, and skiers. This is due to their proximity to Bozeman as well as their classic alpine beauty. The Hyalites are to the summer visitor what the southern part of the range is to the winter recreationist. Here the more gentle parks, plateaus, and open meadows combine with ample deep, dry snow to provide a ski-touring paradise. For many the chance to experience solitude in the steep, narrow canyons or to see wildlife in wild country is reason enough to explore the Gallatins.

It may be that the least-visited portion of the range lies along its northern flank above Paradise Valley in the Eightmile and Fridley Creek drainages. Private landowners have historically prevented direct access to this area of some 30,000 roadless acres. Fortunately, Congress has recently approved a land exchange combining public land in the Porcupine Creek drainage, thereby protecting this critical elk habitat from roading and logging in the former Plum Creek checkerboard inholdings.

The Bozeman Ranger District rents out three cabins within or close to the study area. The two-person capacity Fox Creek cabin is available December 1 to October 15. It is 14 miles south of Bozeman on the northwest boundary. Winter access varies with snow conditions. The four-person capacity Window Rock cabin, just south of Hyalite Reservoir, is rented throughout the year. Again, winter access distance is variable. The four-person Windy Pass cabin is just below the main Gallatin Divide in the central part of the roadless area. The trail access from the road is 2.5 miles with a 1,300 foot elevation gain. It is rented out from June 1 to October 15.

The Livingston District rents the ten-person capacity Big Creek Cabin throughout the year. The cabin is only 0.5 mile from the east-central edge of

39B GALLATIN RANGE-SOUTH

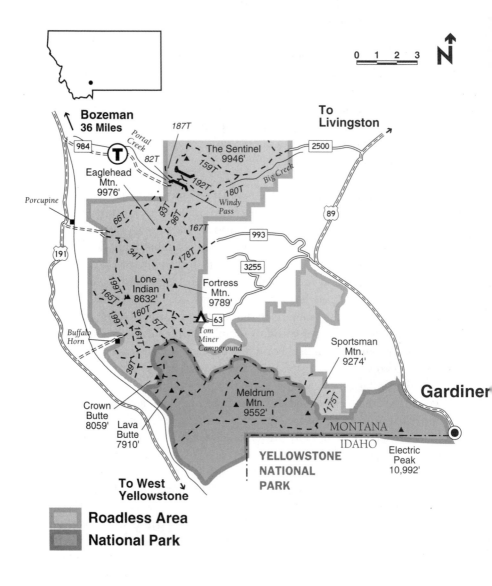

0 1 2 3 **N**

Bozeman
36 Miles

To
Livingston

984

Portal
Creek

187T

82T

159T

The Sentinel
9946'

2500

Eaglehead
Mtn.
9976'

192T

180T

Big Creek

Porcupine

66T

93T

96T

Windy
Pass

89

167T

191

34T

178T

993

3255

199T

Lone
Indian
8632'

Fortress
Mtn.
9789'

165T

160T

199T

57T

63

Buffalo
Horn

161T

Tom
Miner
Campground

Sportsman
Mtn.
9274'

39T

Gardiner

175T

Meldrum
Mtn.
9552'

Crown
Butte
8059'

Lava
Butte
7910'

MONTANA

IDAHO

YELLOWSTONE
NATIONAL
PARK

Electric
Peak
10,992'

To West
Yellowstone

Roadless Area

National Park

the study area on the Big Creek road, which is plowed to within 0.5 mile of the cabin. The cabin is 35 miles south of Livingston on US 89, then 5 miles west on the Big Creek road.

The Gallatins are accessed from numerous forest roads leading from US 191 between Bozeman and West Yellowstone on the west side, or from US 89 between Livingston and Gardiner through Paradise Valley on the east. After reaching the trailhead of your choice you'll find a well-distributed trail system, although some of the trails are in need of repair or reconstruction. Prominent pinnacles include the 10,333-foot summits of Boles Peak and Mount Chisholm (tying for highest point in the range), Mount Blackmore, Hyalite Peak, Eaglehead, and Fortress mountains, all of which offer pleasurable scrambles to the top.

It is best to avoid the overcrowded Hyalite Peaks during the summer season unless you're specifically planning to hike the entire range from Hyalite Reservoir south to Yellowstone Park. If so, plan for at least eight days, lots of up and down, and some careful routefinding in a few stretches where the divide trail leaves the crest for parts unknown. The centerpiece of the range is east-flowing Big Creek—the largest unroaded drainage in the Gallatins—12 miles long from the trailhead up to the crest.

The most popular fishing lakes are most of the Hyalite lakes as well as Ramshorn Lake, the Buffalo Horn lakes, and Golden Trout and Hidden lakes, which harbor 8- to 10-inch goldens.

HYALITE PEAKS, IN THE NORTH END OF THE GALLATIN RANGE.

WINDY PASS, ALONG THE GALLATIN DIVIDE, OFFERS HIGH-COUNTRY SKIING AT ITS BEST.

The Gallatin Petrified Forest covers about 19,200 acres of the southern part of the range near Specimen Ridge, with most of the forest extending into Yellowstone Park. Rockhounding here is popular even though the petrified wood is not of lapidary quality. Permits are required.

HOW TO GET THERE: *West-central/winter access:* Head south on US 191 about 36 miles south of Bozeman to the Portal Creek road (FR 984) turnoff. Turn left (east) and park next to the highway at the gated road closure, which is in effect between January 1 and June 30.

OUT-AND-BACK SKI TOUR OR OVERNIGHTER

Windy Pass
Distance: 20-mile out-and-back day ski tour or 2-to-3 day overnighter.
Difficulty: Strenuous.
Topo Maps: Hidden Lake-MT and The Sentinel-MT.

By March the snow is well consolidated and the days are getting noticeably longer—a good time to head for Windy Pass in the central reaches of the wild Gallatins. Actually, Windy Pass is a sort of non-pass—part of a 15-mile-long plateau along the high crest of the range. The pass requires a 3,500-foot climb up 7 to 8 miles of logging roads in Portal Creek and 2.5 miles of steep trail on Trail 82. The final 1,300-foot pitch will require climbing skins and more than a little determination. An advanced, well-conditioned skier can make the 20-mile round-trip to Windy Pass via Portal Creek in a single day with an early start late in the season. But it makes a lot more sense to put in a snow camp for the night and really make a trip out of it. Find a clump of sheltered whitebark pine at around 9,200 feet on the lee side of the divide near the Windy Pass cabin. The high plateaus and open meadows of the Windy Pass area from The Sentinel south to Eaglehead Mountain offer about 6 north-south miles of ideal ski-touring between 9,000 and 10,000 feet. There are thousands of acres of perfect slopes adorned with dry powder created by constant cold temperatures—a telemarker and diagonal skier's paradise! Hold onto your hat though; Windy Pass is well named.

Looking north to The Sentinel and beyond is a lot easier than trying to get there, in that the peak drops abruptly to a saddle before climbing along a sharp ridge. An advanced skier on stable snow could traverse the west side to the saddle. In stable snow conditions it is also possible to drop into the head of Big Creek, although the route quickly becomes steep and densely forested.

Absaroka-Beartooth Wilderness Complex

40

Location: 5 miles south of Livingston (Absaroka Range); and 8 miles southwest of Red Lodge (Beartooth Range).
Size: 1,208,734 acres (Montana-portion).
Administration: USDAFS—Gallatin, Custer, and Shoshone national forests; NPS—Yellowstone National Park.
Management status: Absaroka-Beartooth Wilderness (920,310 acres); the northeastern edge of Yellowstone National Park; remainder is national forest roadless non-wilderness, some of which is allocated to future development in the forest plans.
Ecosystems: Middle Rocky Mountain coniferous forest-alpine meadow province, Yellowstone Highlands section, characterized by complex and high, steep, strongly glaciated mountains with sharp alpine ridges, cirques, and moraines along with narrow-to-broad valleys; Precambrian metamorphic and granitic rocks; Douglas-fir and western spruce-fir forest types and extensive areas of alpine vegetation; abundant perennial streams, wet meadows, and lakes throughout (the east is a high, uplifted plateau with a dense network of perennial streams and lakes; the west is distinguished by sharper peaks and more narrow valleys).
Elevation range: 5,200 to 12,799 feet.
System trails: 850 miles.
Maximum core to perimeter distance: 13 miles.
Activities: Hiking, backpacking, mountaineering, horseback riding, cross-country skiing, fishing.
Modes of travel: Foot, horse, and skis.
Maps: 1986 Absaroka-Beartooth Wilderness Map (5/8-inch/mile contour); 1991 Gallatin National Forest Visitor Map; and 1986 Custer Forest/Beartooth Visitor Map (see appendix D for a listing of the 52 1:24,000 scale topographic maps covering the complex).

OVERVIEW: On the northeast side of Yellowstone National Park rises the enormous uplift of the Absaroka and Beartooth ranges, one of the highest and most austere alpine expanses on the continent. For 65 miles across its widest boundary on the south, only a couple of short low-standard roads penetrate these mountains. The north-flowing Boulder River is the dividing line between the Absaroka Range on the west and the Beartooth Mountains to the east. With a unified Wilderness core of a million acres, the Absaroka-Beartooth is the second largest contiguous roadless area in Montana, and includes the northeast edge of Yellowstone.

40 ABSAROKA-BEARTOOTH WILDERNESS COMPLEX

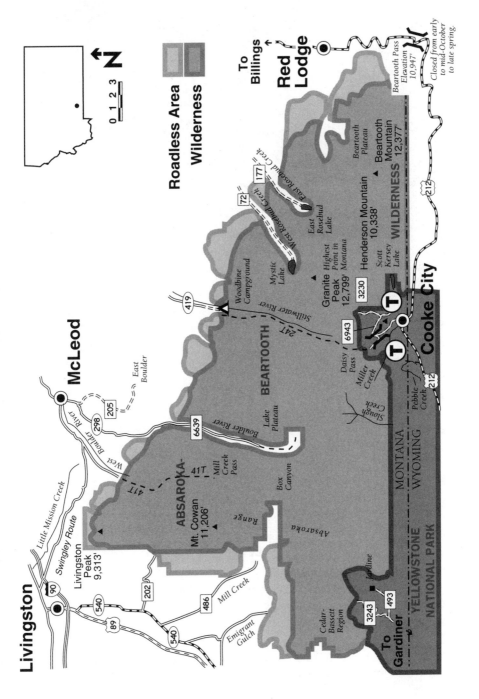

GLACIER PEAK—ONE OF THE 12,000-FOOTERS IN THE HEART OF THE
BEARTOOTH WILDERNESS.

The Beartooths, named after a sharp point jutting from the ragged jaw of
Beartooth Mountain, contain twenty-nine peaks above 12,000 feet, including
Montana's highest and wildest mountain—12,799-foot Granite Peak. The
names of nearby summits reflect the ever-changing mood of this harsh moon-
scape: Froze-to-Death, Tempest, Thunder. Lofty tundra-clad plateaus form the
largest contiguous landmass above 10,000 feet in the United States. The range
is derived from a Precambrian base that, at 4 billion years, is among the oldest known rock on Earth. This foundation was covered with thousands of feet
of sediments and then uplifted 70 million years ago. Thick ice scoured the
southern side of the Beartooth Plateau, leaving a rolling landscape. The highest peaks are islands of sedimentary rock that escaped the ice. On the northern flank the ice gouged out U-shaped valleys and created the distinct, alternating plateau-canyon topography. With an amazing 386 plant species discovered thus far, the Beartooths display the richest flora of any mountain range
in North America. This may be due to the considerable height of the range in
combination with its unusual east-west orientation.

An incredible abundance of water in all its forms is the dominant impression one gets when visiting the Absaroka-Beartooth. Three-hundred-foot
waterfalls plunging to snowbound cirque lakes, countless cascades, remnant
glaciers on high north slopes, and 1,000 deep blue lakes remind us that these
wild mountains are, first and foremost, an undisturbed watershed for
America's longest undammed river—the free-flowing Yellowstone.

In stark contrast to the Beartooths, the Absaroka Range is made of softer sedimentary rock that has eroded some of the peaks into gentler, more rounded mountains. However, many exceptions exist, such as jagged Mount Cowan with its ring of vertical spires. The southern reaches of the range are particularly productive for grizzly bears, moose, bighorn sheep, and summering elk and deer. Soaring golden eagles are common—swept by the wind and bathed in mountain light.

Due to moist microclimates, foothills and canyons along the northwest face of the Absarokas nurture plants unusual east of the Continental Divide, such as bear grass, rare ferns, and the state's only population of high-bush cranberry. Grassy foothills and parks with aspen groves along the north face of the range provide winter forage for elk, deer, and bighorn sheep.

RECREATIONAL USES: About one-fourth of the high lakes contain fish—golden, rainbow, brook, and cutthroat trout, as well as grayling. The fishing varies from good to excellent during the fleeting summer, which averages only four to six weeks from late July to early September. Winter is always close at hand in the harsh, subarctic climate of the "A/B." Violent thunderstorms occur almost daily during warm summer afternoons. Sudden drops in the mercury to fifty degrees below zero are common at least six months of the year. The east-west trend of the Beartooths means less summer sun, with resultant lingering snowfields, slow runoff, and lots of swampy areas.

As the nation's fourth most heavily used wilderness, portions of the A/B are being loved to death by visitors. Sheer numbers of people have made pollution from human waste the most pressing wilderness management problem. In much of this lofty land there is simply little or no soil for absorption. One can even identify the "human browse line" around the more popular alpine lakes where people have left signs of firewood gathering. A proliferation of fire rings near most of the fishable lakes is also of concern. To safeguard water quality and wilderness values, camping is banned within 200 feet of lakes and streams. Party size is limited to no more than fifteen people.

With more than a half million visitor days annually, finding solitude here may be the ultimate challenge. In reality, ample opportunities for solitude await those willing to expend the extra effort. You must first accept the fact that the main line trails, such as Alpine to Cooke City, are transportation corridors and will not offer solitude. For example, there are often more than one hundred people camped around the trail side of Rainbow Lake on East Rosebud Creek during a weekend night in July or August.

Good roads and trails facilitate the growing use of the A/B with access provided from Billings, Big Timber, Livingston, and Cooke City. In fact, about two-thirds of the users live in these and other nearby Montana communities. Once the visitor reaches the wilderness boundary there are 32 major signed

SKIING AT SHEEP BASIN, IN THE SOUTHCENTRAL BEARTOOTHS, NORTH OF COOKE CITY.

trailheads and more than 700 miles of well-maintained trails to choose from. The steep, rugged terrain channels most of the visitation into narrow canyon corridors and at alpine lakes accessed by trail. Most of the use is in the lower 4 to 6 miles of each major canyon, with two-thirds being weekend day use.

The most heavily visited trailheads (more than 5,000 entries per year) are Woodbine (Stillwater Trail 24), East and West Rosebud Creek (trails 15 and 19), Lake Fork and West Fork of Rock Creek (Trail 1), and the popular Cooke City-Alpine Trail 567 to Trail 15. Trailheads receiving a middle range of use include the West Fork Stillwater (Trail 90) and Glacier Lake (trails 66 and 3). In the fall, an army of elk hunters converges on Slough Creek, Hellroaring, the West and Main Boulder, and Buffalo Fork drainages.

Comparatively few people wander more than a half mile off developed trails. Those who trek cross country to reach the hundreds of isolated lakes and trailless peaks are unlikely to encounter many, or any, other visitors. There are many trails which lead directly to the plateaus without following a stream or passing by lakes. These lesser-used trails offer more wilderness solitude.

The Big Timber Ranger District rents several Forest Service cabins along the edges of the complex. The five-person capacity Fourmile cabin is in the main Boulder River canyon 42 miles south of Big Timber and is rented from October 1 to May 30. Cross-country skiers can access the cabin during winter, but avalanche conditions must be carefully checked before skiing up side drainages, such as Fourmile Creek. The four-person Deer Creek cabin is rented year-round. The cabin is 33 miles south of Big Timber with the last 4 miles by trail on foot or horseback. The six-person West Boulder cabin is available from December 1 to May 30. It is 30 miles southwest of Big Timber on the West Boulder River adjacent to the campground. During winter a short ski may be necessary on the county road.

The Livingston Ranger District rents the three-person capacity Mill Creek Guard Station from December 1 to April 30. The road is plowed to the adjacent Snowbank campground. The Gardiner Ranger District rents the ten-person capacity Kersey Lake cabin from June 15 to September 15 and from December 15 to March 15. The cabin is situated on the wilderness boundary 4 miles east of Cooke City and can be reached on skis during winter. The cabin is a good base from which to ski eastward to several of the larger lakes in the country.

HOW TO GET THERE: From Yellowstone National Park Headquarters at Mammoth take US 212 east across the north end of the park for about 50 miles to Silver Gate and Cooke City, Montana, which is 4 miles east of Silver Gate.

From Silver Gate-Cooke City there is virtually an endless variety of winter ski tour/mountaineering possibilities, ranging from easy to strenuous day trips or extended overnighters.

DAY SKI TOURS

Daisy Pass
Distance: 7 to 8 miles out-and-back.
Difficulty: Moderately strenuous.
Topo map: Cooke City-MT.

For starters, drive as far as you can up the Miller Creek/Daisy Pass road, which heads northwest about 0.5 mile east of Cooke City. The upper basin is broad, open, and big enough to accommodate both skiers and snowmobilers. For a vigorous side excursion from the upper basin climb 1,000 feet through scattered open forest to the top of 10,338-foot Henderson Mountain. You can then work your way along the windswept ridge northwest to Chimney Rock, which boasts a commanding view of an alpine snowscape in every direction. For a bit of a loop descend about 550 feet to Daisy Pass and from there glide back down Miller Creek through open parks and stringers of trees. This trip will take you near the site of a controversial gold mine which, if developed, could seriously degrade a portion of the Greater Yellowstone Ecosystem.

Curl Lake
Distance: 3.5 miles out-and-back.
Difficulty: Moderate.
Topo map: Fossil Lake-MT.

With the Kersey Lake cabin (at 8,070 feet) as a base, ski north up the Broadwater River. Trail 564 reaches the wilderness boundary after about 1 mile of wandering through subalpine forest. Continue another 0.75 mile along the east side of Curl Lake to where the trail ends below a steep rocky slope.

Russell Lake
Distance: 7 to 8 miles out-and-back.
Difficulty: Moderate.
Topo maps: Fossil Lake-MT/WY.

Another excellent choice is a 1.5-mile ski southeast to Rock Island Lake (at 8,166 feet) on Trail 566. For a bit more adventure head northeast up Russell Creek on Trail 567. After about 1.5 miles the canyon narrows and then opens up just south of Twin Lakes. If you're on well-consolidated late-season snow take a short side trip north for the 400-foot climb to these tiny twin tarns.

Another 0.5 mile up the main drainage the Russell Creek canyon narrows to steep avalanche-prone sideslopes just below Russell Lake at 8,732 feet. This is a good place to turn around, making the trip a half-day tour of the forested lake country that borders the uplifted Beartooth plateaus to the north.

Pebble Creek
Distance: 15 to 16 miles point-to-point.
Difficulty: Strenuous.
Topo maps: Cutoff Mountain-MT/WY; and Abiathar Peak-WY.

This is one of the classic *long* day ski tours in northeast Yellowstone Park. Post an exit car at the Pebble Creek campground about 14 miles southwest of Cooke City on US 212. Begin the trip at the other trailhead to the northeast, which is located along Soda Butte Creek about 2 miles west of the northeast entrance to the park (at 7,270 feet). The hard work is at the start. Switchback and contour up forested sideslopes, gaining 1,000 feet in 1 mile, with the steepest slopes leveling out into a broad saddle at 8,300 feet. From here it's an easy 300-foot drop to the spacious meadows of upper Pebble Creek. The meadows narrow but continue uninterrupted for 6 to 8 miles, dropping at a moderate grade. This is the payoff, with a delightful cruise down Pebble Creek for miles, surrounded by majestic peaks and ridges exceeding 10,000 feet on both sides of the drainage. The valley closes in during the final 3 to 4 miles. The trail contours on steep sidehills and finally switchbacks down to the trailhead at 6,830 feet. Get an early start for what will surely be a long but rewarding day in the mountains. Pack a headlamp for a probable after-dark slog to the trailhead. Save this one for March or April when the base is good and the days are longer.

Crazy Mountains

41

Location: 15 miles northwest of Big Timber and 21 miles north of Livingston.
Size: 136,547 acres.
Administration: USDAFS—Gallatin and Lewis & Clark national forests.
Management status: Roadless non-wilderness, with some peripheral lands allocated to future development in the forest plans.
Ecosystems: Northern Rocky Mountain coniferous forest-alpine meadow province, characterized by high, isolated, strongly glaciated mountains surrounded by plains and rolling hills; Precambrian metamorphic and cretaceous soft sedimentary rocks; Douglas-fir forest type with extensive areas of alpine vegetation; a dendritic drainage pattern of many perennial streams with numerous high lakes.
Elevation range: 5,590 to 11,214 feet.
Trail system: 66 miles.
Maximum core to perimeter distance: 5 miles.
Activities: Hiking, backpacking, mountaineering, horseback riding, cross-country skiing, fishing.
Modes of travel: Foot, horse, and skis.
Maps: 1991 Gallatin National Forest Visitor Map and 1988 Lewis & Clark National Forest/ Jefferson Division Visitor Map; Cinnamon Peak-MT; Cinnamon Spring-MT; Virginia Peak-MT; Loco Mountain-MT; Rein Lake-MT; Campfire Lake-MT; Crazy Peak-MT; Amelong Peak-MT; Ibex Mountain-MT; Fairview Peak-MT; and Raspberry Butte-MT (1:24,000 topo maps).

OVERVIEW: From the low benches of the Yellowstone River to the jagged 11,214-foot summit of Crazy Peak, the land rises more than 7,000 feet in what is perhaps the most dramatic transition from prairie to mountains in Montana. The highest stark shapes of 23 rugged peaks exceed 10,000 feet, showing strong signs of the glaciation that forced these crags in different directions simultaneously. Legend has it that a white woman driven crazy when Indians killed her family wandered into the mountains here. The origin of the name can also be explained topographically by the convoluted geological formations. They comprise one of the largest exposed blocks of igneous rock on the planet.

Volcanic in origin, the core of the higher southern Crazies is a gigantic igneous intrusion from which spectacular wall-like dikes radiate, some of which are more than 50 feet thick. This is one of the few central Montana montane islands high enough to have held large glaciers during the last Ice Age. As such, the range is a maze of nearly vertical peaks, sawtooth ridges, arêtes, talus fields streaming from broken cliffs, and lush alpine cirques with forty snow-fed lakes.

41 CRAZY MOUNTAINS

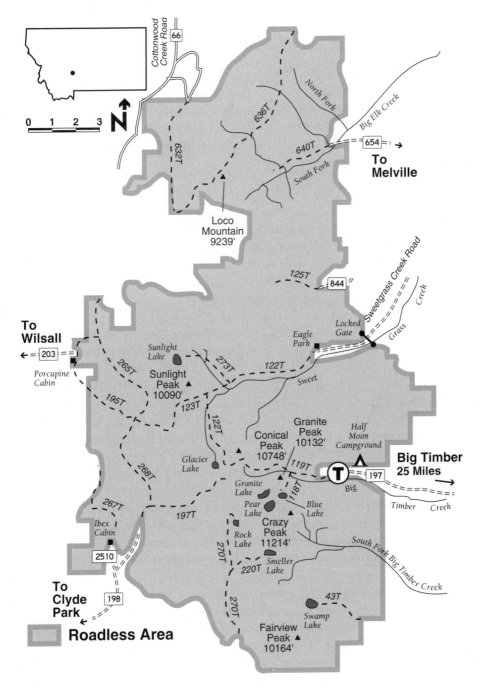

Cottonwood Creek Road

66

0 1 2 3

N

632T

636T

North Fork

640T

South Fork

Big Elk Creek

654

To Melville

Loco Mountain 9239'

125T

844

Sweetgrass Creek Road

Grass Creek

To Wilsall

203

Porcupine Cabin

265T

Sunlight Lake

Sunlight Peak 10090'

273T

122T

Eagle Park

Locked Gate

Sweet

195T

123T

122T

Granite Peak 10132'

Conical Peak 10748'

Half Moon Campground

268T

Glacier Lake

119T

Big Timber 25 Miles

197

267T

197T

Granite Lake

118T

Big

Timber   Creek

Ibex Cabin

Pear Lake

Blue Lake

2510

Rock Lake

Crazy Peak 11214'

270T

Smeller Lake

220T

South Fork Big Timber Creek

To Clyde Park

198

270T

43T

Swamp Lake

Fairview Peak 10164'

Roadless Area

This is an austere land of mountain goats on barren ridges, eagles soaring high overhead, and elk, black bear, and mountain lion dwelling in stringers of forest along the stream bottoms. In the north, the range is lower and gentler, breaking into groups of tree-clad hills and canyons that drain into the Musselshell.

Sometime around 1857, Plenty Coups, the last great pre-reservation chief of the Crow Indians, realized a vision on top of Crazy Peak with which to guide his people. The continued wildness of these sacred mountains inspires modern-day members of his tribe to practice traditional religion here—from purification in lakeside sweat lodges to vision quests on lofty pinnacles towering above the prairie.

RECREATIONAL USES: The Crazy Mountains are incredibly wild and rugged, with some of the most startling topography in Montana. Massive peaks with columns of igneous rock rise hundreds of feet above more than forty sparkling alpine lakes nestled in glacial cirques and hanging valleys. With country like this, hiking and backpacking into the remote high lakes with fishing pole in hand are among the more popular activities. Horseback riding and hunting in the backcountry are also popular. Gaining in popularity is rock climbing and peak scrambling in this challenging terrain. Although cross-country skiing is enjoyable in some of the peripheral foothills, serious avalanche danger in the steep, narrow canyons discourages most skiers from penetrating very deep into the roadless area. For an expanse of public land as large as the Crazies access is minimal; surrounding private landholders have a long history of restricting the public. The major public access is via Cottonwood Road (FR 198) from the west and the Big Timber Canyon Road (FR 197) on the east. The Crazies can also be reached from the Porcupine Guard Station and the Shields River road system.

The Livingston Ranger District rents two cabins bordering the west side of the Crazies throughout the year. The five-person capacity Ibex cabin, 15 miles northeast of Clyde Park, is just barely within the southwest corner of the roadless area. The Cottonwood Creek Road is plowed to within 5 miles. Farther north, the eight-person Porcupine cabin touches the west-central boundary. FR 203 is plowed to within 1.5 miles. Skiers can traverse Bald Ridge into the South Fork of the Shields River but should be alert to avalanche conditions.

HOW TO GET THERE: From Interstate 90 at Big Timber, head 11 miles north on US 191 to Big Timber Canyon Road (FR 197). Turn left (west) and stay on FR 197 heading west to northwest for about 14 miles across private land and through two gates to the Forest Service Half Moon Campground on Big Timber Creek. The campground is also the trailhead for Trail 119, which begins as a reclaimed exploratory mining road now closed yearlong to motorized travel.

BACKPACK OR BASE CAMP HIKE

Half Moon Campground to the South Fork of Sweet Grass Creek

Distance: 15 miles round-trip, plus side trips into lake basins.
Difficulty: Moderately strenuous.
Topo maps: Campfire Lake-MT and Crazy Peak-MT.

The first 1.5 miles of Trail 119 from Half Moon Campground are a reminder of a 1981 gold mine that turned out to be a scam and was later stopped by outraged citizens and the Forest Service. In the future this track might be used as a wheelchair route. Don't miss Big Timber Falls within the first mile just to the south. Between mile 2 and 3 are two very sturdy bridges across raging Big Timber Creek. At the base of Granite Peak consider taking a 1-mile side trip up Trail 118 to Blue Lake, crossing Big Timber Creek on a logjam. This heavily visited lake provides a stunning view of 11,214-foot Crazy Peak. From the lake there are several nontechnical, though difficult, ways to ascend the peak with perhaps the best route on the southwest ridge.

Continuing up Big Timber Creek the trail breaks out into lush meadows below Lower Twin Lake about 6 miles above the campground. Dry but rocky campsites are available at both the lower and upper lakes. From the upper lake the trail climbs 2,000 feet in 1 mile to a 10,000-foot pass next to Conical Peak. Take a short side scramble north to the summit. Then drop a steep mile into

ABOVE SUNLIGHT LAKE ON A NOT-SO-SUNNY JULY DAY IN THE CRAZIES.

the head of the South Fork of Sweet Grass Creek to Glacier Lake, which is often frozen into mid-July. There are no campsites around the exposed rocky shoreline but stay awhile and soak up the inspiring view of waterfalls and high cliffs. Then drop down the South Fork another couple of miles and look for a campsite in the meadows near the stream. This is a beautiful setting in which to set up a base camp for day trips into nearby lake basins, such as Campfire Lake at the head of the Middle Fork on Trail 123 and Sunlight Lake at the upper end of the North Fork on Trail 273. Another excellent and somewhat closer base camp to the high lake basins would be another 1.5 to 2 miles downstream at the confluence of the Middle and South forks of Sweet Grass Creek.

Castle Mountains

42

Location: 5 miles southeast of White Sulphur Springs.
Size: 29,900 acres.
Administration: USDAFS-Lewis & Clark National Forest.
Management status: Roadless non-wilderness with a timber-wildlife emphasis on about 19,000 acres.
Ecosystems: Middle Rocky Mountain steppe-coniferous forest-alpine meadow province, characterized by isolated mountains surrounded by plains and rolling hills; igneous spires in the west and dry, porous limestone soils in the east; foothills prairie and Douglas-fir forest type; perennial streams with dendritic drainage pattern.
Elevation range: 5,800 to 8,566 feet.
System trails: 33 miles.
Maximum core to perimeter distance: 2.5 miles.
Activities: Hiking, backpacking, horseback riding, cross-country skiing.
Modes of travel: Foot, skis, and horse.
Maps: 1988 Lewis & Clark National Forest/Jefferson Division Visitor Map; Pinchout Creek-MT; Fourmile Spring-MT; Manger Park-MT; and Castletown-MT (1:24,000 topo maps).

OVERVIEW: Formed by granite intrusion, the western side of the igneous Castles are lush and moist—unlike the dry, porous limestone mountains of the adjacent east Castles and Little Belts. The highpoint—centrally located 8,552-foot Wapiti Peak—offers a grand overview of almost all of the Castle Mountains roadless area as well as many other island mountain ranges in central Montana. "Castle turrets" of 50-foot igneous spires grace the west slopes. Higher elevations are dominated by a central cluster of peaks above 8,000 feet, along with extensive grassy parks of several square miles surrounded by lodgepole and limber pine. Primitive trails from the early mining days wind through a blend of wet meadows and dark, thick forest ideal as hiding cover for the wily wapiti.

RECREATIONAL USES: Although open for snowmobiling and trail biking, such uses are light within the roadless area. The Castles offer excellent early season hiking and horseback riding as well as cross-country ski touring. These mountains are lightly visited, the exception being during the fall hunting season. Some commercial outfitting is permitted in the Castles during the spring bear and lion hunting seasons, but there is no outfitting here during the fall big-game season. Camping and hiking are increasing slightly.

42 CASTLE MOUNTAINS

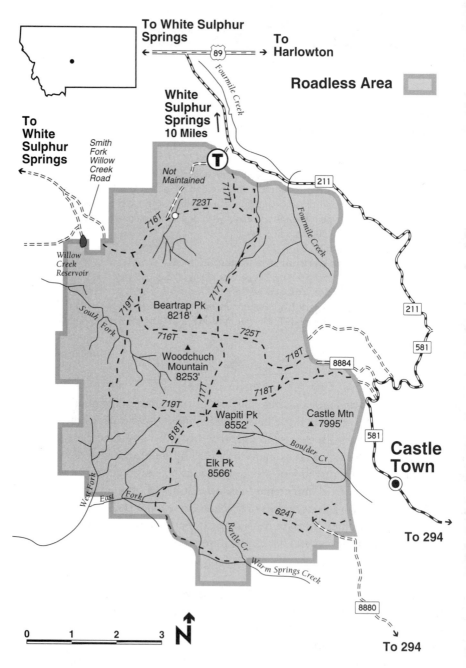

To White Sulphur Springs

US 89

To Harlowton

Roadless Area

White Sulphur Springs ↑ 10 Miles

To White Sulphur Springs

Smith Fork Willow Creek Road

Not Maintained

211

723T

716T

717T

Fourmile Creek

Willow Creek Reservoir

719T

South Fork

Beartrap Pk 8218' ▲

716T

725T

717T

718T

8884

211

581

Woodchuch Mountain 8253' ▲

717T

718T

719T

Wapiti Pk 8552' ▲

Castle Mtn ▲ 7995'

581

618T

Boulder Cr

Castle Town ●

Elk Pk 8566' ▲

West Fork

East Fork

Rattle Cr

624T

To 294

Warm Springs Creek

8880

To 294

0   1   2   3   **N ↑**

The developed Grasshopper and Richardson Creek campgrounds border the roadless area on the north, with Grasshopper receiving the heavier use. Both campgrounds are great for car camping and provide trailhead access to Trails 716 and 717; Trail 717 is the main backcountry route. Late spring to early summer is an especially good time to explore the Castles when wildflowers are at their peak.

HOW TO GET THERE: From White Sulphur Springs drive 6 miles east on US 12. Turn right and drive 4 miles south on FR 211 to Grasshopper Creek Campground and the trailhead for Trail 717.

DAY HIKE OR OVERNIGHTER

Castle Mountains Loop
Distance: 14- to 15-mile loop.
Difficulty: Moderately strenuous.
Topo maps: Pinchout Creek-MT; Fourmile Spring-MT; and Manger Park-MT.

From the south end of Grasshopper Campground follow Trail 717 as it climbs steadily through a dense lodgepole pine forest interspersed with small meadows along the East Fork of Fourmile Creek. Cross over to Horse Park where cattle will be grazing by June. Continue south toward the secluded head of Richardson Creek where you'll find good campsites in a lush meadow ablaze with shooting stars and pasque flowers during early summer. As you continue south you'll pass tiny streams and grassy openings frequented by elk right at first light. After passing the forested slopes that lead west to 8,218-foot Beartrap Peak keep going south on Trail 717 to 8,552-foot Wapiti Peak. A short uphill side trip on Trail 718 leads to the apex of the Castles—8,566-foot Elk Peak—which provides the best view of any of the higher points. On a clear day expect to see the nearby igneous Castle turrets, the Crazies, Big Belts, Little Belts, Big Snowies, Bridgers, and more. The elevation gained from the campground to the peaks is about 2,600 feet.

Continuing the loop, head north for about 3 miles on Trail 719 through a thick doghair forest of spindly lodgepole pine to Manger Park, a mile-long grassy ridge overlooking the wide Smith River Valley to the west. Mule deer are abundant along the forest edges surrounding the park. About 1.5 miles north of the park you'll cross the fair-sized South Fork of Willow Creek—municipal water supply for White Sulphur Springs. Climb steeply up the lightly used and infrequently cut-out Trail 716 to the trail junction just south of Beartrap Peak. Fresh elk sign, and maybe even the critters who made it, will be seen along this stretch. Head north back to camp on Trail 717 and you've completed a rewarding 14- to 15-mile round-trip through the heart of this com-

HEAD OF BOULDER CREEK FROM WAPITI PEAK IN THE SOUTH CASTLES.

pact mountain island. Shorter variations are also possible by wrapping around centrally located Beartrap Peak, bypassing the longer loop to the higher summits in the south. Along the way watch for the crumbling historic remains of old miners' cabins and diggings.

The trails and old "troads" from the early mining days are well signed throughout the Castles and are generally well-maintained.

Elkhorn Mountains 43

Location: 12 miles southeast of Helena.
Size: 89,585 acres.
Administration: USDAFS—Helena and Deerlodge national forests; Bureau of Land Management—Headwaters Resource Area.
Management status: National forest wildlife management unit with roadless management; BLM Wilderness Study Area of 3,585 acres on the southwest corner.
Ecosystems: Middle Rocky Mountain steppe-coniferous forest-alpine meadow province, characterized by isolated mountains surrounded by plains and rolling hills, glaciation evident in the south with alpine cirques and lakes; volcanics, Boulder Batholith granitics, and sedimentary rocks; foothills prairie and Douglas-fir forest type; and many perennial streams and wet meadows.
Elevation range: 5,000 to 9,414 feet.
System trails: 112 miles.
Maximum core to perimeter distance: 8 miles.
Activities: Hiking, backpacking, cross-country skiing, horseback riding, mountain biking, fishing.
Modes of travel: Foot, skis, horse, and mountain bike.
Maps: 1991 Helena National Forest Visitor Map; Clancy-MT; Casey Peak-MT; Winston-MT; Elkhorn-MT; Crow Creek Falls-MT; and Giant Hill-MT (1:24,000 topo maps).

OVERVIEW: The Elkhorn Range is a vast, uplifted block defined by major faults on the north, east. and south. Here the mountains rise 1,000 to 2,000 feet above and immediately east of the Continental Divide, thereby picking up much more moisture from prevailing storms than do the lower, surrounding mountains.

The range is made up of three distinct subregions. First, the high Elkhorn/Crow Peaks ascend above 9,400 feet in the southern end, providing panoramic vistas, alpine lakes, and a rugged landscape formed when long-ago glaciers carved striking rock walls at the head of Tizer Creek. To the north is the expansive Tizer Basin, with carpets of lodgepole pine, subalpine fir, and spruce, along with small clearings, primitive jeep trails, old mining buildings, and large grassy meadows. Thirdly, the upper reaches of McClellan and Beaver creeks contain the most undeveloped part of the Elkhorns with thickets of young trees, high rocky ridges, and deep secluded canyons. Much of this country burned in the 1988 Warm Springs fire.

The lushness and large elevation differences account for an amazing assemblage of 148 known species of mammals, birds, amphibians, and reptiles. With

43 ELKHORN MOUNTAINS

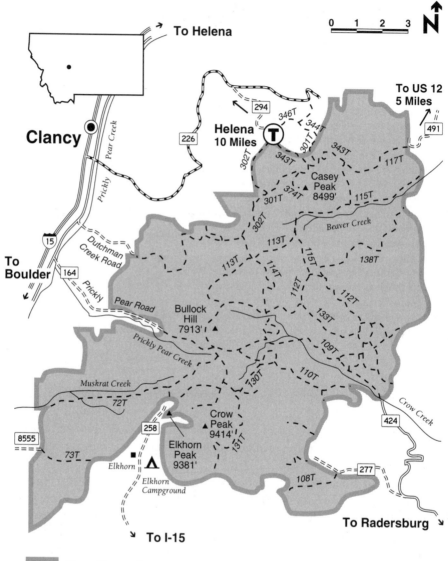

To Helena

Clancy

Helena
10 Miles

226

294

To US 12
5 Miles

491

346T

344T

301T

343T

117T

302T

343T

Casey
Peak
8499'

115T

301T

374T

115T

Beaver Creek

113T

302T

113T

114T

115T

112T

138T

To
Boulder

164

Dutchman
Creek Road

Pear Creek

Prickly

Pear Creek

15

112T

Prickly Pear Road

Bullock
Hill
7913'

133T

Prickly Pear Creek

109T

Muskrat Creek

130T

110T

Crow Creek

72T

258

Crow
Peak
9414'

424

8555

73T

Elkhorn

Elkhorn
Peak
9381'

131T

277

108T

Elkhorn
Campground

To Radersburg

To I-15

Roadless Area

an abundance of eight of Montana's big-game species, the Elkhorns are among the most productive and heavily hunted elk areas in the state. Unlike most other elk habitat, about 80 percent of the winter range in the Elkhorns is publicly owned.

RECREATIONAL USES: At one time the Elkhorn island mountain range was one of the most heavily hunted elk districts in Montana. Although still hunted hard in a closely monitored elk management program, hunting use has leveled off. With proximity to Helena, the Elkhorns are also popular for hiking, backpacking, mountain biking, fishing, and cross-country skiing. The country is large, rugged, and diverse enough to absorb a lot of recreational use without sacrificing solitude. Anyone who wants to be alone can certainly do so in the deep canyons, dense forests, and on distant peaks. There is a good system of trails and old jeep roads from past mining, but the expansive parks and open ridges lend themselves to cross-country travel. Skiers can readily access lofty Elkhorn and Crow peaks by climbing 4 miles up the Iron Mine Road from the historic community of Elkhorn on the south end. Skiers can also ski up the Prickly Pear jeep road (FR 164) about 7 or 8 miles into the Tizer Basin where heavy snow and moderate terrain combine to form a backcountry skier's paradise. On the north end of the range Casey Meadows can be reached during winter for an enjoyable day tour.

LOOKING SOUTH TO CROW AND ELKHORN PEAKS.

There are seven mountain lakes in the Elkhorns, each one worth a visit. The most remote and hardest to get to are Glenwood and Hidden lakes. Stocked with cutthroat, both offer spotty fishing in a classic alpine setting. Several streams in these lush mountains hold pan-sized brook and cutthroat trout, notably Beaver, Blacker, Crow, Prickly Pear, Tizer, and Wilson creeks.

HOW TO GET THERE: From Helena drive 4 miles south on I-15. Take the Montana City exit and turn left (east) and then right (south) on Saddle Mountain Drive at the Montana City School. Drive about 4 miles south (and 0.5 mile past the national forest boundary). Turn left toward Crystal Creek on FR 4017 and drive about 2 miles to Jackson Creek Road 294. Turn right and drive through a mile or so of private land. Shortly after re-entering national forest land take the first spur road to the left and park at the locked gate. Trail 343 bypasses the private land and climbs up the East Fork of Jackson Creek to Casey Meadows.

DAY HIKE OR SKI TOUR

Casey Meadows
Distance: 4 miles out-and-back.
Difficulty: Easy.
Topo map: Casey Peak-MT.

In the big fire year of 1988 the Casey Meadows-Beaver Creek country was burned in the 48,000-acre Warm Springs fire, providing an opportunity to observe post-fire plant succession. Trail 343 climbs gradually for 2 miles to Casey Meadows, up the once-forested East Fork of McClellan Creek. The large, steep grassy meadows are about 1,000 feet above the trailhead.

DAY HIKE OR OVERNIGHTER

Casey Peak Loops
Distance 10 to 11 miles, or a 15-mile loop.
Difficulty: Strenuous.
Topo map: Casey Peak-MT.

If you've got the time and energy after reaching Casey Meadows as described above, go for Casey Peak, which rises to 8,499 feet directly to the south. Take Trail 301 through the trees on the right, climbing for another mile to the Casey Peak junction for Trail 374. Take this trail for the easy walk up the northwest summit ridge, gaining the final 1,200 feet in about 1 mile. The top contains the burned remnants of an old fire lookout. Return options include going back the way you came or dropping down Teepee Creek on Trail

CROW CREEK FALLS.

301 and joining McClelland Creek Trail 302 back down to the trailhead. The latter would be a 10- to 11-mile loop. If you want even more adventure and have plenty of daylight you can hike cross-country about 1.5 miles southwest on the main divide to 8,534-foot High Peak. You'll drop into a heavily forested saddle and then climb a false summit before reaching the peak. After soaking up the view, drop about 500 feet down the southeast ridge and pick up Trail 113, which heads southwest on the contour to a saddle with a four-way trail junction. Go north on Trail 302 for another mile and then bear right on the same trail into upper McClellan Creek continuing all the way down the drainage for about 5 miles to the trailhead. This longer loop with two peak climbs is 15 miles with an elevation gain of more than 4,000 feet—an honest day in the mountains by anyone's standard. You may want to break up the trip by camping along McClellan Creek below the mouth of Teepee Creek, although at this point you're only 3 miles from your car.

Gates of the Mountains Wilderness Complex

44

Location: 15 miles north of Helena.
Size: 69,607 acres.
Administration: USDAFS—Helena National Forest; Bureau of Land Management—Headwaters Resource Area; Montana Department of Fish, Wildlife & Parks.
Management status: Gates of the Mountains Wilderness (28,562 acres); BLM Sleeping Giant Wilderness Study Area (10,414 acres); national forest roadless land (Big Log); and MDFW&P Beartooth Wildlife Management Area.
Ecosystems: Middle Rocky Mountain steppe-coniferous forest-alpine meadow province, Belt Mountains section, characterized by isolated mountains surrounded by plains and rolling hills; Madison limestone and Paleozoic shales, deep canyons, limestone cliffs, peaks and sharp ridges; foothills prairie and Douglas-fir forest type; many streams are intermittent with a dendritic drainage pattern.
Elevation range: 3,600 to 7,980 feet.
System trails: 66 miles.
Maximum core to perimeter distance: 5 miles.
Activities: Hiking, backpacking, cross-country skiing, horseback riding.
Modes of travel: Foot, ski, and horse.
Maps: 1983 Gates of the Mountains Wilderness Map-1-1/4"/mile contour; 1991 Helena National Forest Visitor Map; Sheep Creek-MT; Beartooth Mountain-MT; Candle Mountain-MT; Middle Creek Lake-MT; Upper Holter Lake-MT; Nelson-MT; and Hogback-MT.

OVERVIEW: When Meriwether Lewis and William Clark first entered the Rocky Mountains, it seemed as though the gigantic limestone cliffs along the Missouri River would block their passage. But then the river turned through a narrow gorge and the mountains appeared to open like a gate. Hence the name of the Wilderness core of a diverse 70,000-acre wildlands complex in the north end of the Big Belt Range.

West of the Missouri, the Sleeping Giant—officially known as Beartooth Mountain—resembles a huge fellow on his back with his feet toward the Continental Divide and the distinctive profile of his craggy face toward the Gates

44 GATES OF THE MOUNTAINS WILDERNESS COMPLEX

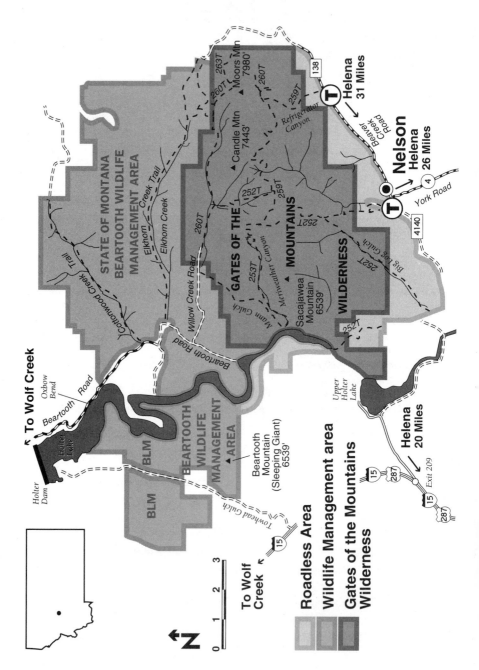

of the Mountains. The 6,792-foot giant's massive barrel chest is open grass-land with slow-growing ponderosa pine, limber pine, and Douglas-fir draping his sides and the lower ridges that form his arms. Nimble mountain goats climb the giant's huge nose and other facial features, which are the "bear teeth" of vertical rock outcroppings.

Here the effects of 300 million years of erosion on sedimentary rock beds have left an intriguing landscape of sheer cliffs, shallow caves, and spires. Dramatic folding and faulting of the limestone exposes fossil beds where animal and plant remains from the Mississippian period have been preserved in the most intricate detail. The jagged terrain of plunging canyons and bold knife ridges contrasts with higher-elevation parks where the landscape smooths into sloping meadows and open bald ridges. A rough-hewn character is left by the scars of past fires, such as the disastrous Mann Gulch fire of 1949 that left thirteen men dead, and the 1984 North Hills fire.

Osprey are common along the Missouri, as are surefooted goats on sheer cliffs above the river. Bighorn sheep were successfully transplanted onto the adjacent Beartooth Wildlife Management Area—an undeveloped expanse of winter range and deep canyons that was largely burned over in the fall of 1990.

RECREATIONAL USES: Compared to most other wilderness areas, recreational use is low in the dry, relatively small Gates of the Mountains Wilderness. Hunt-

CANDLE MOUNTAIN, A REMOTE NORTHERN SENTINEL OF THE GATES.

THE LIMESTONE SPIRES OF WILLOW CREEK IN THE GATES OF THE MOUNTAINS
WILDERNESS.

ing for big game and grouse accounts for about half of the use, with hiking,
backpacking, and horseback riding starting by mid- to late May. Most of the
recreation occurs between June and November. Wildflowers, a star attraction,
peak out by around mid-June. The rugged terrain confines most of the travel
to designated trails, most of which are well maintained annually. Water and
feed for horses are scarce, so most of the overnight horse use is concentrated
next to the two major springs and the four flowing creeks. The availability of
water determines the season and location of use. The fairly low visitation combined with the numerous steep, rugged limestone canyons provides exceptional
solitude close to existing roads. While hiking, one of the more interesting activities is the exploration of ancient limestone fossils beds.

There is little winter use of the Gates because of lack of snow at lower elevations. However, there is usually at least once or twice during the winter
when the hearty backcountry adventurer can cross-country ski or snowshoe
around 7,980-foot Moors Mountain, usually by way of Porcupine Creek on
the east side. Most of the access to the wilderness is via national forest land.
But two trailheads, Porcupine Creek and Grant Gulch, are on private land. It
is essential that visitors respect private property and close all gates. Three
trailheads are equipped with stock unloading facilities. Hunters Gulch Trail
255 has a corral, hitching rack, and unloading ramp at Nelson. A hitching rail
and unloading ramp are also available at the Refrigerator Canyon trailhead for
Trail 259.

On the northwest side of the complex, just west of Holter Lake, sits the BLM Sleeping Giant Wilderness Study Area—home to one of Montana's most distinctive landmarks. The open southern exposures of the giant are hikeable throughout much of the year, although forested ridges and protected draws will hold a couple of feet of snow into early April. Public access is limited to the shoreline of Holter Lake or from the frontage road along I-15 to the BLM Wood Siding Gulch road, which ends just west of the Sheep Creek/Sleeping Giant WSA boundary. For boaters on Holter Lake, a cove just northeast of the giant in section 2 gives access to a short hike through history to a picturesque early homestead, complete with log cabin, frame house, barn, shed, and root cellar.

How to get there: From the north end of Helena head northeast on MT 280, past Hauser Lake, for the 18 mile drive to York. Turn north at York on FR 4 and drive 8 miles to Nelson on Beaver Creek, which flows along the south edge of the Gates of the Mountains Wilderness. Turn right on Beaver Creek Road 138 for the remaining 5 winding miles to the Refrigerator Canyon trailhead for Trail 259.

For river access go about 17 miles north of Helena on I-15. Take the Gates of the Mountains exit and drive 2 miles to the Gates of the Mountains Boat Club on the north end of Upper Holter Lake.

DAY HIKE OR OVERNIGHTER

Refrigerator Canyon - Hunters Gulch

Distance: 15 miles point-to-point.
Difficulty: Moderate.
Topo maps: Candle Mountain-MT; Middle Creek Lake-MT; Nelson-MT; and Hogback Mountain-MT.

On Trail 259 (see above) climb into refreshing Refrigerator Canyon and then switchback up another 3 miles to the Moors Mountain junction. Turn left, continuing on Trail 259 another 5 miles to the aspen-parkland-meadow of centrally located Bear Prairie. En route, a short 500-foot scramble to the top of 7,443-foot Candle Mountain offers a magnificent open vista of rugged limestone ridges and canyons radiating in every direction. Water can normally be found at Bear Prairie and nearby Kennedy Springs, which partly explains why both sites have been heavily impacted in the past by camping. From just west of Kennedy Springs go south on the Big Log Trail 252, branching off to the left after a couple of miles on Trail 255 down scenic Hunters Gulch. You'll end up at Nelson about 5 miles below your vehicle. Unless you've arranged for a car shuttle, someone will need to walk, run, hitch, or mountain bike back to the Refrigerator Canyon trailhead.

DAY HIKE

Sleeping Giant

Distance: 14 to 16 miles round-trip.
Difficulty: Strenuous.
Topo map: Sheep Creek-MT and Beartooth Mountain-MT.

Although trailless, the Sleeping Giant offers enjoyable ridgeline hiking. Begin the climb from the Towhead Gulch Road, which provides the only public access from land to this remarkable geologic feature. The up-and-down route winds along a series of ridges above 6,000 feet at the head of Sheep Creek, crossing the Towhead/Falls Gulch divide at the powerline. Continue southeast on the main ridge to the top of the giant's great barrel chest, which rises to 6,792-foot Beartooth Mountain with a 900-foot ascent during the last mile. Look for mountain goats on the big fellow's craggy facial features, as well as a superb view east across the Missouri River to the adjacent Big Belt Range.

Mount Baldy

45

Location: 16 miles northeast of Townsend.
Size: 18,700 acres.
Administration: USDAFS—Helena National Forest.
Management status: Roadless non-wilderness with a small portion of area on north end allocated to future development in the forest plan.
Ecosystems: Middle Rocky Mountain coniferous forest-alpine meadow province, Belt Mountain section, characterized by high, isolated, glaciated mountains surrounded by plains and rolling foothills; Madison limestone and granite spires; Douglas-fir forest type and smaller areas of alpine vegetation; and a complex pattern of perennial streams with numerous lakes at higher elevations.
Elevation range: 6,025 to 9,467 feet.
System trails: 13 miles.
Maximum core to perimeter distance: 2.5 miles.
Activities: Hiking, backpacking, horseback riding, cross-country skiing, fishing.
Modes of travel: Foot, horse, and skis.
Maps: 1991 Helena National Forest Visitor Map; Gipsy Lake-MT; Mount Edith-MT (1:24,000 topo maps).

OVERVIEW: South of Duck Creek Pass, the Big Belt Mountains reach monumental proportions as they stretch a vertical mile from the Missouri River to more than 9,400 feet atop Mount Baldy and Mount Edith. More than 80 percent of this unroaded enclave rises above 7,000 feet, giving the country a distinctive alpine flavor. The main divide wraps around lush, north-facing Birch Creek basin, a huge glacial cirque holding a dozen jewel-like lakes.

On the north end of the basin a series of jagged granite spires known as The Needles guard an open meadow enclosed by lodgepole pine with hidden elk wallows. Wildlife here abounds, as illustrated by an early fall excursion some years back. While roaming the tundra plateaus of the Baldy-Edith ridge, I came across a dozen mountain goats in a high saddle. Like an apparition they vanished instantly into the swirling mountain mist. Continuing east I found myself in the midst of a golden eagle migration of at least 100 of the giant birds of prey circling over the rock-strewn tundra tabletop of Mount Edith.

RECREATIONAL USES: Birch Creek basin in the Mount Baldy Roadless Area is one of the few areas on the Helena National Forest where summer recreational

45 MOUNT BALDY

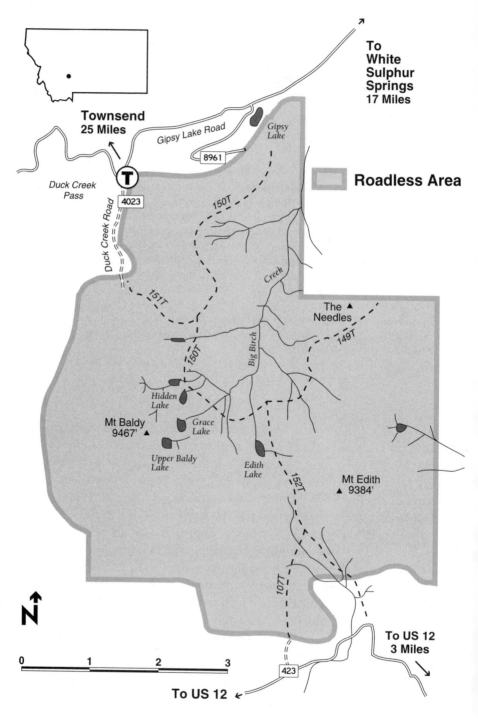

use exceeds hunting use. Hikers and backpackers are drawn to the classic mountain beauty of this pocket-sized alpine gem of glacial lakes and challenging terrain. Cutthroat trout inhabit Birch Creek, Gypsy Creek, and the four largest and deepest of the twelve sparkling high lakes. Small size and ease of access make the Birch Creek roadless area popular for short family outings. There is some late spring and late fall cross-country skiing, but caution is called for in the avalanche-prone Birch Creek basin below the main divide. Duck Creek pass is closed during winter and it may be a 6- to 8-mile ski or slog just to reach the pass before skiing into the roadless area.

HOW TO GET THERE: From Townsend, 32 miles southeast of Helena on US 12, drive 2 miles east on US 12 and turn left (north) on MT 284. Continue north 11 miles to the well-signed Duck Creek Road, turn right (east), and stay on the main road for about 12 miles to Duck Creek Pass. To reach the pass from White Sulphur Springs, head west out of town on MT 360 for 1.5 miles and go straight west when MT 360 turns north. Continue west on the main road another 16 miles to Duck Creek Pass. A new trail has been constructed from the pass bypassing the old jeep trail (FR 4023). The trail heads south from Duck Creek Pass along the main Big Belt Divide.

DAY HIKE OR OVERNIGHTER

Hidden Lake - Baldy Grand Tour
Distance: 8 miles out-and-back to Hidden Lake, or a 20- to 25-mile loop.
Difficulty: Moderate to strenuous.
Topo map: Mount Edith-MT.

From 7,515-foot Duck Creek Pass there are a number of out-and-back or loop trip options for either long day hikes or overnight backpacks.

From the pass climb steeply for about 1.5 miles to the microwave station where Trail 151 drops into lush springs and joins Trail 150 to Hidden Lake. The trail continues through the broad forested basin past Grace Lake and branches off on Trail 152 to Edith Lake. One choice is to make a base camp near any one of the lakes and hike to a new lake every day for as much time as you have available. You may want to avoid the more heavily impacted Hidden Lake as a campsite. The other, more strenuous option is to continue cross country along the main divide. After another mile with a bit of scrambling on talus rock you'll reach north Baldy at around 9,300 feet. This point opens up to a fantastic view of the hanging valleys of the basin all the way northeast to the protruding granite formation of The Needles. Already in this short distance you've achieved a fast way to really see the country and to get a good feeling for its alpine flavor. Two higher, more rugged Baldy peaks rise to the south,

MOUNT BALDY, AS SEEN FROM THE MAIN BIG BELT DIVIDE NORTH OF DUCK CREEK PASS.

whereas north Baldy is more rounded with a rocky tundra summit. After reaching the 9,467-foot top of Mount Baldy, drop into a broad saddle and make the easy 4-mile half-circle traverse to 9,384-foot Mount Edith. This is prime mountain goat country as well as an important golden eagle migration route in the early fall. Backtrack a short distance from Edith and follow the rock cairns down to Edith Lake. After soaking up the splendor of this sparkling high-country gem drop down 1 mile below the lake and either take a right on Trail 149 for a 3-mile side trip through dense forest to The Needles, or go left on the main Trail 150 through the basin to Hidden Lake, switchbacking back up to the main divide on Trail 151 to Duck Creek Pass and the trailhead.

Tenderfoot/ Deep Creek

46

Location: 28 miles south of Great Falls and 25 miles north of White Sulphur Springs.
Size: 98,500 acres.
Administration: USDAFS—Lewis & Clark National Forest.
Management status: Roadless non-wilderness, with some portions of the area allocated to future development in the forest plan.
Ecosystems: Middle Rocky Mountain coniferous forest-alpine meadow province, Belt Mountain section, characterized by high, isolated mountains surrounded by plains and rolling hills; Precambrian metamorphic and Cretaceous soft sedimentary rocks with widespread limestone outcroppings along water courses; foothills prairie and Douglas-fir-eastern ponderosa forest types; and widely spaced perennial streams with a dominantly dendritic drainage pattern.
Elevation range: 3,800 to 7,595 feet.
System trails: 101 miles.
Maximum core to perimeter distance: 3.5 miles.
Activities: Hiking, backpacking, river floating, cross-country skiing, horseback riding, mountain biking, fishing.
Modes of travel: Foot, horse, skis, mountain bike, boat (canoe, kayak, and raft are most popular on the Smith River).
Maps: 1988 Lewis & Clark National Forest/Jefferson Division Visitor Map; The Smith River from Fort Logan to the Missouri River, No. 9 in the Montana Afloat series of floater's maps; Millegan-MT; Deep Creek Park-MT; Blankenbaker Flats-MT; Lingshire NE-MT; Bald Hills-MT; Monument Peak-MT; and Bubbling Springs-MT (1:24,000 topo maps).

OVERVIEW: The largest expanse of unroaded country in the Little Belt Mountains, Tenderfoot-Deep Creek has 24 miles of the wild Smith River as its western boundary. The 61-mile stretch of the Smith from Camp Baker to Eden Bridge is Montana's premier overnight float, with 400-foot limestone walls, an easy gradient of S-curves, and good fishing when the water clears for native cutthroat and rainbow upstream and brown trout downstream. The deepest, most impressive canyons enclose the river from just above the mouth of Tenderfoot Creek north and downstream to where Deep Creek empties into the Smith.

Other attractions include the 25-mile Deep Creek loop national recreation trail, a series of 20- to 30-foot waterfalls on Tenderfoot Creek, and a blend of large meadows and dense forests favored by elk, deer, moose, and black bear.

46 TENDERFOOT/DEEP CREEK

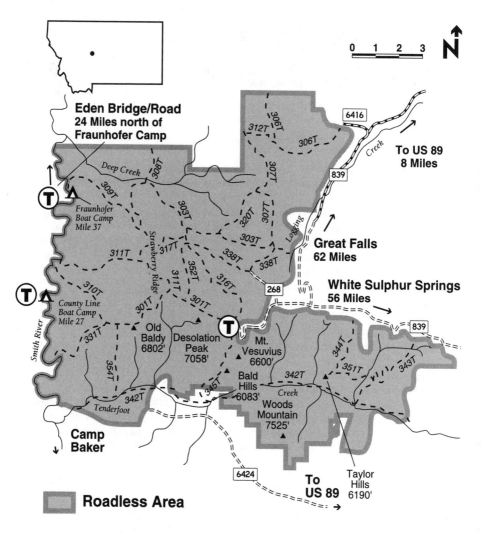

Eden Bridge/Road
24 Miles north of
Fraunhofer Camp

0 1 2 3 N

6416

To US 89
8 Miles

839

Deep Creek

Fraunhofer
Boat Camp
Mile 37

Great Falls
62 Miles

White Sulphur Springs
56 Miles

268

839

Smith River

County Line
Boat Camp
Mile 27

Old
Baldy
6802'

Desolation
Peak
7058'

Mt.
Vesuvius
6600'

Bald
Hills
6083'

Creek

Woods
Mountain
7525'

Tenderfoot

Camp
Baker

6424

To
US 89

Taylor
Hills
6190'

Roadless Area

Tepee rings, pictographs, tools, and arrowheads along the Smith bring to life images of prehistoric Indians hunting, camping, and traveling along this tributary of the Missouri. The Smith was named by Lewis and Clark in 1805 in honor of Thomas Jefferson's secretary of the Navy.

RECREATIONAL USES: The star attractions in these western Little Belt Mountains are big-game hunting in the fall, along with fishing and floating. Indeed, the serpentine Smith River is one of Montana's most popular overnight float trips, so popular that the Montana Department of Fish, Wildlife & Parks has instituted a much-needed permit-reservation system. Up to nine groups per day can launch from Camp Baker, only one of which can be an outfitted party. Each party must pay $15/person, which goes into the river management fund. At the time of the launch each group must declare its campsites for the nights they'll be on the river. Reservations must be made well in advance with the Great Falls office of the department. The relatively short floating season, normally from April to early July, is booked solid early in the year. Most people complete the 60-mile journey to Eden Bridge in three to four days by raft, canoe, or kayak but adding an extra day allows for fascinating side hikes and a more leisurely pace. The cultural enthusiast can search for pictographs, tepee rings, and other evidence of prehistoric use of what was likely a major Native American travel corridor. Numerous rock gardens and S-curves make for a challenging float, especially in high water. There are two class II/III rapids at

FRAUNHOFER BOAT CAMP ON THE NORTHWEST CORNER OF THE TENDERFOOT-DEEP CREEK.

mile 49. For the most part the river follows a gentle gradient, cutting through a spectacular 300- to 400-foot deep limestone canyon. Often by June irrigation reduces the flow to the point where floaters must drag their boats in places.

One road penetrates the roadless area. From the west this low-standard road crosses the Smith and goes east about 4 miles to Deep Creek Park. Another road touches the east-central boundary to access Daisy Spring and an abandoned fire lookout on Monument Peak. The country has a large, well-distributed trail system along major drainages and ridges; the routes are ideal for hiking, backpacking, and horseback riding. All of these trails are accessible from Forest Service roads along the eastern boundary, which are also used by mountain bikers. The higher ridgetop trails would be excellent for cross-country skiing but long distances from plowed roads limit winter use. The highest summits are forested mountains in the south-central reaches—Desolation Peak, Old Baldy, and Mount Vesuvius.

How to get there: From Great Falls head southeast for 36 miles, first on US 87 past Belt, then south on US 89 to Monarch Canyon. Turn right (west) on FR 839, which reaches the national forest boundary after about 5 miles. Continue on FR 839 to Logging Creek and then up Logging Creek for about 15 miles to FR 268. Turn right (west) and go another 6 miles to Daisy Spring, passing the Monument Peak Lookout en route. Daisy Spring is the trailhead for Trail 345 to Tenderfoot Creek. The trailhead for two trails leading toward Deep Creek, trails 301 and 316, is located at a switchback on FR 268 about 0.5 mile before reaching Daisy Spring.

From White Sulphur Springs, take US 89 north for 18 miles. Turn left (west) on FR 119 and go about 4 miles to Moose Creek Road (FR 204). Turn right and drive 10 miles northeast up Moose Creek to FR 839. Go left and drive west-northwest for about 18 miles to FR 268. Turn left on FR 268 and go 6 miles west to Daisy Spring.

The country may also be accessed directly from the Smith River during a float trip where the roadless area meets the right (east) bank between river miles 16 and 40. The most popular and feasible float in terms of public access and water levels is the 60-mile stretch from Camp Baker to Eden Bridge. To reach Camp Baker take the Fort Logan road northwest from White Sulphur Springs for about 15 miles to the well-signed Camp Baker turnoff. Head north on this good gravel road. After about 10 miles turn left onto a winding lower standard road and drive about 1 mile, crossing the Smith River, to the spacious Camp Baker camping area and launch site.

DAY HIKE OR OVERNIGHTER

Upper Deep Creek
Distance: 12- to 13-mile loop.
Difficulty: Strenuous as a day hike; more moderate as an overnighter.
Topo maps: Deep Creek Park-MT; Blankenbaker Flats-MT; and Monument Peak-MT.

Begin at an elevation of 6,440 feet by taking Trail 301 west to 7,058-foot Desolation Peak. Continue across a broad, open saddle to the high point of 7,222 feet. Just below the rise take the right-hand Trail 352, which drops evenly down a north-running ridge to the South Fork of Deep Creek at about 4,550 feet. There is a good campsite 0.5 mile down where the North Fork joins the South Fork. To complete the loop take Trail 316 up the South Fork all the way back to where you began, gradually gaining 1,900 feet over a distance of 5 to 6 miles of forested canyon and rocky slideslopes. This loop from the central-east boundary is an excellent sampler of the mountainous heart of this Montana expanse of undeveloped wildlife habitat.

SMITH RIVER DAY HIKES

County Line Boat Camp
Distance: 2 to 6 miles out-and-back.
Difficulty: Moderate.
Topo map: Millegan-MT.

From the County Line Boat Camp at river mile 27 on the right (east) bank climb to the prominent limestone cliffs immediately upriver. Using game trails and bushwhacking up through Douglas-fir forest and limestone ledges, climb 600 feet above the river to the overlook for one of the most spectacular views of any of the countless short hikes above the Smith. Continuing, this hike will lead you to a series of points that narrow to a sharp ridge which eventually connects to the higher peaks to the east. After 2 miles the ridge intersects Trail 310, which climbs above sheer cliffs that plummet into Bear Gulch.

DEEP CREEK OVERLOOK

Fraunhofer Boat Camp
Distance: 4 miles.
Difficulty: Moderate.
Topo maps: Millegan-MT and Deep Creek Park-MT.

From the Fraunhofer Boat Camp at river mile 37 climb 400 feet through open forest to an obvious gap on a narrow ridge. Drop into the gully on the

LIMESTONE WALLS TOWER 400 FEET ABOVE THE SMITH RIVER.

other side and pick up an old trail leading up the drainage. Continue climbing on this trail another 600 feet to a grassy park along the main south ridge above Deep Creek. Walk out to the overlook at an unnamed 4,902-foot point for a grand vista of the incredibly rugged limestone cliffs towering above the streambed of Deep Creek. Ironically, Deep Creek is usually dry here.

It's worth ambling southeast another 0.3 mile to a high point at 4,995 feet for a slightly different angle on Deep Creek. This is a moderate 4-mile round-trip with a 1,100-foot gain in elevation. The old jeep track (Trail 309) continues southeast 3 miles to the expansive Deep Creek Park, which has several developments for livestock grazing, such as drift fences and stock ponds. At Deep Creek Park it is possible to connect with several trails for more extended loop trips through the center of the roadless area.

Middle Fork Judith

47

Location: 21 miles northeast of White Sulphur Springs and 19 miles southwest of Stanford.
Size: 92,145 acres.
Administration: USDAFS—Lewis & Clark National Forest.
Management status: Congressional Wilderness Study Area.
Ecosystems: Middle Rocky Mountain coniferous forest-alpine meadow province, Belt Mountain section, characterized by high, isolated mountains surrounded by plains and rolling hills; Precambrian metamorphic and cretaceous soft sedimentary rocks with limestone outcroppings along major water courses; foothills prairie and Douglas-fir-eastern ponderosa forest types; and widely spaced perennial streams with a dominantly dendritic drainage pattern.
Elevation range: 4,960 to 8,801 feet.
System trails: 130 miles.
Maximum core to perimeter distance: 4.5 miles.
Activities: Hiking, backpacking, horseback riding, cross-country skiing, mountain biking, fishing.
Modes of travel: Foot, skis, horse, mountain bike.
Maps: 1988 Lewis & Clark National Forest Visitor Map; Yogo Peak-MT; Bandbox Mountain-MT; Kings Hill-MT; Sand Point-MT; Ettien Spring-MT; Indian Hill-MT; and Hoover Spring-MT (1:24,000 topo maps).

OVERVIEW: The heart of the eastern Little Belt Mountains is the wild country draining into the Middle Fork of the Judith River—one of only two Montana Wilderness Study Areas east of the main range of the Rockies. This circular expanse of unroaded elk range stretches for 17 miles from the striking headwall basins of the Middle and Lost forks to lower foothills and canyons, with a north-south span of 13 miles. Broad, moderately rolling ridges rise above thickets of elk-hiding lodgepole interspersed with limestone outcrops and grassy parks.

The Middle Fork Judith is the only year-round stream flowing east from the Little Belts. A small pure-strain population of cutthroat trout inhabits the upper Lost Fork despite a high natural silt load. Roadless security and prime habitat combine to make the Middle Fork elk herd one of the most prolific in Montana, with a cow-calf ratio often surpassing 50 percent. Chalk white limestone cliffs pocketed with caves guard the lower 4 miles of the Middle Fork as it leaves the mountains for its journey through the plains.

47 MIDDLE FORK JUDITH

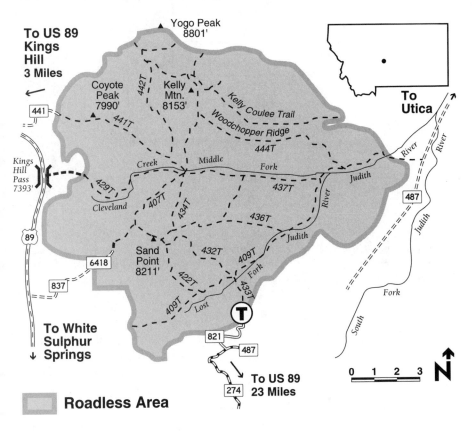

Roadless Area

RECREATIONAL USES: The remote Middle Fork Judith country offers its relatively few visitors ample solitude. As with most of the island ranges, the most popular activity is the fall pursuit of big game. Motorized recreation is fairly widespread, even though many of the trails are closed to motorized vehicles during hunting season. The Middle and Lost forks offer spotty fishing for native cutthroat trout. The winter enthusiast can rent the Forest Service cabin atop Kings Hill on US 89 on the western edge of the roadless area. From there day ski tours can be taken along the high ridges at the head of the Middle Fork along with several trails that drop steeply into the main drainage. Each winter a few experienced skiers spend three to four days traversing down the Middle Fork from Kings Hill.

YOGO PEAK—HIGHEST AND NORTHERNMOST POINT OF THE MIDDLE FORK JUDITH.

The following low-standard jeep roads skirt the edge of the wilderness study area and are not suitable for low-clearance vehicles: Grendah Mountain primitive Road 437; Ettien Ridge primitive Road 821; and primitive Road 251 across a 4-mile section of Yogo Peak. These primitive tracks are excellent for mountain biking to the start of several steep trails that can then be hiked into the heart of the roadless area. Several other peripheral roads can be used in dry weather by passenger cars, including Weatherwax Creek Road 2056; Yogo Creek Road 266 (from Utica and US 200); Memorial Way Road 487; South Fork Deadman Road 837 (from US 89); Jefferson Creek roads 3328/3356 (from US 89); and the Dry Wolf Road 251 from about midway between Tepee Butte and Yogo Peak.

HOW TO GET THERE: From White Sulphur Springs drive about 18 miles east on US 12 to Checkerboard. Continue another 6 miles east of Checkerboard, turn north on Spring Creek Road (FR 274), and drive about 20 miles to FR 487. Turn right onto FR 487 and continue 1 mile northeast to where FR 487 joins FR 821 at Big Hill. Turn left (north) on FR 821 and go about 2 miles to the Holiday Camp trailhead for Trail 433, which drops steeply to the Burris Cabin on the Lost Fork. This trailhead can also be reached by way of FR 487 (Memorial Way Road) from Utica on the east side of the Little Belts.

BACKPACK

Middle Fork - Lost Fork Loop

Distance: 30-mile loop (3 days).
Difficulty: Moderate.
Topo maps: Sand Point-MT and Ettien Spring-MT.

Unlike most backcountry journeys, this one begins by dropping rather than climbing. The Burris Trail 433 descends 3 miles from the ridgetop to the Burris cabin on the Lost Fork of the Judith. There are lots of good campsites along this lovely stream. From the old homestead site of the cabin take Trail 409 1.5 miles up the Lost Fork and turn right on Trail 422 for a 4-mile climb through rolling uplands on up to the open knob of 8,211-foot Sand Point. From here the 11,000-acre Sand Point fire of 1985 presents an excellent opportunity to observe the ever-changing natural effects of fire on plant communities, with its profusion of new grasses, forbs, and lodgepole pine seedlings. From Sand Point go northwest for about 0.5 mile to a trail junction. Take a right and head north down Doerr Creek on Trail 407 for the enjoyable 3-mile roll to the Middle Fork Judith ranch. This is private land so before camping take a right and continue downstream at least 3 miles to where the primitive jeep track again enters national forest land. From here on down there are ample camping spots along the river.

As you continue down to the confluence with the Lost Fork, towering limestone cliffs surround the trail. The Lost Fork comes in about 7 miles below the Middle Fork ranch. From this point you will have dropped about 3,300 feet from Sand Point over a distance of about 11 miles. Take a right on Trail 409 and head up the Lost Fork for about 7 miles back to the Burris Cabin, crossing the stream four or five times en route. From the cabin retrace your route back up to the trailhead, thereby completing a 30-mile loop through one of the largest and most diverse roadless areas in central Montana.

Big Snowy Mountains

48

Location: 15 miles south of Lewistown.
Size: 104,755 acres.
Administration: USDAFS—Lewis & Clark National Forest; and Bureau of Land Management—Judith Resource Area.
Management status: Congressional Wilderness Study Area of 97,885 acres and adjacent BLM Twin Coulees Wilderness Study Area of 6,870 acres.
Ecosystems: Middle Rocky Mountain coniferous forest-alpine meadow province, Belt Mountain section, characterized by high, isolated mountains surrounded by plains and rolling hills; Precambrian metamorphic and cretaceous soft sedimentary rocks with limestone ridges, tabletops, and outcroppings along some watercourses; foothills prairie and Douglas-fir/eastern ponderosa forest types; widely spaced perennial streams with some streams being intermittent. An unusual stand of Englemann spruce grows in the Twin Coulees area on the southeast corner of the roadless area.
Elevation range: 5,200 to 8,681 feet.
System trails: 80 miles.
Maximum core to perimeter distance: 5 miles.
Activities: Hiking, backpacking, spelunking, horseback riding, and cross-country skiing.
Modes of travel: Foot, skis, and horse.
Maps: 1988 Lewis & Clark National Forest/Jefferson Division Visitor Map; Crystal Lake-MT; Jump Off Peak-MT; Half Moon Canyon-MT; Alaska Bench-MT; Yaple Bench-MT; Snow Saucer Coulee-MT; Green Ashley Gulch-MT; and Patterson Canyon-MT.

OVERVIEW: The tilted limestone beds of the Big Snowy Mountains thrust 3,000 feet above a sea of dry grasslands just south of Montana's geographical center at Lewistown. From a distance, the east-west crest looks bare and level above steep, heavily forested faces separating narrow avalanche chutes. Up close the summit ridge is indeed a flat tundra-covered plain for nearly half of a 22-mile corridor of wild country that occupies almost all of this high mountain island. The north side of the range is moist enough to support lodgepole pine, spruce, and Douglas-fir. Bowl-shaped headwalls are carved into the dry craggy southern face of the arching Big Snowies.

Folding and warping of the sedimentary rock have given these mountains their distinctive personality—a broad, relatively flat crest with limestone cliffs, steep cirques, and U-shaped canyons draining to the Great Plains. On

48 BIG SNOWY MOUNTAINS

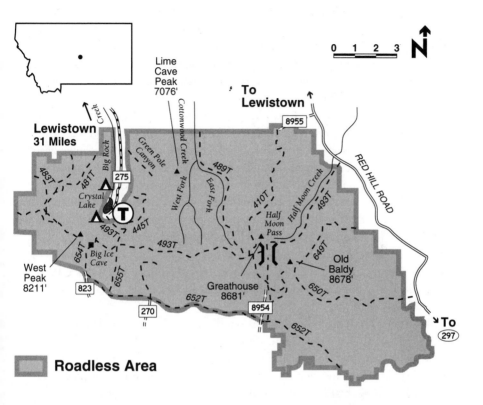

☐ **Roadless Area**

the east end, Knife Blade Ridge becomes easier to negotiate for mountain goats than for hikers; it follows a precipice that drops sharply on both sides. On a clear day vistas from the high point of the range—8,681-foot Greathouse Peak—encompass the entire width of Montana from Canada to Yellowstone. On the west end, spelunkers are attracted to the Devil's Chute and Ice Cave, as well as to other as yet unexplored limestone caverns. The frozen-walled room of Ice Cave is typically 40 degrees cooler than the outside summer temperature.

RECREATIONAL USES: Day hiking and hunting are the most popular activities in the Big Snowies along with some early season backpacking and peripheral cross-country skiing in several of the canyon bottoms. Lack of water, especially along the high crest of the range, limits extended backpacking trips after about the first of July. The only campground adjacent to the wilderness study area is at Crystal Lake on the northwest corner. The six-person capacity Crystal Lake cabin can be rented from October 15 to April 30; contact the Judith Ranger District. Crystal Lake Road (FR 275) on Rock Creek is plowed to within 6 miles of the cabin, but early and late-season snow conditions are usually marginal for ski touring. The 80 miles of maintained trails throughout the area are primarily horse and hiker trails. Half Moon and Swimming Woman trails are part of the NeeMePoo National Recreation Trail, which commemorates the route taken by the Nez Perce Indians in their flight toward Canada.

Almost every canyon bottom has a low-standard road that reaches the edge of the roadless area, although access through private land is extremely limited. Major attractions include Ice Cave and Devil's Chute Cave on the west end of the main ridge, and Crystal Cascades southeast of the campground. There are several unexplored caves in the limestone formations, some of which drop vertically from the top of the main ridge. Excellent fossil specimens have been found on the uplifted plateaus. Canyon walls, cliffs, unique rock formations, and alpine tundra along the crest are among the scenic attractions. The isolation of the narrow valleys and canyons leading to the crest provide a high degree of solitude. The west end of the Big Snowies receives the most day use because of public access from Crystal Lake. In addition to the Crystal Lake Road there is legal public access via the Cottonwood Creek Road (Trail 489), and up Timber Creek (FR 270), Niel Creek, and the Big Snowy Trail 650. Red Hill Road provides undeveloped public access along the east end of the range.

How to get there: From Lewistown drive 9 miles west on US 87/MT 200. Turn south on Crystal Lake/Rock Creek Road and drive about 16 miles to the national forest boundary where the road designation changes to FR 275. Continue another 6 miles, past Crystal Lake, to the campground which is also the trailhead for Trail 493.

Day Trip

Ice Cave Loop
Distance: 12-mile loop.
Difficulty: Moderate.
Topo map: Crystal Lake-MT.

Begin at the trailhead for Uhlhorn Trail 493 at the south end of Crystal Lake near the campground. The trail gains 2,000 feet to the crest of the Big Snowies in only 3 miles. From here the steep pull turns into mellow hiking in both directions across high, open tundra on fractured limestone table rock interspersed with windswept jumbles of gnarled trees. To explore the unusual Ice Cave take West Peak Trail 493 about 1.5 miles west to Trail 654. Take Trail 654 downhill 0.2 mile through scattered rocks and trees to the ice cave, which is a single large room full of ice. For a loop back to Crystal Lake double back to Trail 493 and head back down the trail about 1.5 miles to Trail 445. Go right on this trail, past the Crystal Cascades, ending up about 2 miles below the Crystal Lake campground.

UPPER HALF MOON CREEK, BELOW THE MAIN EASTERN CREST OF THE BIG SNOWIES.

OVERNIGHT BACKPACK

Knife Blade Ridge
Distance: 27 miles out-and-back.
Difficulty: Moderate.
Topo maps: Crystal Lake-MT; Jump Off Peak-MT; and Half Moon Canyon-MT.

For a grand overnight backpack, hike the 10 miles of relatively flat crest east from the junction of trails 493 and 490 to the high point in the range—8,681-foot Greathouse Peak. Water is the limiting factor, but early summer camping is usually feasible by melting water from intermittent snow banks. Find a level tent site on the lee side of a tree thicket next to a snowbank and you'll have an unparalleled "top of the world" experience. The crestline Trail 493 heading east is marked by cairns, but for the most part a trail isn't needed across this alpine prairie. The wide crest narrows to only a few feet along the Knife Blade Ridge at the head of the vast amphitheater of Careless Creek. On the east end of the ridge the trail drops into a little pass where trails take off in four directions. Stay on Trail 410 along the main ridge for the remaining 0.5-mile easy walk to the top. On a clear day you can almost see the breadth of Montana—from Canada to Yellowstone! The plateau summit also offers a bird's-eye view of the rugged limestone canyons of Half Moon, Swimming Woman, and the east forks of Cottonwood and Big Spring creeks.

Highwood
Mountains

49

Location: 25 miles east of Great Falls.
Size: 39,900 acres.
Administration: USDAFS—Lewis & Clark National Forest.
Management status: Roadless non-wilderness, with some lands allocated to future development in the forest plan.
Ecosystems: Middle Rocky Mountain coniferous forest-alpine meadow province, Belt Mountain section, characterized by high, isolated mountains surrounded by plains and rolling hills; igneous volcanic rocks; foothills prairie and Douglas-fir forest type; and widely spaced perennial (some intermittent) streams.
Elevation range: 4,540 to 7,670 feet.
System trails: 20 miles.
Maximum core to perimeter distance: 2 miles.
Activities: Hiking, backpacking, horseback riding, small stream fishing, cross-country skiing, mountain biking.
Modes of travel: Foot, skis, horse, and mountain bike.
Maps: 1988 Lewis & Clark National Forest/Jefferson Division Visitor Map; Highwood Baldy-MT; Arrow Peak-MT, and Palisade Butte-MT (1:24,000 topo map).

OVERVIEW: The exposed rock walls of an igneous dike connect distinctive Square Butte to the main range of the Highwood Mountains east of Great Falls. Geologists believe that this tight cluster of 7,000-foot volcanic peaks blocked the advance of continental glaciers 30,000 years ago. The Highwoods are a compact blend of meadows, forest, and talus slopes split by a low-standard road that fords Highwood Creek a half dozen times, slicing the unroaded lands into a western third and eastern two-thirds. Narrow coulees with aspen groves lead to spacious, gently sloping meadows ringed by mature lodgepole pine and Douglas-fir that originated from a large turn-of-the-century fire. The land is uncommonly lush for "east of the divide" central Montana country, which partially explains why a sizable herd of 800 elk thrive in this montane island in a sea of prairie and cultivated farmland.

RECREATIONAL USES: The Highwood Range is the closest national forest land, as well as forested land, to Great Falls and therefore attracts lots of local use. The most popular recreation is big game and upland bird hunting, hiking, fishing, camping, and horseback riding. Firewood gathering also brings many visitors here. The country is heavily hunted for elk with both archery and rifle. The east half of the Highwoods receives the greater amount of recreational use

49 HIGHWOODS

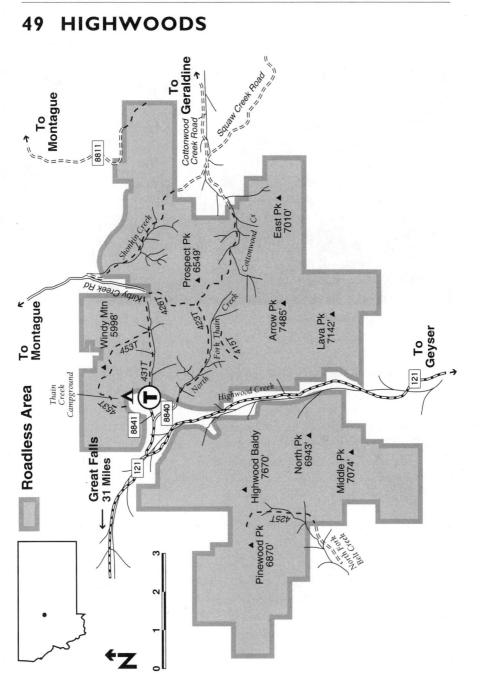

SOUTH SIDE OF THE HIGHWOODS.

because it has more water sources and more trails, as well as an adjacent camp-ground. The upper reaches of the mountains offer gentle hiking with moder-ate slopes and good trail access, and are within 2 to 3 miles of a road. There is little overnight backcountry use because of the nearby Thain Creek Camp-ground, which is heavily used by RV campers. Despite the small size of the two rectangular roadless units, solitude is provided by narrow, steep-sided coulees. Aspen groves are common in the bottoms, exploding into dazzling yellows and golds by late September, which is an excellent time to visit this isolated moun-tain island.

HOW TO GET THERE: From just east of Malmstrom Air Force Base at Great Falls, take CR 228 about 12 miles to Fox Corners. Continue straight ahead (east) across Belt Creek and on to North Willow Creek. After about 7 miles turn left (northeast) onto the main road to Highwood Creek. In another 3 miles the road crosses Highwood Creek and joins Highwood Creek Road 121. Turn right and head east up Highwood Creek about 7 miles to the national forest boundary where the road splits. Take the left-hand fork, FR 8841, and con-tinue east for the final 1.5 mile to Thain Creek campground on Briggs Creek, which is just south of the low-standard road that leads onto Thain Creek Trail 453.

DAY HIKE OR OVERNIGHTER

Windy Mountain Loop
Distance: 12-mile loop.
Difficulty: Moderate.
Topo map: Arrow Peak-MT.

Begin the trip from either Thain Creek Campground or about 0.5 mile up the primitive Thain Creek Road to where it turns into Trail 453 to Windy Mountain. As it climbs into the head of Thain Creek the trail winds east along the south slopes of the volcanic mound of 5,998-foot Windy Mountain, which is well worth a quick side scramble for the view. Continue south into Grant Creek, meeting Trail 431 at the head of the drainage. After about 1 mile the trail briefly enters private land on Kirby Creek. Turn right and head up Kirby Creek on Trail 426 where it quickly re-enters national forest. There are grassy meadow campsites on both Kirby Creek and in the upper reaches of the North Fork of Highwood Creek where Trail 423 joins in. A 3-mile round-trip hike to the top of 6,549-foot Prospect Peak affords a grand view east to the prominent volcanic laccoliths of Round Butte and Square Butte. Trail 423 down the North Fork eventually becomes the low-standard FR 8840 for a mile or so to its intersection with the main road, FR 8841. Turn right on FR 8841 for the 0.5-mile walk back to Thain Creek campground, thereby completing a 12-mile exploratory loop through the northern Highwood Mountains. During summer you'll likely be sharing the country with cattle and a few trailbikers; trailbikes are allowed on these Highwood trails until October 15.

Missouri Breaks
Complex

50

Location: West End—77 river miles downstream from Fort Benton to The Wall; and 50 miles north of Lewistown to the Judith River.
Central—the James Kipp State Park on the Missouri is 70 miles southwest of Malta and 63 miles northeast of Lewistown.
East End—33 miles south of Glasgow to Sheep Creek.
Size: 407,492 acres.
Administration: Bureau of Land Management—Judith, Phillips, and Valley resource areas; and U.S. Fish & Wildlife Service—Charles M. Russell and UL Bend national wildlife refuges.
Management status: National Wild & Scenic River status for 149 miles of the Upper Missouri from Fort Benton to the James Kipp State Park on the Charles M. Russell NWR; UL Bend Wilderness of 20,819 acres on the UL Bend NWR; BLM Wilderness Study Areas (Six WSA's totaling about 97,000 acres); nearly 200,000 acres of National Wildlife Refuge roadless lands; plus additional BLM roadless non-wilderness lands lacking formal designation or protection.
Ecosystems: Great Plains dry steppe province, Northwestern glaciated plains section, characterized by gently rolling to steep, dissected continental glacial till plains and rolling hills on the Missouri Plateau with steep breaks and badlands along the Missouri River and tributary valleys; Mesozoic shales covered by glacial till with non-marine sediments in the south; grama-needlegrass-wheatgrass vegetative type with eastern ponderosa forest; a high-density dendritic drainage pattern on areas of exposed marine shales, most streams seasonal.
Elevation range: 2,247 to 3,450 feet.
System trails: There are no formal trails, although numerous primitive (unconstructed and unmaintained) vehicle ways exist in some of the BLM lands, which facilitate travel by foot, mountain bike, or horse.
Maximum core to perimeter distance: 5 miles.
Activities: Hiking (canyoneering in a few places), backpacking, horseback riding, mountain biking (on some vehicle ways in dry conditions), floating, and fishing.
Modes of travel: Foot, horse, mountain bike, boat.
Maps: BLM Upper Missouri Wild & Scenic River Maps 1 & 2 and 3 & 4 (1"/mile contour); Charles M. Russell National Wildlife Refuge-MT Guide Map (showing road designations and closures); 1:100,000 topographic series ownership maps (BLM) or Woodland Area (US Geological Survey); Winifred-MT; Zortman-MT; Fort Peck Lake West-MT; and Fort Peck Lake East-MT. (See Appendix D for a listing of the 52 1:24,000 topographic maps covering the complex).

50 MISSOURI BREAKS COMPLEX

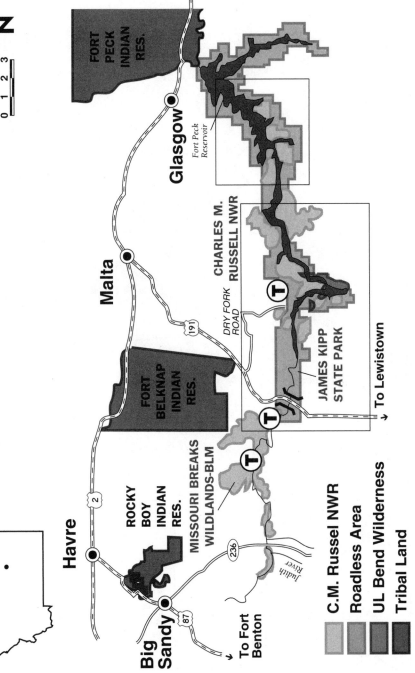

50A MISSOURI BREAKS COMPLEX-
CENTRAL

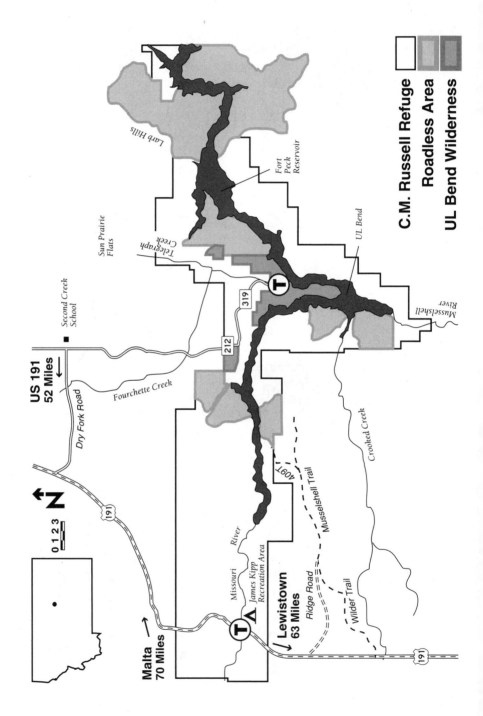

OVERVIEW: The last wild 7 percent of the Missouri is a National Wild and Scenic River for 149 miles, from historic Fort Benton downstream to the Fred Robinson Bridge on the west end of the Charles M. Russell National Wildlife Refuge. The Charlie Russell stretches another 120 miles, enveloping Fort Peck Reservoir. From the Judith River country downriver, twenty-one roadless areas are managed by the Bureau of Land Management (BLM) and the U.S. Fish & Wildlife Service (FWS). Actually, this Missouri Breaks wildland complex of 407,492 acres is really ONE magnificent 160-mile linear west-to-east wilderness from the Judith country to the east end of the Charlie Russell. Although separated from each other by mostly low-standard roads and jeep tracks that are impassable when wet, these twenty-one unroaded tracts share the common thread of the wild Missouri River, making them in total the fifth-largest roadless and undeveloped complex in Montana.

A person can stand on the cultivated benchlands above the Missouri and have no idea that the wild breaks are below. Conversely, when deep in the breaks visitors have a profound sense of being completely cut off from the rest of the world.

Mule deer are the most abundant large mammals in the breaks. Mature big-bodied bucks display high sweeping racks, as opposed to the wider sets of antlers more common elsewhere. Whitetails are limited from Cow Island downstream, where heavy brush adjoins crop lands near the river. Several transplants since 1951 have restored thriving herds of elk to densely forested parts of the breaks. The last of the Audubon bighorns was killed near Billy Creek in 1916. In 1979, twenty-seven bighorn sheep were planted at Chimney Bend. The sheep have gradually expanded both numbers and territory upstream as far as Stafford, and are readily visible from the river. Sharp-tailed grouse thrive where grasslands rise into brushy coulees. Pheasant are found on islands and in river bottoms of impenetrable rosehips. The Missouri supports a warm-water fishery of sauger, catfish, walleye, and paddlefish—prehistoric relics that often exceed 100 pounds.

Let us begin a hypothetical canoe voyage down the wild Missouri with a brief look at each of the roadless components of the Missouri Breaks wildland complex—from The Wall on down to Sheep Creek.

The Wall is a narrow 12,200-acre strip touching 15 miles of the north shore. Cottonwoods parallel the river with the rugged, dissected face of The Wall appearing as an almost vertical mat of prairie grasses and sagebrush. Sheltered coulees hide tiny pockets of juniper and pine, with tepee rings on the bluffs overlooking an old homestead.

Immediately downriver from the historic PN Ranch, BLM's 5,150-acre Dog Creek South Wilderness Study Area (WSA) borders 5 miles of the south bank. Heavily eroded open clay slopes plummet from sharp, barren ridges. The long, thin 4,800-acre Stafford WSA extends for 9 miles directly across the river from Dog Creek. Flat ridges drop almost vertically with soils too loose to support

50B MISSOURI BREAKS COMPLEX-EAST

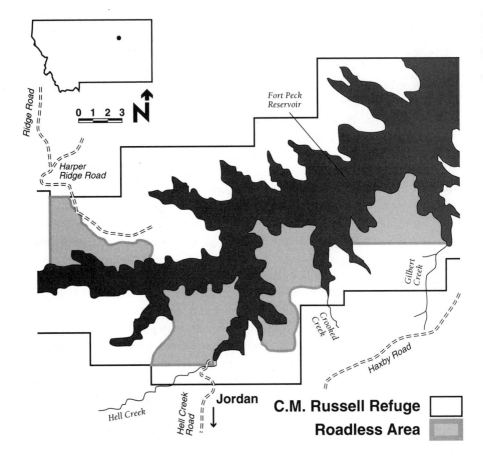

vegetation. The more moderate slopes are covered with grasses, sagebrush, and greasewood. The east boundary is an old wagon road once used to salvage a grounded steamboat.

Nearly 30 miles of the Wild Missouri serve as the northern boundary of the combined 30,000-acre Chimney Bend-Woodhawk roadless area. Here the rugged, deeply dissected terrain and scattered but dense pockets of ponderosa pine and Douglas-fir offer outstanding solitude. Colorful geological formations are matched by an equally colorful history. Woodhawkers cut timber to fuel steamboats; today their woodlots have regrown except in several large burns. The country was likely traversed by Chief Joseph's Nez Perce in their attempted 1877 escape to Canada.

Across the river from Chimney Bend, the 12,880-acre Ervin Ridge WSA has some of the more rugged badlands in the breaks. Differential erosion has created a jumbled maze of mushroom-shaped rocks, castles, monuments, and arches along the river. Narrow bare ridges are flanked by steep clay sides with short prairie grasses and sagebrush. The more remote east end has scattered ponderosa and lodgepole pine, juniper, and Douglas-fir at the heads of protected draws.

Separated from Ervin Ridge by a low-standard road, the lower 10,000 acres of the Bullwhacker and Little Bullwhacker drainages are a wild continuation of the breaks. The country is heavily dissected with tight coulees that feed into broad bottoms.

An undeveloped 50,000-acre expanse surrounds the lower reaches of Cow Creek. Sandstone cliffs form walls above Bull Creek and Hay Coulee with the most impressive being 4 miles of sheer sandstone on the west side of Winter Creek. Over the eons water and wind have chiseled this face into castlelike formations. The Nez Perce traversed the Cow Island WSA on the west boundary during their 1877 flight toward Canada, and rifle pits dug by the waiting calvary can be found nearby. A box canyon above Winter Creek called Horse Thief Pass was used as a natural wild horse corral at the turn of the century.

The 17,900-acre Antelope Creek WSA is a series of deeply eroded coulees dropping into the refuge portion of the breaks. Ponderosa pine and three species of juniper grow in the short prairie grass bottoms of lower Antelope Creek. Kid Curry's outlaw hideaway is concealed in the northwest corner.

The south shore of the refuge is bordered by the 9,210-acre Fort Musselshell WSA, where the Missouri changes from river to reservoir. In an unusual twist, drainages parallel the Missouri instead of running at right angles.

When the displaced Missouri River channel was carved along the southern face of the glaciers, it detoured around the "thumb" of ice that overlaid the preglacial valley of UL Bend. Today, the 20,819-acre UL Bend Wilderness is scattered among five unconnected tracts that adjoin 33,824-acres of the refuge and BLM wildlands around Mickey Butte and East and West Beauchamp. The UL Bend peninsula is the most striking feature of this north-shore segment of the breaks. The May 21, 1805, journal of the Lewis and Clark expedition describes UL Bend:

> In its course the Missouri makes a sudden and extensive bend toward the south . . . the neck of land thus formed, though itself high, is lower than the surrounding country and makes a waving valley . . . with a fertile soil which, though, without wood, produces a fine turf of low grass, some herbs, and vast quantities of prickly pear.

Across the river from the west side of UL Bend rises a series of isolated breaks in the refuge's 14,340-acre Crooked Creek WSA. Both the lengthy Crooked Creek drainage and the adjacent 7,990-acre Alkali Creek WSA have a dense pattern of heavily forested coulees interspersed with small, grassy parks. Due south of Mickey Butte lies the 11,500-acre Lost Creek WSA where

FLOATING THE WILD MISSOURI NEAR THE MOUTH OF BULLWHACKER CREEK DEEP IN THE MISSOURI BREAKS.

steep, open coulees on the west change to densely forested hills to the east.

The combined BLM/FWS Burnt Lodge WSA on the north shore encompasses 42,930 acres of the most rugged and scenic country in the complex. Here severe erosion reveals sheer sandstone walls and castle turrets suitable for climbing. Most notable is a 75-foot vertical sandstone face extending more than 100 yards above Wyatt Coulee, known locally as The Wall. Directly across the reservoir to the south stretches 50,400 acres in the Seven Blackfoot WSA. A jumble of sharp shale ridges studded with ponderosa pine and Douglas-fir and "gumbo sharks' teeth" open up to a vast space bounded by rugged breaks. The existence of Douglas-fir this far east is unusual. A central basin is molded by erosion, leaving stark cliffs and rolling prairies, and exposing formations with fossilized dinosaurs, early mammals, and marsupials.

To the immediate east are the deep breaks of the 13,700-acre Billy Creek WSA where the exposed Hell Creek and Tullock formations have yielded the skeletons of dinosaurs and smaller reptiles. Flat, open prairie falls into rugged breaks on the reservoir's north side in the 11,088-acre Wagon Coulee WSA. Elk and deer are abundant throughout the forested benches and canyons of this refuge wildland. The breaks become even more rugged to the immediate south in the 6,760-acre Snow Creek WSA, where patches of ponderosa pine cling to steep canyon walls. The remote 6,400-acre Duck Creek roadless area is a dry block of treeless BLM prairie where two deep, steep-walled canyons converge at the north boundary of the refuge.

On the south shore of the reservoir the 13,480-acre West Hell Creek WSA is an atypical blend of breaks reminiscent of the Missouri west of the refuge and of badlands further east. The land is mantled with grasses, sagebrush, and a few pine trees. The East Hell Creek WSA, along with BLM roadless lands to the south in Crooked Creek, make up 22,514 acres of badlands with a maze of carved and stratified buttes. Gumbo knobs, sandstone formations, multicolored sediment layers, and dramatic cliffs combine with unobstructed expanses to create a forbidding but spectacular landscape.

The eastern-most Missouri Breaks wildland is the 13,080-acre Sheep Creek WSA, where inconsistent erosion patterns in the shale have made this stark, hidden place a true badlands. The heavily dissected terrain is covered with grasses, some sagebrush, bare ground, and very few trees.

RECREATIONAL USES: To really experience the Upper Missouri Wild and Scenic River and adjacent wildlands launch a canoe at Fort Benton (mile 0) and spend at least 5 to 7 days floating the 149 miles to the Kipp State Park in the Charles M. Russell NWR. In actuality, wild, undeveloped country begins just upstream from Judith Landing at The Wall (mile 77) and continues downstream for about 68 river miles. Therefore, a canoe trip focusing on wildlands should begin at the Judith with enough time for exploration along the way.

Historically, the most popular uses have been fishing in the Missouri River and mule deer hunting from the benchlands along the upper edges of the roadless areas above the breaks. Six bighorn sheep hunting permits are issued for the Missouri Breaks as well. Float trips, mostly by canoe, are increasing with several thousand people floating all or part of the 149-mile corridor each year. Of these, few get out and really hike back into the rugged breaks. Those who do hike and climb in the breaks and coulees are well rewarded by a prairie badlands landscape unlike anywhere in the mountainous western third of Montana.

The most popular campsites are in the limited number of cottonwood groves along the floodplain. Due to chemical pollution the water in the Missouri should not be used for drinking, even if treated. Those floating through the wildest badlands stretch must carry drinking water, in that there is no potable water between Judith Landing Campground and Kipp State Park.

The BLM has produced an excellent mile-by-mile History Digest which can be checked out and used along the river. It provides historical glimpses of early homesteads, Lewis and Clark journal entries, and fascinating tales of steamboats, outlaws, and Native Americans. The Upper Missouri National Wild and Scenic River is also a major segment of the Lewis and Clark National Historic Trail.

The slow-moving current and mostly sunny weather make the Upper Missouri ideal for family trips and beginning canoeists. However, unexpected strong gusts of wind can occur anytime and, of course, there is the proverbial east wind that can bring canoes to a standstill, or even force them back upstream! The prescription here is to head for shore and wait for the winds to calm. Rattlesnakes are common from spring through summer in the canyonlands and sagebrush-covered river terraces. Heavy thunderstorms with hail can move in quickly during spring and summer, where temperatures may exceed 100 degrees F. Spring is an especially enjoyable time to float the river where a profusion of nesting geese, pelicans, owls, bald eagles, and hundreds of other avian species constitute a bird and wildlife watcher's paradise.

A short overnight backpack is possible into one of the secluded side canyons, but at least a gallon of water per person per day would have to be carried. Another sort of "fringe" activity is mountain biking, which would be limited to low-standard vehicle ways in dry conditions. Rainfall transforms the clay soil into a gluey gumbo which makes it impossible for any wheeled vehicle to move, whether it be a four-wheel-drive rig or a mountain bike.

Downstream on the Charles M. Russell NWR wildlands, visits are negligible outside of the hunting season. Some motorboaters on Fort Peck Reservoir beach and hike along the shore or a short distance up a side canyon. As with the Upper Missouri, late spring is the perfect time to catch the prairie in full bloom with the bright colors of yellow pea and penstemon. Low visitation is largely attributable to lack of drinking water and great distance from population centers.

HOW TO GET THERE: To reach Judith Landing (west end) from Lewistown drive 14 miles north on US 191 to Hilger. Turn left on CR 236 for the 49-mile drive to the Missouri River (good gravel-based road for the 26 miles north of Winifred). Cross the bridge to a campground on the north shore just above the bridge. The best boat launching site is on private land just below the bridge where vehicles can be parked due to the good graces of the landowner.

Judith Landing can also be reached from Big Sandy by driving southeast for 42 miles on CR 236. The road is graveled except for one short stretch of gumbo on a hill a few miles north of the Missouri.

To reach the central portion of the complex at James Kipp State Park, which is on the Missouri just downstream from the Robinson Bridge, take US 191 northeast from Lewistown for 63 miles, or US 191 from Malta southwest for 70 miles.

To get to the UL Bend NWR and Wilderness on the central north shore of Fort Peck Reservoir, head east from US 191 on the Dry Fork Road, which takes off opposite the Zortman turnoff. Continue about 28 miles east on the gravel-based Dry Fork Road to Second Creek School. Turn right (south) on the county road and go about 13 miles, crossing Fourchette Creek, to the UL Bend NWR boundary where the road becomes Refuge Road 212. Continue south

One of the countless twisting coulees on the west end of the Missouri Breaks complex.

2 miles and turn left (east) on Refuge Road 319. After another 5 to 6 miles angle right (south) on Road 319 and drive 3 to 4 miles to the end of the road/ jumping-off point leading into Jim Wells Creek within the UL Bend-portion of the Wilderness.

DAY HIKE

Bullwhacker Creek
Distance: 7-8 mile loop.
Difficulty: Moderately strenuous.
Topo map: Sturgeon Island-MT.

By far the best way to explore the Upper Missouri wildlands is to canoe the 60-mile stretch from Judith Landing to Kipp. The river segments with the wildest adjacent badlands and breaks are mile 90 to 101 with Stafford on the north bank and Dog Creek South to the south; mile 103 to 132 with Rock Ridge/ Ervin Ridge/Bullwhacker/Cow Creek on the north side and Chimney Bend-Woodhawk along the south shore; and mile 135 to 143 with Antelope Creek along the north bank. For a wilderness-quality day trip you can't go wrong by hiking up any of the countless coulees dissecting the breaks along any of these stretches of the river. As an example, stop and set up camp in the cottonwood grove on the left bank (north shore) just below the mouth of Bullwhacker Creek (mile 122.5). Hike past the old ranch buildings and head northwest up the broad Bullwhacker Creek valley using well-worn cow paths. Continue about 2 miles up to the first major junction, take the right-hand fork for a way, and then climb to the right up a side ridge, gaining about 600 feet to a broad, grassy, pine-studded plateau. Look for an easy ridge on which to descend to the main west fork of Little Bullwhacker Creek. Follow the streambed and adjacent banks about 0.5 mile down to Little Bullwhacker, where you'll find large conglomerate chunks of fossilized sea shells. The canyon narrows and widens amidst rugged breaks to create a deep feeling of solitude. You'll wonder how the Bureau of Land Management could possibly have determined that this wild country lacked "wilderness characteristics" during its wilderness review in the early 1980s.

After a twisting 1 to 2 miles the bottom intersects a gumbo road; follow this about 1.5 miles back to the river. Fascinating discoveries of sandstone formations, landslides, and geologic contrast await, along with a good chance to see coyotes, mule deer, prairie dog towns, raptors, and more. When hiking this unstable, highly erodible country look for solid footing. In particular, beware of strange, deep vertical shafts in the ground called "pipes." Give them a wide berth to insure that you don't slip down into one of these black holes. Prickly pear cactus is usually thick on the flats and can penetrate light footwear. It's advisable to wear sturdy boots and, as always, keep a wary eye out for slow-moving but potentially lethal rattlesnakes from late spring to early fall.

There is no such thing as straight-line travel in these deeply eroded badlands, so allow plenty of time and take lots of water for this exploratory loop.

DAY HIKE

UL Bend

Distance: 14 to 15 miles out-and-back.
Difficulty: Moderate but long.
Topo maps: Locke Ranch-MT; Mickey Butte-MT; Germaine Coulee West-MT; and Germaine Coulee East-MT.

For birding, photography, and enjoying the solitude and expanse of prairie wilderness, take a late spring or early fall hike across the length of UL Bend from the end of Refuge Road 319 to the tip of the peninsula 7 or 8 miles to the south. The trailless travel is over fairly easy terrain. Carry ample water and leave early in the morning so as to avoid as much of the heat of day as possible. An early departure is also the way to see more wildlife.

Bitter Creek

51

Location: 25 miles northwest of Glasgow and 18 miles south of the Canadian border.
Size: 62,940 acres.
Administration: Bureau of Land Management—Valley Resource Area.
Management status: BLM Wilderness Study Area.
Ecosystems: Great Plains dry steppe province, northwestern glaciated plains section, characterized by level to gently rolling continental glacial-till plains and rolling hills on the Missouri Plateau; glacial till underlain by soft cretaceous marine shale; grama-needlegrass-wheatgrass vegetative type; a medium-to-high density drainage pattern with seasonal streams.
Elevation range: 2,378 to 3,120 feet.
System trails: None.
Maximum core to perimeter distance: 5 miles.
Activities: Hiking, horseback riding, limited mountain biking in dry conditions on the interior low-standard roads, limited backpacking, limited reservoir fishing.
Modes of travel: Foot, horse, mountain bike.
Maps: 1985 BLM edition, Opheim-Montana/Saskatchewan, 1:100,000 contour map (5/8"/mile); Last Chance Reservoir-MT, Dodge Reservoir-MT, Gay Dam-MT, Kerr Cow Dam-MT; and Laundry Hill-MT (1:24,000 topo maps).

OVERVIEW: As long ago as 12,000 years, hunter-gatherers used what is today known as the Bitter Creek country—nearly 63,000 acres of undeveloped public land in northeastern Montana. Today this area is divided in three parts by low-standard roads. The land is flat to gently rolling with about 700 feet of elevation separating the lower coulees from the higher benches. In places extensive glaciation has formed barren badlands. Advanced erosion caused by a crack in the ice during late Pleistocene explains the "blowout" scenery of sand/shale "waves." Although classified ecologically as shortgrass prairie, Bitter Creek is likely closer to being a mixed-grass prairie of wheatgrass, blue grama, native legumes, silver sage, creeping juniper, aspen, and chokecherry. Difficulty of access accounts for Bitter Creek's population of magnum-sized mule deer. This remote prairie is also visited, though rarely, by wandering elk from the Missouri Breaks and gray wolves from Canada.

Conservationists have proposed Bitter Creek as part of a vast prairie complement to the recently established Canadian Grasslands National Park bordering Montana in southern Saskatchewan. The west unit of the Canadian

51 BITTER CREEK

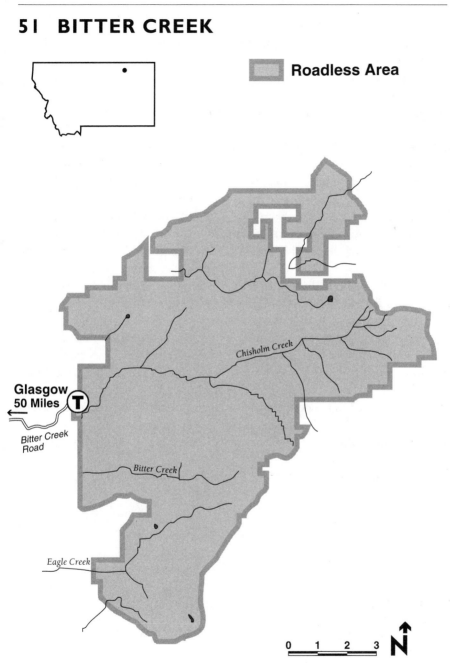

Roadless Area

Glasgow
50 Miles **T**

Bitter Creek
Road

Chisholm Creek

Bitter Creek

Eagle Creek

0 1 2 3 N

park consists of upper Frenchman Creek, which drains south into the large BLM Frenchman Creek wildland. Bitter Creek sits less than 15 miles southeast of Frenchman Creek and is part of the same shortgrass prairie ecosystem. The proposal calls for BLM to designate the Frenchman Creek-Bitter Creek complex as an Area of Critical Environmental Concern so its natural values may be specially recognized and protected.

RECREATIONAL USES: Big game, upland, and waterfowl hunting on reservoirs are the major forms of recreation in Bitter Creek. Many of the hunters use a number of the two-wheeled tracks for vehicular access. The country is known locally as a good place for trophy mule deer. One of the reservoirs (Gay) is a trout fishery and receives light-to-moderate use. Many of the descendants of local homesteaders enjoy visiting ancestral homesteads. Hiking across this rare, undeveloped expanse of rolling plains and prairie is best during early spring and fall. Camping, backpacking, and nature study haven't yet caught on, although there is potential for these activities as people increasingly seek opportunities for solitude.

HOW TO GET THERE: From Glasgow, drive 26 miles northwest on US 2 (the "High-line") to Willow Creek Road. Turn right (north) and stay on the main road for about 20 miles to the Bitter Creek turnoff. Go right (east) for about 3.5 miles to where the road angles left (straight north), which is also where the road briefly touches the boundary of public land and the west-central edge of the Wilderness Study Area. At this point you are on a bench overlooking Chisholm Creek, which is also known as the North Fork of Bitter Creek.

OFF-TRAIL DAY HIKE

Chisholm Creek Prairie
Distance: 5 to 10 miles, out-and-back.
Difficulty: Moderate.
Topo map: Gay Dam-MT.

From the point referred to above it is an easy 0.5-mile, 100-foot descent east to the bottom of Chisholm Creek, angling around the fairly rough mouth of a northern tributary. Follow your nose northeast up the main (and very winding) Chisholm Creek drainage for as long as you have time and energy. Small sandstone formations add variety to your travels in this aptly named "Land of the Long Look." Although formal trails are lacking, there are countless paths made by deer and livestock which both follow the main bottom and cut it at right angles. After 5 or 6 miles, and perhaps almost as many hours, you'll find yourself in the heart of this remnant of a once vast, intact grasslands ecosys-

BITTER CREEK—WILD PRAIRIE DEEP IN THE "LAND OF THE LONG LOOK."

tem. Take plenty of drinking water and keep a sharp eye out for the occasional rattlesnake, especially from May to September.

Outside of hunting season this land is seldom visited by humans, so solitude should be ample, with only the unceasing wind to keep you company. Abundant opportunities for loop trips exist by turning up side coulees, benching out, then dropping back into the main drainage. Good compass and topographic map skills are needed here. Head west back down Chisholm to your point of origin.

Medicine Lake
Wilderness

52

Location: 27 miles north of Culbertson and 25 miles south of Plentywood.
Size: 11,366 acres.
Administration: U.S. Fish & Wildlife Service.
Management status: Designated Wilderness within a National Wildlife Refuge.
Ecosystems: Great Plains dry steppe province, northern glaciated plains section, characterized by gently undulating to rolling continental glacial till with kame and kettle topography; wheatgrass-needlegrass vegetative type; prairie pothole lake, marsh, and heavily glaciated rolling plains supporting mixed-grass prairie plant and animal communities.
Elevation range: 1,935 to 2,025 feet.
System trails: None.
Maximum core to perimeter distance: 1 mile (and portion of area).
Activities: Hiking, wildlife viewing, non-motorized boating, and fishing from November 15 through September 15.
Modes of travel: Foot, non-motorized boat.
Maps: Medicine Lake National Wildlife Refuge maps and brochures; Medicine Lake-MT; and Capeney's Lake-MT (1:24,000 topo maps).

OVERVIEW: More than 10,000 years ago the prehistoric bed of the Missouri River wound through what is now Medicine Lake in the extreme northeast corner of Montana. Then like a giant plow the glaciers smoothed out the land and pushed the course of the Missouri southward. As the glaciers retreated, buried ice melted in place to form Medicine Lake and the surrounding prairie potholes. Over time, the winds carried and shaped sand from the shores of the lake into the dune of nearby Sand Hills.

Today, the shallow 8,700-acre Medicine Lake and 2,320-acre Sand Hills comprise a designated Wilderness within a National Wildlife Refuge. Medicine Lake is the smallest, flattest, and lowest of Montana's wilderness areas, with vertical relief of only 90 feet. The rolling dunes of the Sand Hills are adorned with a blend of mixed prairie grasses, chokecherry, and buffalo berry.

Each spring, nearly 3,500 white pelicans power their 9-foot wingspans to the islands of Medicine Lake to form one of North America's largest pelican nesting colonies. Medicine Lake is a way station for hundreds of thousands of birds during spring and fall migrations—a dazzling display of more than 200 avian species. Probably the rarest migrant to Medicine Lake is the endangered

52 MEDICINE LAKE WILDERNESS

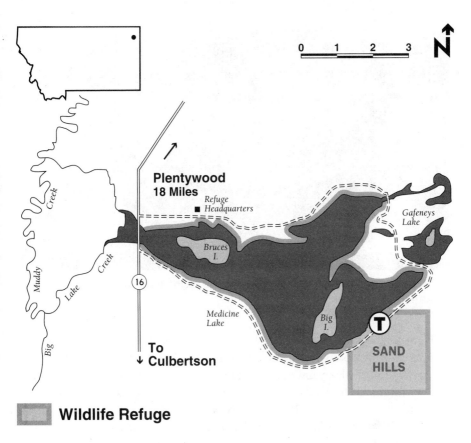

0   1   2   3   **N**

Plentywood
18 Miles
Refuge
■ Headquarters

Gafeneys
Lake

Creek

Muddy

Creek

Bruces
I.

16

Medicine
Lake

Big
I.

T

**To
↓ Culbertson**

**SAND
HILLS**

Lake

Big

Wildlife Refuge

whooping crane—a magnificent bird that can reach a height of 5 feet with a 7.5-foot wingspan.

The lake is closed to public use from mid-September to mid-November to protect staging waterfowl. This is a refuge where visitors can stroll quietly, listening to the lonesome call of the wild goose or perhaps, just maybe, to the far-away trumpeting of the whooping crane calling us to our wild origins.

RECREATIONAL USES: At least half of the recreation visits to the refuge are for a self-guided auto tour. Wildlife viewing and photography takes place from vehicles on an 18-mile, ten-stop, 1-to-2 hour self-guided auto tour along the north shore of Medicine Lake. People typically begin the tour at the refuge headquarters by climbing up a 100-foot tower for a grand overview of this prairie lake wilderness.

SAND HILLS — THE LAND-PORTION OF THE MEDICINE LAKE WILDERNESS ON ITS SOUTHEAST CORNER.

Hunting for waterfowl, upland birds, and deer is also popular; ringnecked pheasant and sharptail grouse attract the most attention. Bridgerman Point on the east end of the lake and the Sand Hills are the only portions of the refuge open to hunting. The Medicine Lake component of the Wilderness is closed to public use from September 16 through November 14 to protect staging waterfowl. The Wilderness islands in the lake are closed to public use year-round for the security of the colonial birds that depend on them for undisturbed habitat.

A boat landing and picnic area are situated on the west end of the lake. Medicine Lake is open to non-motorized fishing from November 15 through September 15. Canoeists should stay close to shore because high winds can suddenly whip the surface into a frenzy of deadly whitecaps. Unlike any other Wilderness in Montana, camping is not allowed at Medicine Lake due to the lack of suitable campsites and the need to minimize disturbance to wildlife. Thus, all public use of the Wilderness is limited to the daylight hours.

HOW TO GET THERE: From US 2 at Culbertson drive 27 miles north on MT 16. Turn east at Road 515 and go about 2.5 miles to Refuge Headquarters. Continue around the lake on the main road for another 12 to 13 miles, ending up on the dirt patrol road on the northern edge of the Sand Hills in the southeast corner of the refuge.

DAY CANOE OUTING AND HIKE

Medicine Lake - Sand Hill Ramble
Distance: 2 to 4 miles on foot; easy canoe.
Difficulty: Easy.
Topo map: Capeney's Lake-MT.

You can't go wrong, during spring or summer, exploring the shoreline of Medicine Lake by canoe, followed by a short hike across the Sand Hills. There are no established trails, but deer paths are abundant and easy to follow in this rolling country. You need walk only 1 mile into these gentle mounds to be surrounded by low dunes in the heart of the Sand Hills, with an ensuing feeling of remoteness and solitude.

During April and May check at the refuge headquarters to learn where to go at dawn to see the primeval courtship dance of sharptail grouse.

Pryor Mountains Complex

53

Location: 27 miles southeast of Bridger; 45 miles south of Billings.
Size: 95,020 acres.
Administration: USDAFS—Custer National Forest; National Park Service—Bighorn Canyon National Recreation Area; Bureau of Land Management—Billings Resource Area; and Crow Indian Reservation.
Management status: Roadless non-wilderness, roadless tribal preserve lands, National Recreation Area, BLM Wilderness Study Areas, and Wild Horse Range.
Ecosystems: Southern Rocky Mountain steppe-coniferous forest province, Bighorn Mountain section, characterized by high mountains and rolling uplands cut by narrow, steep canyons; unglaciated sedimentary formations dominated by Madison limestone; wheatgrass-needlegrass-shrub steppe and Douglas-fir forest type; a medium density dendritic drainage pattern with many intermittent streams.
Elevation range: 4,361 to 8,776 feet.
System trails: None.
Maximum core to perimeter distance: 2 miles.
Activities: Hiking (including canyoneering), backpacking, spelunking, horseback riding, limited stream fishing, mountain biking on high mesas on four-wheel-drive roads.
Modes of travel: Foot, horse, mountain bike.
Maps: 1986 Custer National Forest/Beartooth Division Visitor Map; Big Ice Cave-MT; East Pryor Mountain-MT; Dead Indian Hill-MT; Red Pryor Mountain-MT; and Mystery Cave-MT (Montana public lands portion 1:24,000 topo maps).

OVERVIEW: The Pryors conjure images of thundering wild horses running free where the eastern edge of the Rockies meet the prairie. In fact, our nation's first wild horse range encompasses 32,000 acres in the Pryor Mountains, which overlap much of a four-agency wildland complex. A primitive, lightly visited Crow Tribal Reserve of about 45,000 acres is closed to non-tribal members to protect cultural and religious sites. The remaining 50,000 acres are shared by three federal agencies: the Forest Service, Park Service, and Bureau of Land Management.

Bighorn Canyon NRA includes 17,000 acres of buttes, reefs, and mesas. A central 21,000-acre core of three BLM Wilderness Study areas consists largely of broken foothills and sonoran landforms on the wild horse range. To the northwest, the Forest Service manages 12,020 acres of higher country within and surrounding pristine Lost Water Canyon. From semi-arid deserts to sub-

53 PRYOR MOUNTAINS COMPLEX

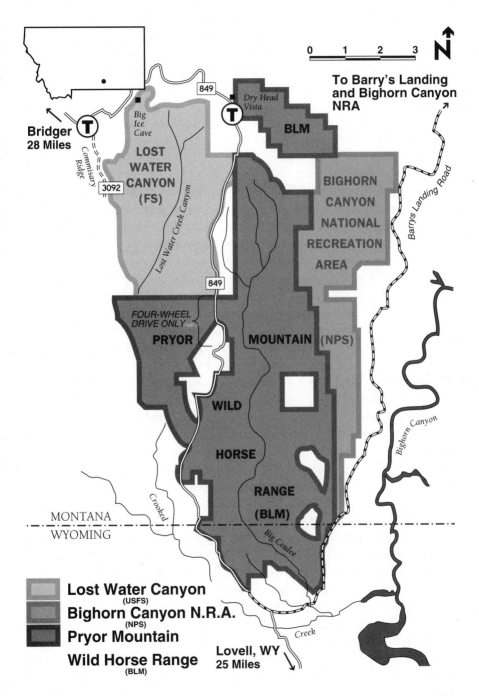

alpine plateaus approaching 9,000 feet, the topographic and vegetative diversity of the Pryors is unequalled. On the southern flanks, dry limestone canyons in high desert—such as Big Coulee and Burnt Timber Canyon—form an ecosystem not found elsewhere in Montana. Exposed marine fossil beds display a rainbow of blues, greens, grays, and Chugwater formation reds.

The Pryors developed from vertical uplift, causing upfoldings of rock that often ruptured into faults on their northeast corners. The uplift, along with erosion, accounts for today's varied landforms of deep limestone canyons pocketed with caves, overhanging ledges, alcoves, and bottoms difficult to negotiate because of dense underbrush and steep, rocky talus. On higher ground, thick forests of Douglas-fir are one of the eastern-most populations of the species. The range also contains the most northerly growth of mountain mahogany.

Regardless of whether the wild horses are relict descendants of seventeenth-century Spanish stock, as many believe, or are of more recent lineage, they coexist well with native wildlife. Mule deer and black bears are numerous in these nearly inaccessible canyons and buttes, along with less abundant elk and bighorn sheep. Most of the streams are seasonal, but short perennial stretches of Lost Water Canyon and Crooked Creek may harbor an isolated pure strain of cutthroat trout.

In spite of the tough terrain, prehistoric peoples used the country extensively for camps, chert quarries, rock art, vision quests, and travel routes. Ancient cave dwellers may have hunted mountain sheep here as long ago as 30,000 years.

RECREATIONAL USES: This is dry country with wide temperature swings from as low as minus 40 degrees F. in winter to 100 degrees F. during summer. With the prevailing storms coming from the northwest the higher north end of the range is wetter than the desertlike southern portion. In general, expect lots of sunshine, low relative humidity, strong winds, and not much precipitation. Keep an eye out for rattlesnakes from early spring to late summer. Steep limestone cliffs and narrow, brushy canyon bottoms provide for both challenge and solitude.

With no trails or lakes the Pryors are lightly visited most of the year, but hunting, hiking, and camping are increasingly popular here. The chance to see wild horses draws many visitors, especially on low-standard jeep roads into and along the edge of the BLM's Pryor Mountain Wild Horse Range near the Wyoming border. All of the major canyons, including Crooked Creek and Burnt Timber Canyon, offer hiking, backpacking, rock climbing, spelunking, and nature study. Crooked Creek contains fishable populations of small brook and rainbow trout, along with what may be an isolated pure strain of cutthroat in the creek's upper reaches. The Crooked Creek Natural Landmark is a site for vertebrate fossils. The Forest Service plans to designate 1,800 acres in the pristine upper Lost Water Canyon as a Research Natural Area to protect natural values and processes.

WILD HORSES ON COMMISSARY RIDGE.

How to get there: From Bridger, drive 2.5 miles south on US 310 to Pryor Mountain Road. Turn left (east) and drive about 33 miles to Dry Head Vista, which is within Custer National Forest on the north edge of the public-lands portion of the complex. The Sage Creek segment of the road on the Crow Reservation can be somewhat greasy when wet, but with care the road can usually be negotiated without difficulty. Upon entering the national forest the road becomes FR 3085. About 9 miles from the national forest boundary watch for a road junction; take the left-hand fork, FR 849. Go another 2 miles to Commissary Ridge. From Commissary Ridge continue past the Big Ice Cave and on to Dry Head Vista.

DAY TRIP (ON FOOT, HORSE, OR MOUNTAIN BIKE)

Commissary Ridge
Distance: 8 miles out-and-back.
Difficulty: Easy.
Topo maps: Big Ice Cave-MT and Red Pryor Mountain-MT.

Hike, horseback ride, or mountain bike down broad, open Commissary Ridge beginning at first on a set of jeep tracks, taking off from the end of spur Road 3092. The ridge is negotiable for about 4 miles to the cliffs above the confluence of Crooked and Commissary creeks. There is a good chance of seeing wild horses along this stretch. The painted red hues of a remote desert landscape extend southward to infinity.

DAY HIKE

Lost Water Canyon
Distance: 16 miles out-and-back.
Difficulty: Strenuous.
Topo maps: Big Ice Cave-MT and Red Pryor Mountain-MT.

If you're traveling on foot and have a thirst for adventure, consider a canyoneering loop from the turnaround point described above. The 800-foot drop from the point of the ridge to the bottom is marked by steep limestone cliffs on the east side and a dense Douglas-fir type forest to the west. With care a safe route can be negotiated. Once on the bottom work your way downstream another mile to Cave Canyon. Turn up this canyon or continue down Crooked Creek another 0.5 mile to the mouth of pristine Lost Water Canyon. At this point you've dropped 2,200 feet from where you started on the top of Commissary Ridge. The slow going in the extremely rugged Lost Water Canyon allows the visitor to more carefully observe the intricate small limestone caves and ledges. There is an occasional small opening along the bottom just wide enough for one or two tents for those few who would actually take a backpack into this rough country. Water can be found intermittently. The better choice is to make a long day hike by backtracking down Lost Water, back up Crooked Creek, and then up Commissary Creek a short way to where the west side of the canyon can be climbed back to Commissary Ridge.

DAY HIKE

Dry Head Vista Rim
Distance: 4 to 5 miles out and back.
Difficulty: Easy.
Topo maps: East Pryor Mountain-MT and Mystery Cave-MT.

Another easier choice for exploration is to drive past the Big Ice Cave on FR 849 and go about 5 miles east to 8,644-foot Dry Head Vista. From the vista point just northeast of the 8,776-foot high point (the southeast end of East Pryor Mountain) hike to the southeast along the rim for a couple of miles, skirting around the private inholding. This is an easy, open hike with views of a varied land of plateaus, cliffs, and high plains.

LOOKING FROM COMMISSARY RIDGE SOUTHWARD TO A MAZE OF HIGH MESAS AND HIDDEN CANYONS.

Tongue River Breaks
Complex

54

Location: 2 miles east of Birney; 4 miles northeast of Ashland and 8 miles south of Ashland.

Size: 49,278 acres.

Administration: USDAFS—Custer National Forest and Bureau of Land Management—Powder River Resource Area.

Management status: USDAFS Hiking and Riding Areas; BLM Wilderness Study Area.

Ecosystems: Southern Rocky Mountain steppe-open woodland province, Bighorn Mountains section, characterized by low mountains and rolling uplands cut by narrow, steep V-shaped valleys and severely eroded breaks; Cretaceous sandstones, siltstones, and shales; Douglas-fir and eastern ponderosa forest types along with wheatgrass-needlegrass-shrub steppe; and a medium density dendritic drainage pattern with mostly seasonal flows.

Elevation range: 3,100 to 4,369 feet.

System trails: 7 miles (South Fork of Poker Jim Creek).

Maximum core to perimeter distance: 2 miles (Tongue River Breaks unit).

Activities: Hiking, backpacking, horseback riding, and mountain biking.

Modes of travel: Foot, horse, mountain bike.

Maps: 1983 1/2"/mile Custer National Forest/Ashland Division contour map; Cook Creek-MT; Birney Day School-MT; Green Creek-MT; King Mountain-MT; Browns Mountain-MT; and Poker Jim Butte-MT.

OVERVIEW: The Tongue River Breaks are a maze of steep, deeply eroded canyons that, collectively, contain four roadless areas on both sides of the Tongue River. Wind and water erosion have undercut sandstone walls, forming small caves and protected spaces that were used by Stone Age people for as long as 10,000 years. At the edge of an ancient plateau, the land plunges into V-shaped gullies that send water to the Tongue River after snowmelt and heavy summer thunderstorms. Tiny springs seep from cracks in the rock only to quickly disappear into the sandy soils of a near-desert prairie of juniper and sagebrush. Most of this country is important mule deer summer habitat and each of the four areas provide a winter home for deer, antelope, turkey, and a few sharptail grouse.

On the north end of the plateau the gentle slopes of the 11,700-acre Cook Mountain area fall north from Cook Mountain, the highest point in these breaks. The 11,900-acre King Mountain unit is mostly made up of west- or northwest-facing buttes supporting ponderosa pine and bunchgrass along a 4,100-foot divide.

54 TONGUE RIVER BREAKS COMPLEX

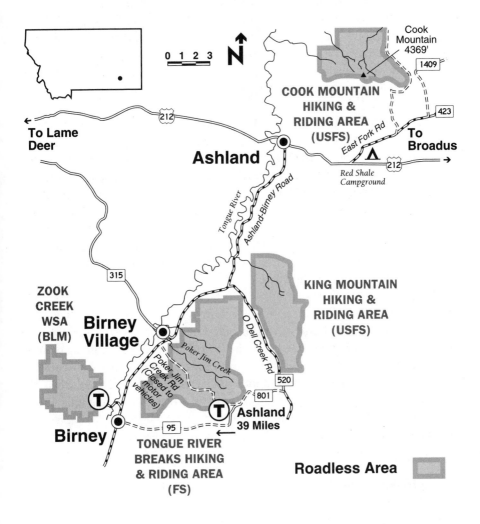

The 16,600-acre Tongue River Breaks area is distinguished by rugged, deeply dissected terrain. These breaks and higher plateaus contain cultural sites of concern to the Northern Cheyenne. The expansive flower-studded ponderosa pine parks of Poker Jim Flat provide a panorama of the breaks bordering both sides of the river valley. Folklore has it that when his boss caught him playing cards back in the 1880s, Poker Jim left without a job but his name stuck to these rambling meadows.

Much of BLM's 9,078-acre Zook Creek WSA on the west side of the river is covered by the reddish pink of clinker—sandstone baked hard by burning coal seams. Chippings from early Indian tools are sometimes found along the broken faces of formations, where bright red bands contrast with buff-colored sandstone. About two-thirds of the wide-open Zook Creek drainage is dotted with ponderosa pine on a northern plateau that sends seasonal streams to every direction. At least two sharptail grouse leks, or courting grounds, are contained here.

RECREATIONAL USES: Despite the name, "hiking and riding area," trails are basically nonexistent in this lightly visited breaks country. The only real trail is a cow path down the South Fork of Poker Jim Creek. Fortunately, these mostly open pine-studded hills lend themselves to trailless tramping. The exceptions to light use are fall big game hunting and spring and fall turkey hunting. Once beyond the roads you'll almost certainly find all the solitude you could possibly hope for. The best seasons to visit the Tongue River country are late spring and fall when the canyons blaze with autumn foliage. The extremes of heat or cold keep most people away during summer and winter. Keep a watchful eye out for rattlesnakes, especially from mid-spring on as temperatures rise.

Despite canyon depths of up to 500 feet along the western face of the breaks, you'll never have to gain more than 1,000-feet of vertical elevation while traversing this country. And this modest relief is spread over miles of gently-rising ridges. When you get to the top of wherever you're going, you're only a little over 4,000 feet above sea level. Snow is too spotty in this country to count on cross-country skiing, although there are occasional times when it's possible to hike up some of the lower canyons and ski the rolling uplands. A rare mountain biker will sometimes skirt around the edges of the roadless areas on low-standard jeep roads. The prime activity here is cross-country day hiking through gentle, remote country.

HOW TO GET THERE: From Ashland drive 1 mile west on US 212 and go about 20 miles south on the Tongue River Highway to Birney Day School. Then drive about 1.5 miles southwest to the Poker Jim Creek junction. Turn south on the Birney road for another 8 miles to Birney, and take the road southeast out of Birney another mile to FR 95. Turn left (east), drive 3.5 miles, and turn left again (north) on the Timber Creek Road (FR 801) for the final 5 miles to Poker Jim Lookout and Picnic Area.

To access Zook Creek, continue south beyond Birney Day School for another 5 miles to a road junction located about 0.5 mile past Black Eagle Creek. Turn right and head northwest across the Tongue River, continuing 1 mile to a road junction. Turn left (south) and drive 2.5 miles to where the road touches the southeastern corner of the Zook Creek WSA at Browns Gulch. Hike up the gulch for an enjoyable introduction to this small but varied pocket of wild badlands.

DAY HIKE

Poker Jim Creek

Distance: 12- to 14-mile loop.
Difficulty: Moderate.
Topo maps: Birney Day School-MT; Green Creek-MT; Browns Mountain-MT; and Poker Jim Butte-MT.

In the Tongue River Breaks, largest of the four roadless units in the complex, start at the Poker Jim Lookout and picnic area. Hike 6 to 7 miles down the cow path trail along the South Fork of Poker Jim Creek to its confluence with the North Fork. Then work your way back up the North Fork about 3 miles to the first major canyon on the right (south). Take either this coulee or the pine-studded bench between the forks straight south another 1.5 miles back to the lookout, thereby completing an exhilarating exploration of this remote wildland. The elevation loss and gain is about 1,000 feet. The canyons are surprisingly rugged with strange rock formations, and with side coulees that offer several trip variations. Carry plenty of water with you when wandering these dry breaks, buttes, bluffs, and benches.

THE TONGUE RIVER BREAKS FROM THE GRASSY EXPANSE OF POKER JIM FLATS.

Terry Badlands

55

Location: 3 miles west of Terry.
Size: 47,797 acres.
Administration: Bureau of Land Management—Big Dry Resource Area.
Management status: BLM Wilderness Study Area.
Ecosystems: Great Plains-dry steppe province, Powder River Basin section, characterized by steeply sloping badlands and flat-topped, steep-sided buttes; cretaceous and Lower Tertiary non-marine sedimentary rocks; grama-needlegrass-wheatgrass vegetative type with some eastern ponderosa forest type containing an unusual stand of eastern limber pine; and deeply eroded drainages with seasonal flows along with large, shallow head basins underlain by coal or scoria.
Elevation range: 2,180 to 2,900 feet.
System trails: There are no actual trails but there are eleven low-standard primitive vehicle ways totaling 23 miles within the WSA that can be used for walking and horseback riding.
Maximum core to perimeter distance: 2.5 miles.
Activities: Hiking, horseback riding, and mountain biking.
Modes of travel: Foot, horse, and mountain bike.
Maps: Terry-MT USGS topographic map-1:100,000 scale; "Terry/Miles City-Montana" BLM Recreation Access Map-1:100,000 scale; McClure Reservoir-MT; Calypso-MT; Kinsey NE-MT; and Zero-MT (1:24,000 topo maps).

OVERVIEW: The Terry Badlands are characterized by twisted tunnels of tortured topography in which soft sedimentary rocks are continuously eroded by wind and water into strange, chaotic shapes: bridges, table tops, battlements, pinnacles, spires, scoria escarpments, and haystack buttes.

The badlands are separated into an eastern third and western two-thirds by the Calypso Trail, which is actually a road. The BLM is considering whether to close this lightly used road to vehicular use. Closure would unify the roadless area with a resulting increase in wilderness values.

Emptying to the southeast into the Yellowstone River, deep parallel drainages are lined with colorful, banded cliffs above rolling prairie grasslands dotted with scattered juniper. The more open southeast corner touches the Yellowstone and rises 700 feet on undulating benches on up to extremely rough badlands pocketed with sunken gullies and bounded by eroded side slopes.

55 TERRY BADLANDS

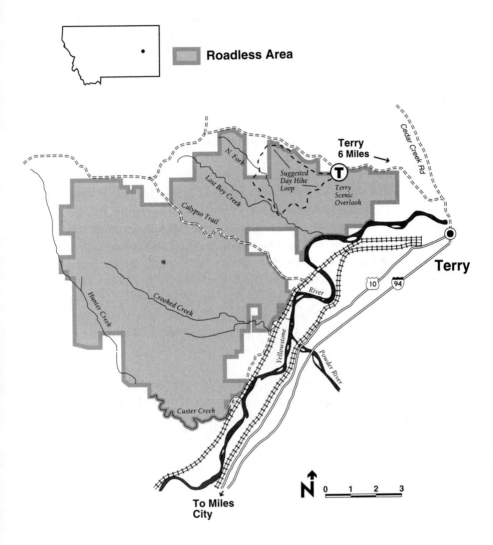

Roadless Area

During spring, summer, and fall mule deer and grouse are abundant, along with a few wild turkeys. One of the easternmost stands of limber pine, a close but lower elevation relative of whitebark pine, grows atop some 800 acres of northern rims. Of perhaps some historic value, U.S. Cavalry troops carved graffiti on Sheridan Butte in the Badlands during the 1870s, and dug rifle pits on a butte just north of the study area.

RECREATIONAL USES: The extremely rugged Terry Badlands are used mostly for deer hunting and sightseeing from vehicles on peripheral roads. There is one established overlook, the Terry Scenic Overlook, on the northeastern end of the wilderness study area. The Badlands are accessible on the north by country roads, from the east by the Yellowstone River, and in the center by the Calypso Trail. Most of the roads are gumbo and aren't passable in wet weather. The terrain and harsh winters with little snow limit winter recreation. An occasional rattlesnake poses another hazard that the traveler must be alert for spring through summer. There are several good places for overnight camping. However, drinking water is not available, thereby limiting the length of stay and hiking range of backpackers. The large size of the Badlands along with the steep, deeply dissected landscape give the visitor a true sense of solitude. Day hiking is perhaps the most enjoyable activity for the scenery buff, the rock and fossil collector, or for the kind of person who simply wants to be alone in undeveloped backcountry.

HOW TO GET THERE: From I-94 at Terry head north on the Cedar Creek Road, which crosses the Yellowstone River just north of town. Turn left (west) about 1 mile north of the river and proceed another 4.5 miles to the Terry Scenic Overlook.

DAY HIKE

Terry Badlands
Distance: 7- to 8-mile cross-country loop.
Difficulty: Moderately strenuous.
Topo maps: Calypso-MT; Terry-MT.

From the Terry Overlook hike west on a red rock rim, drop into a grassy plateau, and then climb a prominent sandstone pinnacle topped with a pyramid rock cairn, which is about 0.5 mile southwest of the overlook. Then proceed southwest down steep gumbo slopes into one of the north forks of Lost Boy Creek, and head down the coulee for about 2 miles to the main broad bottom of the drainage. Turn back up the drainage to the northwest for about 0.75 mile to the main North Fork shown on the map. Keep going up the in-

HAYSTACK BUTTES IN THE TERRY BADLANDS NEAR THE TERRY SCENIC OVERLOOK.

creasingly narrow twisting bottom for about a mile to the first major forks. Turn up either fork but within 0.5 mile begin working up to your right across a series of benches to the north toward the top of the rim. En route you'll see a wonderland of sandstone ledges, overhangs with arches, spires, and small buttes eroded into every grotesque shape imaginable. Upon reaching the top you can either hike the rim or the road east back to the overlook. Despite the ruggedness of the country it is possible to hike with relative ease for long distances with careful routefinding. You may flush a wild turkey at close range one minute only to catch a grand vista of the free-flowing Yellowstone River from a high butte the next. Be sure to carry ample water, a compass, and a topographic map for this off-trail excursion through the badlands.

EPILOGUE

Montana has been discovered. Big time. A river is not all that "runs through it." Enough tourists run through Montana to more than double the state's population each summer, along with an unprecedented number of new residents who, to paraphrase the late Pulitzer Prize-winning Montana author A. B. Guthrie, Jr., are coming to Montana to get away from it all and, in so doing, bring it all with them. The big draws are Montana's relatively abundant wild country and all that brings to mind: uncluttered space, scenic grandeur, plentiful wildlife, clean air and water, solitude, and quality outdoor recreation.

With our bigger-name wilderness areas already being loved to death by an ever-increasing number of visitors, one could argue that the last thing we need is another guidebook to our backcountry. Certainly this was my first reaction as I pondered my own ethics and motivations. But then I remembered the words of wilderness writer and eccentric Ed Abbey who said wilderness needs no defense, just more defenders. Actually, both are needed, but the defense of wild country comes from defenders who have a heartfelt feeling for the land they love. This feeling can be developed vicariously by those with a broad understanding of the ecological need for wilderness. It can also be derived from the personal experiences folks have when they paddle, ski, hike, climb, horseback ride, or mountain bike through wild country.

Wilderness will only endure in our industrialized society if there is public support. And so, this book is presented in hopes that you will join or increase your involvement with the ranks of wilderness defenders, regardless of whether you ever set foot in any of the fifty-five Montana wild areas featured in the previous pages. Wilderness defense can take many forms, from political advocacy to a leave-no-trace camping ethic to quietly setting the example of respect for wildland for others to follow.

My second justification for writing this book and believing that it should be written is my belief that redistribution of recreational use of our wildlands is desirable. The overwhelming majority of backcountry recreation takes place on a very small percentage of the wildland base, with many of the same locations getting more use with each passing year. Most people would agree that the Chinese Wall in the heart of the Bob or many of the high lakes in the Beartooth don't need more visitors. If this book helps some of these backcountry enthusiasts find new places to explore, especially for those activities such as mountain biking that don't depend on Wilderness, it will have served an important purpose. Indeed, most of the suggested trips described are to seldom-visited places that can absorb sensitive use without losing their essential wildness.

It all boils down to respect for the land, for those wild creatures that live there, for other visitors, and for those yet unborn who will retrace the journeys we make today into the next century and beyond.

APPENDIX A:

RECOMMENDED EQUIPMENT LIST FOR HIKING, SKIING, AND BACKPACKING BEYOND THE ROADS

Core essentials for day trips:

Gear/Accessories

—day pack (or "day-and-a-half" climbing style pack if needed).
—water bottle (filled, 1-2 liter capacity).
—matches in a waterproof case/fire starter.
—small first aid kit.
—pocket knife.
—mirror (for emergency signaling).
—whistle.
—compass (adjusted for magnetic declination)
—area topo map(s).

Clothing

—sturdy well-broken-in boots (normally light-to-medium weight).
—shirt, sweater, pants, and jacket suited to the season.
—socks: wool outer; light cotton, polypro, or nylon inner.
—rain gear that can double for wind protection (Gore-tex brand fabric or 60-40 parka and/or rain suit with pants or chaps).
—ski-type hat (balaclava, headband, or stocking cap).
—hat with brim (for sun protection).
—belt and/or suspenders.

If you're staying over for one night or longer add the following:

Gear/Accessories

—backpack/pack cover/extra set of pack straps (internal or external frame is a matter of personal preference).
—tent with fly and repair kit (to include ripstop tape).
—sleeping bag (rated to at least 10 degrees F or as season requires).
—sleeping pad (self-inflating type best).
—stove/fuel bottle (filled)/repair kit (include cleaning wire).
—flashlight with extra batteries and bulb.

—candle lantern with spare candle.
—cook kit/pot gripper/cleaning pad.
—eating utensils: bowl (12-15 oz. with cover), cup, fork and spoon.
—several small drawstring grab bags for miscellaneous items.
—trowel.
—toilet paper in plastic bag.
—biodegradable soap and small towel.
—plastic bags (including a large garbage bag) with ties.
—toothbrush/toothpaste/dental floss.
—drugs: prescriptions and antibiotics.
—sunglasses/sunblock.
—zinc oxide (for sunburn).
—chapstick with sunblock.
—eye drops.
—aspirin or ibuprofen.
—throat lozenges.
—laxative.
—anti-diarrhea medicine.
—decongestant medicine.
—antacid tablets.
—salt tablets.
—scissors/safety pins/small sewing kit.
—moleskin (before the blister), second skin (after the blister).
—extra bandages.
—insect repellent (spring-summer trips).
—water filter designed and approved for backcountry use.
—sharpening stone.
—nylon cord (50' to 100' for hanging food, drying clothes etc.).
—snakebite kit and bee sting kit (over the counter anti-histamine or epinephrine by prescription) as needed for area and season.

Clothing

—wading sandals or old running shoes that can double for around camp and wading streams.
—hiking shorts/swim suit (summer).
—gaiters (especially for winter trips).
—undershirt and longjohns (polypropylene or capilene).
—extra shirt.
—extra socks and underwear (3-5 pair for a weeklong trip).
—bandana/handkerchiefs.
—lightweight cotton or polypropylene gloves.

For winter trips add or substitute:

—internal frame backpack (lowers the center of gravity for skiing).
—space blanket.
—ensolite pad (for insulation against the snow).
—pad for stove.
—four season tent.
—sleeping bag rated to at least 20 degrees below zero F (down-filled is best during winter).
—snow shovel.
—ski accessories: extra tip, skins, waxes, cork and scraper.
—avalanche cord.
—special ski poles that can be threaded together to probe for avalanche victims.
—transceivers (at least 2 in the party).
—warm, waterproof clothing that can be layered.

Optional for any day or overnight trip:

—compact binoculars.
—camera/film/lens brush and paper.
—notebook and pencils.
—book.
—field guides.
—fishing tackle (flies and/or spinning gear).

So there you have it—80 pounds of lightweight gear! Actually, most people can get along safely and comfortably with 35 to 50 pounds of gear and food, depending on the duration of the trip. Your pack will weigh 8 to 10 pounds more during winter with four-season gear and heavier clothing.

APPENDIX B:

Public Lands Conservation Groups

The following groups are citizen-based and have offices in Montana. Each has a statewide or broader focus.

Montana Wilderness Association
P.O. Box 635
Helena, MT 59624
(406) 443-7350

The Montana Wilderness Association (MWA) is the oldest statewide wilderness conservation group in the nation, established in Bozeman in 1958—six years before passage of the Wilderness Act. One of the most popular programs of this grassroots advocacy organization is its Wilderness Walks into threatened wildlands, some of which are portrayed in this book. MWA maintains local chapters throughout the state.

Alliance for the Wild Rockies
P.O. Box 8731
Missoula, MT 59807
(406) 721-5420

The Alliance has established a bioregional network and nationwide campaign to protect the remaining publicly owned wildland, wild rivers, and wildlife of the Northern Rockies bioregion, including the roadless lands of Montana.

American Wildlands
40 East Main, Suite 2
Bozeman, MT 59715
(406) 586-8175

American Wildlands is a small, national public lands conservation group focusing on reform of grazing and forest practices, sustainable resource use, training of grassroots activists, and the identification and protection of biological corridors in the Northern Rockies.

Wilderness Watch
P.O. Box 9175
Missoula, MT 59807
(406) 542-2048

Wilderness Watch is a national chapter-based public lands conservation group. It is the only such organization dedicated exclusively to the stewardship of our existing Wildernesses and Wild and Scenic Rivers. Wilderness Watch does not work on wildland allocation issues but, instead, focuses on taking care of what we already have in the Wilderness and Wild and Scenic River Systems.

The Wilderness Society
Northern Rockies Regional Office
105 West Main Street, Suite E
Bozeman, MT 59715
(406) 586-1600

The Wilderness Society was cofounded in 1935 by Bob Marshalland others, and is dedicated to preserving wilderness and wildlife and fostering an American land ethic.

APPENDIX C:
FEDERAL AGENCIES

The wildland areas and complexes covered in this book are administered by one or more of the following agency offices. Check under the "Administration" heading for the area you're interested in, then look below for the address of whom to contact for additional information. For national forest wildlands, the local ranger district office is usually the best source of information on trail conditions, road status, and regulations. The addresses of each ranger district are listed on the visitor map for each of the ten national forests in Montana which are listed here.

USDA Forest Service

Beaverhead-Deerlodge National Forest
Supervisor's Office
420 Barrett Street
Dillon, MT 59725
(406) 683-3900

Bitterroot National Forest
Supervisor's Office
1801 North First Street
Hamilton, MT 59840
(406) 363-3131

Custer National Forest
Supervisor's Office
1310 Main St.
Billings, MT 59103
(406) 248-9885

Flathead National Forest
Supervisor's Office
1935 Third Avenue East
Kalispell, MT 59901
(406) 755-5401

Gallatin National Forest
P.O. Box 130
Bozeman, MT 59771
(406) 587-6920

Helena National Forest
Supervisor's Office
2880 Skyway Drive
Helena, MT 59601
(406) 449-5201

Kootenai National Forest
Supervisor's Office
506 U.S. Highway 2 West
Libby, MT 59923
(406) 293-6211

Lewis & Clark National Forest
Supervisor's Office
1101 15th Street North
P.O. Box 869
Great Falls, MT 59403
(406) 791-7700

Lolo National Forest
Supervisor's Office
Building 24, Fort Missoula
Missoula, MT 59804
(406) 329-3750

National Park Service

Glacier National Park
Superintendent's Office
West Glacier, MT 59936
(406) 888-7000

Yellowstone National Park
Superintendent's Office
P.O. Box 168
Yellowstone National Park, WY 82190
(307) 344-7381

Bureau of Land Management

Billings Field Office
810 East Main
Billings, MT 59105
(406) 238-1540

Butte Field Office
106 N. Parkmont
Butte, MT 59701
(406) 494-5059

Dillon Field Office
1005 Selway Drive
Dillon, MT 59725
(406) 683-2337

Glasgow Field Station
Route 1-4775
Glasgow, MT 59230
(406) 228-4316

Great Falls Field Office
1101 15th St. N.
Great Falls, MT 59401
(406) 791-7700

Lewistown Field Office
Airport Road
Lewistown, MT 59457
(406) 538-7461

Malta Field Office
501 S. 2nd St. E.
Malta, MT 59538
(406) 654-1240

Miles City Field Office
111 Garryowen Rd.
Miles City, MT 59301
(406) 232-4333

U.S. Fish & Wildlife Service

Red Rock Lakes National
Wildlife Refuge
Refuge Manager
Monida Star Route, Box 15
Lima, MT 59739
(406) 276-3347

Charles M. Russell National
Wildlife Refuge
Refuge Manager
P.O. Box 110
Lewistown, MT 59457
(406) 538-8706

Medicine Lake National
Wildlife Refuge
Refuge Manager
223 North Shore Road
Medicine Lake, MT 59247
(406) 789-2305

APPENDIX D:

TOPOGRAPHIC MAP LISTS

Note: all of these 1:24,000-scale topo maps (2 1/2"/mile) are listed line-by-line from right to left beginning on the most northern line and ending with the most southeastern map title covering the area.

1. Northwest Peaks: Northwest Peaks-MT; Canuck Peak-ID/MT.

2. Scotchman Peaks: Benning Mountain-ID/MT; Spar Lake-MT; Scotchman Peak-ID/MT; Sawtooth Mountain-MT; Heron-MT; Smeads Bench-MT.

3. Cabinet Mountains Wilderness Complex: Kootenai Falls-MT; Scenery Mountain-MT; Crowell Mountain-MT; Treasure Mount-MT; Little Hoodoo Mountain-MT; Ibex Peak-MT; Snowshoe Peak-MT; Cable Mountain-MT; Elephant Peak-MT; Howard Lake-MT; Noxon Rapids Dam-MT; Goat Peak-MT.

4. Cube Iron–Silcox: Fishtrap Lake-MT; Mount Headley-MT; Priscilla Peak-MT; Thompson Falls-MT; Eddy Mountain-MT.

5. Ten Lakes: Ksanka Peak-MT; Stahl Peak-MT; MT Marston-MT.

6. North Fork Wildlands: Tuchuck Mountain-MT; Mount Hefty-MT; Trail Creek-MT; Mount Thompson-Seton-MT; Red Meadow Lake-MT; Whale Buttes-MT.

7. Glacier National Park Wilderness Complex: Trail Creek-MT; Kintla Lake-MT; Kintla Peak-MT; Mount Carter-MT; Porcupine Ridge-MT; Mount Cleveland-MT; Gable Mountain-MT; Chief Mountain-MT; Polebridge-MT; Quartz Ridge-MT; Vulture Peak-MT; Mount Geduhn-MT; Ahern Pass-MT; Many Glacier-MT; Lake Sherburne-MT; Babb-MT; Demers Ridge-MT; Camas Ridge West-MT; Camas Ridge East-MT; Mount Cannon-MT; Logan Pass-MT; Rising Sun-MT; Saint Mary-MT; Fox Creek-MT; Huckleberry Mountain-MT; McGee Meadow-MT; Lake McDonald West-MT; Lake McDonald East-MT; Mount Jackson-MT; Mount Stimson-MT; Cut Bank Pass-MT; Kiowa-MT; Hungry Horse-MT; West Glacier-MT; Nyack-MT; Stanton Lake-MT; Mount Saint Nicholas-MT; Mount Rockwell-MT; Squaw Mountain-MT; Pinnacle-MT; Essex-MT; Blacktail-MT; Summit-MT; Nimrod-MT.

8. **Bob Marshall Wilderness Complex:** West Glacier-MT; Nyack-MT; Slake-MT; Doris Mountain-MT; Nyack SW-MT; Mount Grant-MT; Pinnacle-MT; Blacktail-MT; Summit-MT; Hyde Creek-MT; Half Dome Crag-MT; Hash Mountain-MT; Jewel Basin-MT; Pioneer Ridge-MT; Felix Peak-MT; Nimrod-MT; Mount Bradley-MT; Red Plume Mountain-MT; Crescent Cliff-MT; Morning Star Mountain-MT; Swift Reservoir-MT; Fish Lake-MT; Crater Lake-MT; Big Hawk Mountain-MT; Quintonkon-MT; Circus Peak-MT; Horseshoe Peak-MT; Capitol Mountain-MT; Gable Peaks-MT; Gooseberry Park-MT; Gateway Pass-MT; Wailing Reef-MT; Volcano Reef-MT; Swan Lake-MT; Connor Creek-MT; Tin Creek-MT; Spotted Bear Mountain-MT; Whitcomb Peak-MT; Trilobite Peak-MT; Pentagon Mountain-MT; Porphyry Reef-MT; Mount Wright-MT; Cave Mountain-MT; Thunderbolt Mountain-MT; String Creek-MT; Meadow Creek-MT; Cathedral Peak-MT; Bungalow Mountain-MT; Three Sisters-MT; Gates Park-MT; Our Lake-MT; Ear Mountain-MT; Swan Peak-MT; Sunburst Lake-MT; Marmot Mountain-MT; Pagoda Mountain-MT; Amphitheatre Mountain-MT; Slategoat Mountain-MT; Glenn Creek-MT; Arsenic Mountain-MT; Castle Reef-MT; Condon-MT; Holland Peak-MT; Big Salmon Lake west-MT; Big Salmon Lake East-MT; Haystack Mountain-MT; Prairie Reef-MT; Pretty Prairie-MT; Patricks Basin-MT; Sawtooth Ridge-MT; Holland Lake-MT; Shaw Creek-MT; Una Mountain-MT; Pilot Creek-MT; Trap Mountain-MT; Benchmark-MT; Wood Lake-MT; Double Falls-MT; Lake Inez-MT; Morrell Lake-MT; Crimson Peak-MT; Hahn Creek Pass-MT; Danaher Mountain-MT; Flint Mountain-MT; Scapegoat Mountain-MT; Jakie Creek-MT; Steamboat Mountain-MT; Bean Lake-MT; Seeley Lake East-MT; Morrell Mountain-MT; Dunham Point-MT; Spread Mountain-MT; Lake Mountain-MT; Olson Peak-MT; Heart Lake-MT; Caribou Peak-MT; Blowout Mountain-MT; Ovando Mountain-MT; Coopers Lake-MT; Arrastra Mountain-MT; Stonewall Mountain-MT; Silver King Mountain-MT.

9. **Mission Mountains Wilderness Complex:** Cedar Lake-MT; Piper-Crow Pass-MT; Peck Lake-MT; Mount Harding-MT; Hemlock Lake-MT; Saint Marys Lake-MT; Gray Wolf Lake-MT.

10. **Anaconda Hill:** Rogers Pass-MT; Wilborn-MT.

11. **Nevada Mountain:** Lincoln-MT; Swede Gulch-MT; Finn-MT; Nevada Mountain-MT; Granite Butte-MT.

12. **Electric Peak:** Baggs Creek-MT; Bison Mountain-MT; Sugarloaf Mountain-MT; Thunderbolt Creek-MT.

13. **Black Mountain-Mount Helena:** MacDonald Pass-MT; Black Mountain-MT; Helena-MT; Three Brothers-MT; Chessman Reservoir-MT.

14. **Flint Creek Range:** Pikes Peak-MT; Rock Creek Lake-MT; Fred Burr Lake-MT; Pozega Lakes-MT; Mount Powell-MT.

15. **Stony Mountain:** Sawmill Saddle-MT; Quigg Peak-MT; Willow Mountain-MT; Burnt Fork Lake-MT; Stony Creek-MT; Skalkaho Pass-MT.

16. **Quigg:** Grizzly Point-MT; Spink-MT; Quigg Peak-MT; Alder Gulch-MT.

17. **Welcome Creek Wilderness:** Elk Mountain-MT; Iris Point-MT; Cleveland Mountain-MT; Grizzly Point-MT.

18. **Rattlesnake National Recreation Area and Wilderness Complex:** Belmore Sloughs-MT; Upper Jocko Lake-MT; Stuart Peak-MT; Wapiti Lake-MT; Gold Creek Peak-MT; Northeast Missoula-MT; Blue Point-MT.

19. **Reservation Divide:** Knowles-MT; Perma-MT; Stark North-MT; McCormick Peak-MT; Hewolf Mountain-MT.

20. **Mount Bushnell:** Driveway Peak-MT; Table Top Mountain-MT; Thompson Falls-MT; Saltese-MT; Haugan-MT; De Borgia North-MT.

21. **Sheep Mountain-State Line:** Torino Peak-MT; Wilson Gulch-MT; Sherlock Peak-MT; Illinois Peak-MT.

22. **Burdette Creek:** Lupine Creek-MT.

23. **Great Burn:** Hoodoo Pass-ID/MT; Straight Peak-MT/ID; Saint Patrick Peak-MT; Bruin Hill-ID/MT; Schley Mountain-MT/ID; White Mountain-MT; Rhodes Peak-ID/MT; Granite Pass-ID/MT.

24. **Selway-Bitterroot Wilderness Complex:** Dick Creek-MT/ID; Carlton Lake-ID/MT; St. Joseph Peak-MT/ID; St. Mary Peak-MT; White Sand Lake-ID/MT; Gash Point-MT/ID; Blodgett Mountain-ID/MT; Printz Ridge-MT; Tenmile Lake-MT/ID; Ward Mountain-MT; El Capitan-MT/ID; Como Peaks-MT; Tin Cup Lake-ID/MT; Trapper Peak-MT; Burnt Ridge-MT; Watchtower Peak-ID/MT; Mount Jerusalem-MT/ID; Boulder Peak-MT.

25. **Blue Joint:** Nez Perce Peak-ID/MT; Bare Cone-MT; Painted Tocks Lake-MT; Blue Joint-ID/MT; Horse Creek Pass-MT/ID; Alta-MT/ID.

26. **Allan Mountain:** Piquett Creek-MT; Medicine Hot Springs-MT; Sula-MT;

Piquett Mountain-MT; Overwhich Falls-MT/ID; Lost Trail Pass-MT/ID; Henderson Ridge-MT/ID; Allan Mountain-ID/MT; Shoup-ID/MT.

27. **Anaconda-Pintler/Sapphires Wilderness Complex:** Skalkaho Pass-MT; Mount Emerine-MT; Kent Peak-MT; Whetstone Ridge-MT; Moose Lake-MT; Carpp Ridge-MT; Storm Lake-MT; Mount Evans-MT; Gibbons Pass-MT; Kelly Lake-MT; Warren Peak-MT; Long Peak-MT; Lower Seymour Lake-MT; Bender Point-MT; Mussigbrod Lake-MT; Pintler Lake-MT.

28. **Humbug Spires:** Tucker Creek-MT; Mount Humbug-MT; Melrose-MT; Wickiup Creek-MT.

29. **Tobacco Roots:** Waterloo-MT; Manhead Mountain-MT; Old Baldy Mountain-MT; Noble Peak-MT; Potosi Peak-MT; Copper Mountain-MT; Ramshorn Mountain-MT.

30. **East Pioneers:** Vipond Park-MT; Cattle Gulch-MT; Maurice Mountain-MT; Mount Tahepia-MT; Elkhorn Hot Springs-MT; Torrey Mountain-MT; Polaris-MT; Ermont-MT.

31. **West Pioneers:** Pine Hill-MT; Foolhen Mountain-MT; Dickey Hills-MT; Proposal Rock-MT; Shaw Mountain-MT; Stine Mountain-MT; Stewart Mountain-MT; Odell Lake-MT; Maurice Mountain-MT; Jackson Hill-MT; Maverick Mountain-MT; Elkhorn Hot Springs-MT.

32. **West Big Hole:** Big Hole Pass-ID/MT; Isaac Meadows-MT; Jumbo Mountain-MT/ID; Homer Youngs Peak-MT/ID; Miner Lake-MT; Bohannon Spring-ID/MT; Goldstone Pass-MT/ID.

33. **Italian Peaks:** Morrison Lake-ID/MT; Island Butte-MT; Caboose-MT; Cottonwood Creek-ID/MT; Eighteenmile Peak-MT/ID; Deadman Lake-MT/ID; Scott Peak-ID/MT.

34. **Lima Peaks:** Gallagher Gulch-MT; Lima Peaks-MT; Fritz Peak-ID/MT; Edie Ranch-ID/MT; East of Edie Ranch-ID/MT.

35. **Centennial Mountains/Red Rock Lakes Wildland Complex:** Lower Red Rock Lakes-MT; Elk Springs-MT; Corral Creek-MT/ID; Big Table Mountain-MT/ID; Wilson Creek-MT/ID; Slide Mountain-MT/ID; Upper Red Rock Lake-MT/ID; Mount Jefferson-MT/ID; Sawtell Peak-ID/MT.

36. Snowcrest: Home Park Ranch-MT; Swamp Creek-MT; Spur Mountain-MT; Whiskey Spring-MT; Antone Peak-MT; Stonehouse Mountain-MT; Wolverine Creek-MT.

37. Lionhead: Earthquake Lake-MT; Hebgen Dam-MT; Targhee Peak-ID/MT; Targhee Pass-ID/MT.

38. Lee Metcalf Wilderness Complex: Norris-MT; Bear Trap Creek-MT; Ennis Lake-MT; Cherry Lake-MT; Willow Swamp-MT; Beacon Point-MT; Garnet Mountain-MT; Fan Mountain-MT; Lone Mountain-MT; Gallatin Peak-MT; Hidden Lake-MT; Lake Cameron-MT; Sphinx Mountain-MT; Ousel Falls-MT; No Man Peak-MT; Koch Peak-MT; Sunshine Point-MT; Big Horn Peak-MT; Squaw Creek-MT; Hilgard Peak-MT; Pika Point-MT; Upper Tepee Basin-MT; Divide Lake-MT/WY; Earthquake Lake-MT; Mount Hebgen-MT; Richards Creek-MT/WY.

39. Gallatin Range: Wheeler Mountain-MT; Mount Ellis-MT; Mount Blackmore-MT; Fridley Peak-MT; Big Draw-MT; The Sentinel-MT; Lewis Creek-MT; Lone Indian Peak-MT; Ramshorn Peak-MT; Miner-MT; Dome Mountain-MT; Sunshine Point-MT; Big Horn Peak-MT; Sportsman Lake-MT; Electric Peak-MT; Divide Lake-MT.

40. Absaroka-Beartooth Wilderness Complex: McLeod-MT; Ross Canyon-MT; Packsaddle Butte-MT; Brisbin-MT; Livingston Peak-MT; Mount Rae-MT; McLeod Basin-MT; Squaw Peak-MT; Sliderock Mountain-MT; Wildcat Draw-MT; Dexter Point-MT; Mount Cowen-MT; West Boulder Plateau-MT; Chrome Mountain-MT; Picket Pin Mountain-MT; Meyer Mountain-MT; Emigrant-MT; Knowles Peak-MT; The Pyramid-MT; The Needles-MT; Mount Douglas-MT; Tumble Mountain-MT; Cathedral Point-MT; Mount Wood-MT; Emerald Lake-MT; MacKay Ranch-MT; Dome Mountain-MT; Monitor Peak-MT; Mineral Mountain-MT; Mount Wallace-MT; Iron Mountain-MT; Haystack Peak-MT; Pinnacle Mountain-MT; Little Park Mountain-MT; Granite Peak-MT; Alpine-MT; Sylvan Peak-MT; Bare Mountain-MT; Red Lodge West-MT; Electric Peak-MT; Gardiner-MT; Ash Mountain-MT; Specimen Creek-MT; Hummingbird Peak-MT; Roundhead Butte-MT; Cutoff Mountain-MT; Cooke City-MT; Fossil Lake-MT; Castle Mountain-MT; Silver Run Peak-MT; Black Pyramid Mountain-MT; Mount Maurice-MT.

41. Crazy Mountains: Cinnamon Peak-MT; Cinnamon Spring-MT; Virginia Peak-MT; Loco Mountain-MT; Rein Lake-MT; Campfire Lake-MT; Crazy Peak-MT; Amelong Peak-MT; Ibex Mountain-MT; Fairview Peak-MT; Raspberry Butte-MT.

42. **Castle Mountains:** Pinchout Creek-MT; Fourmile Spring-MT; Manger Park-MT; Castletown-MT.

43. **Elkhorn Mountains:** Clancy-MT; Casey Peak-MT; Winston-MT; Elkhorn-MT; Crow Creek Falls-MT; Giant Hill-MT.

44. **Gates of the Mountains Wilderness Complex:** Sheep Creek-MT; Beartooth Mountain-MT; Candle Mountain-MT; Middle Creek Lake-MT; Upper Holter Lake-MT; Nelson-MT; Hogback Mountain-MT.

45. **Mount Baldy:** Gipsy Lake-MT; Mount Edith-MT.

46. **Tenderfoot/Deep Creek:** Millegan-MT; Deep Creek Park-MT; Blankenbaker Flats-MT; Lingshire NE-MT; Bald Hills-MT; Monument Peak-MT; Bubbling Springs-MT.

47. **Middle Fork Judith:** Yogo Peak-MT; Bandbox Mountain-MT; Kings Hill-MT; Sand Point-MT; Ettien Spring-MT; Indian Hill-MT; Hoover Spring-MT.

48. **Big Snowies:** Crystal Lake-MT; Jump Off Peak-MT; Half Moon Campground-MT; Alaska Bench-MT; Yaple Bench-MT; Snow Saucer Coulee-MT; Green Ashley Gulch-MT; Patterson Canyon-MT.

49. **Highwood Mountains:** Highwood Baldy-MT; Arrow Peak-MT; Palisade Butte-MT.

50. **Missouri Breaks Wildland Complex:** Butch Reservoir-MT; John Coulee-MT; Crazyman Coulee-MT; Chase Hill-MT; Ragland Bench-MT; Leroy-MT; Bird Rapids-MT; Sturgeon Island-MT; Cow Island-MT; Shetland Divide-MT; Whiskey Coulee-MT; Smith Coulee-MT; Seventh Point Buttes-MT; Starve Out Flat-MT; PN Ranch-MT; Council Island-MT; Gallatin Rapids-MT; Taffy Ridge-MT; Woodhawk Hill-MT; Reppe Butte-MT; Baker Monument-MT; Grand Island-MT; Bell Ridge West-MT; Lake Reservoir-MT; Karsten Coulee-MT; Indian Lake-MT; Herman Point-MT; Schuyler Butte-MT; Swede Ridge-MT; Wolfe Coulee-MT; Wagon Coulee-MT; Harper Camp-MT; Peterson Point-MT; Little Buffalo Hill-MT; Signal Butte-MT; Gilbert Creek-MT; Hanson Flat-MT; Dry Coulee-MT; Chain Buttes-MT; Locke Ranch-MT; Mickey Butte-MT; Lost Creek-MT; Pine Grove School-MT; Sawmill Creek-MT; Chalk Butte-MT; Trumbo Ranch-MT; Maloney Hill-MT; Germaine Coulee West-MT; Germaine Coulee East-MT; Spring Creek School-MT; Blackfoot School-MT; Brusett-MT.

51. Bitter Creek: Last Chance Reservoir-MT; Dodge Reservoir-MT; Gay Dam-MT; Kerr Cow Dam-MT; Laundry Hill-MT.

52. Medicine Lake Wilderness: Medicine Lake-MT; Capeney's Lake-MT.

53. Pryor Mountains Wildland Complex: Big Ice Cave-MT; East Pryor Mountain-MT; Dead Indian Hill-MT; Red Pryor Mountain-MT; Mystery Cave-MT (Note: this listing covers only the public lands-portion of the complex within Montana).

54. Tongue River Breaks Wildland Complex: Cook Creek-MT; Birney Day School-MT; Green Creek-MT; Browns Mountain-MT.

55. Terry Badlands: McClure Reservoir-MT; Calypso-MT; Kinsey NE-MT; Zero-MT.

Getting the right maps: To explore the country described in this book you need two basic types of maps: one or more of the detailed USGS 1:24,000-scale topographic (contour) maps listed above; and the Forest Service national forest visitor map, which is usually 1/2"/mile planimetric, and/or the applicable wilderness map, which is on a contour base, or the applicable agency map. At this writing the Forest Service maps cost $3 and the USGS topo maps are $4. See Appendix C for where to order the Forest Service maps you need. If you are ordering more than one map from the Forest Service it would be more efficient to purchase them from the Regional Office: Information Assistant, USDA Forest Service, P.O. Box 7669, Missoula, MT 59807 (406) 329-3511. U.S. Geological Survey (USGS) maps may be purchased from: Map Distribution, USGS Map Sales, Box 25286, Federal Center, Bldg. 810, Denver, CO 80225.

ROADLESS AREA UPDATE AND VISITATION RECORD

(Please copy this form as needed for future use and send completed copy to:
Bill Cunningham, c/o Falcon Press, P.O. Box 1718, Helena, MT 59624.)

1) Name of area visited: _____

2) Location of visit (legal description-section, township, range, if possible; name of drainages; trail numbers; etc.):

3) Date of visit:

4) Condition of access to trailhead or beginning of trail:

5) Status and condition of trails used (by name/number):

6) Brief description of area visited:

7) Is the trail (area) used by both motorized and non-motorized recreationists? If yes, is there any evidence of user conflict or resource damage?

8) If the area or trail segment visited has been changed by roads or resource development describe the LOCATION and TYPE of development and its impact on the roadless area:

9) Action taken (if applicable):

10) Name/address/telephone:

Note: this information will serve as a record of your visit to a Montana wildland and may also be used for future updates of this book. Also, with your permission, the information may be shared with the land management agency and a local conservation group in order to assist with the area's protection and stewardship.

ABOUT THE AUTHOR

Bill Cunningham has been a hard-core "wildernut" for longer than he can remember. His lifelong passion has been, and is, the defense and enjoyment of Montana's wildlands. His special joy is teaching about wilderness *in* the wilderness through university-sponsored field courses and guided backpacking trips. Bill has written several books and numerous articles about Montana wild areas based on extensive personal exploration. He lives in Choteau, Montana.

FALCONGUIDES ®Leading the Way™

FALCONGUIDES ® are available for where-to-go hiking, mountain biking, rock climbing, walking, scenic driving, fishing, rockhounding, paddling, birding, wildlife viewing, and camping. We also have FalconGuides on essential outdoor skills and subjects and field identification. The following titles are currently available, but this list grows every year.

HIKING GUIDES

Hiking Alaska
Hiking Arizona
Hiking Arizona's Cactus Country
Hiking the Beartooths
Hiking Big Bend National Park
Hiking the Bob Marshall Country
Hiking California
Hiking California's Desert Parks
Hiking Carlsbad Caverns
    and Guadalupe Mtns. National Parks
Hiking Colorado
Hiking Colorado, Vol.II
Hiking Colorado's Summits
Hiking Colorado's Weminuche Wilderness
Hiking the Columbia River Gorge
Hiking Florida
Hiking Georgia
Hiking Glacier & Waterton Lakes National Parks
Hiking Grand Canyon National Park
Hiking Grand Staircase-Escalante/Glen Canyon
Hiking Grand Teton National Park
Hiking Great Basin National Park
Hiking Hot Springs in the Pacific Northwest
Hiking Idaho
Hiking Maine
Hiking Michigan
Hiking Minnesota
Hiking Montana
Hiking Mount Rainier National Park
Hiking Mount St. Helens
Hiking Nevada
Hiking New Hampshire

Hiking New Mexico
Hiking New York
Hiking North Carolina
Hiking the North Cascades
Hiking Northern Arizona
Hiking Olympic National Park
Hiking Oregon
Hiking Oregon's Eagle Cap Wilderness
Hiking Oregon's Mount Hood/Badger Creek
Hiking Oregon's Three Sisters Country
Hiking Pennsylvania
Hiking Shenandoah National Park
Hiking the Sierra Nevada
Hiking South Carolina
Hiking South Dakota's Black Hills Country
Hiking Southern New England
Hiking Tennessee
Hiking Texas
Hiking Utah
Hiking Utah's Summits
Hiking Vermont
Hiking Virginia
Hiking Washington
Hiking Wyoming
Hiking Wyoming's Cloud Peak Wilderness
Hiking Wyoming's Wind River Range
Hiking Yellowstone National Park
Hiking Zion & Bryce Canyon National Parks
The Trail Guide to Bob Marshall Country
Wild Country Companion
Wild Montana
Wild Utah

■ *To order any of these books, check with your local bookseller or call The Globe Pequot Press ® at **1-800-243-0495**.*

FALCON®

Visit us on the world wide web at:
www.FalconOutdoors.com

FALCONGUIDES® Leading the Way™

FALCONGUIDES® are available for where-to-go hiking, mountain biking, rock climbing, walking, scenic driving, fishing, rockhounding, paddling, birding, wildlife viewing, and camping. We also have FalconGuides on essential outdoor skills and subjects and field identification. The following titles are currently available, but this list grows every year.

MOUNTAIN BIKING GUIDES
Mountain Biking Arizona
Mountain Biking Colorado
Mountain Biking Georgia
Mountain Biking New Mexico
Mountain Biking New York
Mountain Biking Northern New England
Mountain Biking Oregon
Mountain Biking South Carolina
Mountain Biking Southern California
Mountain Biking Southern New England
Mountain Biking Utah
Mountain Biking Wisconsin
Mountain Biking Wyoming

LOCAL CYCLING SERIES
Fat Trax Bozeman
Mountain Biking Bend
Mountain Biking Boise
Mountain Biking Chequamegon
Mountain Biking Chico
Mountain Biking Colorado Springs
Mountain Biking Denver/Boulder
Mountain Biking Durango
Mountain Biking Flagstaff and Sedona
Mountain Biking Helena
Mountain Biking Moab
Mountain Biking Utah's St. George/Cedar City Area
Mountain Biking the White Mountains (West)

■ *To order any of these books, check with your local bookseller or call The Globe Pequot Press* ® *at 1-800-243-0495.*

FALCON®

Visit us on the world wide web at:
www.FalconOutdoors.com

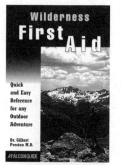

WILDERNESS FIRST AID

By Dr. Gilbert Preston M.D.

Enjoy the outdoors and face the inherent risks with confidence. By reading this easy-to-follow first-aid text, all outdoor enthusiasts can pack a little extra peace of mind on their next adventure. *Wilderness First Aid* offers expert medical advice for dealing with outdoor emergencies beyond the reach of 911. It easily fits in most backcountry first-aid kits.

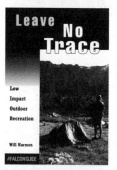

LEAVE NO TRACE

By Will Harmon

The concept of "leave no trace" seems simple, but it actually gets fairly complicated. This handy quick-reference guidebook includes all the newest information on this growing and all-important subject. This book is written to help the outdoor enthusiast make the hundreds of decisions necessary to protect the natural landscape and still have an enjoyable wilderness experience. Part of the proceeds from the sale of this book go to continue leave-no-trace education efforts. The Official Manual of American Hiking Society.

BEAR AWARE

By Bill Schneider

Hiking in bear country can be very safe if hikers follow the guidelines summarized in this small, "packable" book. Extensively reviewed by bear experts, the book contains the latest information on the intriguing science of bear-human interactions. *Bear Aware* can not only make your hike safer, but it can help you avoid the fear of bears that can take the edge off your trip.

MOUNTAIN LION ALERT

By Steve Torres

Recent mountain lion attacks have received national attention. Although infrequent, lion attacks raise concern for public safety. *Mountain Lion Alert* contains helpful advice for mountain bikers, trail runners, horse riders, pet owners, and suburban landowners on how to reduce the chances of mountain lion-human conflicts.

Also Available

Wilderness Survival • Reading Weather • Backpacking Tips • Climbing Safely • Avalanche Aware • Desert Hiking Tips • Hiking with Dogs • Using GPS • Route Finding • Wild Country Companion

To order check with your local bookseller or call The Globe Pequot Press ® at 1-800-243-0495.
www.FalconOutdoors.com